ENCYCLOPEDIA OF GREAT CIVILIZATIONS

This edition produced in 1994 for
Shooting Star Press Inc
230 Fifth Avenue
Suite 1212
New York, NY 10001

© Aladdin Books Ltd 1994

Designed and produced by
Aladdin Books Ltd
28 Percy Street
London W1

Printed in the Czech Republic   ISBN 1-56924-065-5

Some of the material in this book was previously published in the History Highlights and Great Civilizations series

INTRODUCTION — 4

EGYPT — 6
Including a special feature on *The Pyramids* — 36

CHINA — 60

JAPAN — 90
Including a special feature on *The Samurai Warriors* — 120

GREECE — 144

ROME — 174
Including a special feature on *The Roman Forts* — 204

VIKINGS — 226

MEDIEVAL EUROPE — 256

AZTECS and INCAS — 286

INDEX — 316

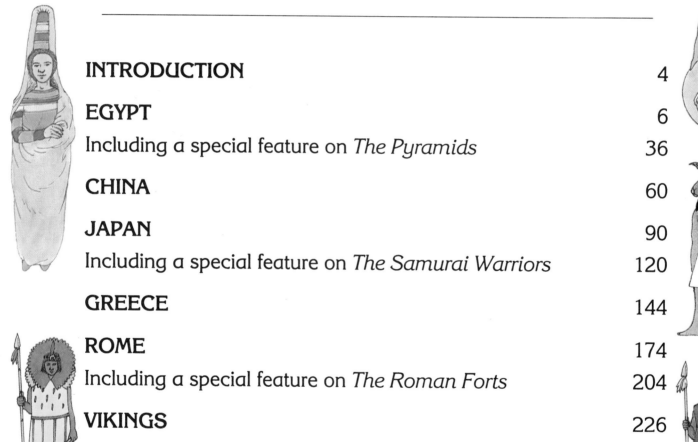

ENCYCLOPEDIA OF GREAT CIVILIZATIONS

Written by

Brian Adams, Penny Bateman, Simon James

Mavis Pilbeam, Anton Powell, Jenny Roberts

Beth McKillop, Anne Millard and Margaret Mulvihill

Illustrated by

Rob Shone, Tony Smith and Gerald Wood

SHOOTING STAR PRESS

INTRODUCTION

Throughout history the people from different countries or regions of the world have developed their own lifestyles and customs. Civilization is a way of life that began after people started to live in cities or organized societies. A civilization is made up of more than just the people, it includes their art, customs, technology, methods of government, agriculture and so on. It is also a term used to describe groups of people, or societies, whose economy, politics and culture are highly developed and successful. Over the thousands of years of our history, individual civilizations have risen and fallen, some having been far more successful than others. The important civilizations of the world have passed on ideas and inventions to other civilizations, many of which we still benefit from today.

The beginnings of agriculture, in about 9000 BC, brought about a great change in human life, as prehistoric people learned to farm and no longer had to roam the land looking for food. They began to settle in one place and some of these settlements grew into the world's first cities. People in these cities learned new skills and developed specialized jobs, such as builders, craftsmen, merchants and priests. Eventually people developed ways of writing and the first civilizations began.

For hundreds of years, the earliest civilizations had little contact with one another and developed independently. Because of this the progress of each civilization depended

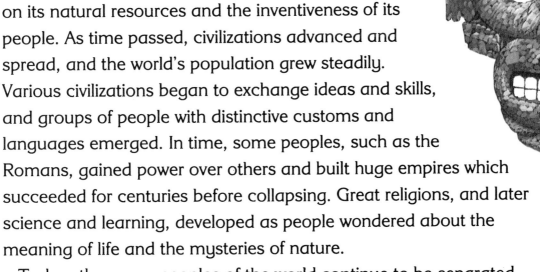

on its natural resources and the inventiveness of its people. As time passed, civilizations advanced and spread, and the world's population grew steadily. Various civilizations began to exchange ideas and skills, and groups of people with distinctive customs and languages emerged. In time, some peoples, such as the Romans, gained power over others and built huge empires which succeeded for centuries before collapsing. Great religions, and later science and learning, developed as people wondered about the meaning of life and the mysteries of nature.

Today, the many peoples of the world continue to be separated by different cultural traditions, but they also have more in common than ever before. Worldwide systems of communication have broken down barriers of time and distance and rapidly increased the exchange of ideas and information.

The *Encyclopedia of Great Civilizations* looks at eight civilizations whose people and their way of life produced some of the most important developments in history. In each section of this book we give a complete overview of a different civilization, from its origins to its influence on today's world. We look at how people lived and examine key incidents and personalities of the time. In three sections of the book, an additional *Special Feature* illustrates, in depth, one important aspect of that civilization. Included in this book are *Special Features* on the Pyramids, Samurai Warriors, and Roman Forts.

CONTENTS

EGYPT

INTRODUCTION   8
UNIFICATION OF EGYPT C3118-2181 BC   10
The Pyramids – The Pharaoh – Life at the Royal Court
A Nobleman's Estate – A Farmer's House – The Farmer's Year
MIDDLE KINGDOM AND AFTER c2181-1567 BC   16
Scribes and Scrolls – Making Papyrus – Hieroglyphs – Education
The Army – Egypt's Wealth – The Hyksos Invasion
EMPIRE AT ITS HEIGHT 1567-1085 BC   22
Egypt at War – Tribute and Trade – Gods and Temples – Akhenaten and Nefertiti
Mummification – The Valley of the Kings – The Village of the Workmen
FOREIGN PHARAOHS 1085 BC-AD 642   28
The Royal Cities – Magic and Medicine – Mathematics and Building – Astronomy
The Nubian Conquerors – Alexandria and the Ptolemies – Egypt Under Rome
THE LEGACY OF ANCIENT EGYPT   34

THE PYRAMIDS

INTRODUCTION   37
WHY PYRAMIDS?   38
A PYRAMID COMPLEX   40
BUILDING PYRAMIDS   42
CRAFTSMEN   44
GROWING UP   46
SCRIBES AND SCHOLARS   48
THE NEXT WORLD   50
THE NILE – EGYPT'S LIFELINE   52
WHAT HAPPENED TO PYRAMIDS?   54
PYRAMIDS WORLDWIDE   56
DATE CHARTS   58

ENCYCLOPEDIA OF GREAT CIVILIZATIONS

EGYPT

Including a special feature on
The Pyramids

INTRODUCTION

The civilization of Egypt is one of the oldest and greatest in the world. We are lucky that so much material from the time of the ancient Egyptians has survived for us to study. We can admire the remains of their huge buildings and get to know individuals from their statues. We can discover details of their daily lives from the paintings in their tombs. From the writings which survive we can learn about what they thought, felt and did. The ancient Egyptians believed that death was just a door to another, eternal life and that they could take all they would need there by putting it in their tombs. Because of this we can handle objects, clothes and furniture that were in daily use thousands of years ago.

Egyptian civilization developed on the banks of the Nile. Herodotus, a clever Greek historian, wrote that Egypt was "the gift of the Nile." Egypt is an area almost entirely without rain and most of the land is stark desert. Every year, heavy rains in the south send water into the Nile. Before the building of modern dams, this caused the Nile to overflow its banks. This was the Inundation, a flood which brought with it rich, fertile mud to renew the soil.

This book divides the story of ancient Egypt into four periods: the unification and the pyramid age; the middle kingdom and its collapse; the empire at its height; and finally the decline of ancient Egypt.

As Egypt was flooded for several weeks every year, the river was the easiest way to move all heavy loads. But water wasn't the only gift of the Nile. Its waters teemed with fish. Reed beds supplied papyrus, used to make a kind of paper, and reeds for building and making a variety of goods from pens to sandals. The reed thickets were also home to many kinds of birds and hippopotami which were hunted by the nobles.

UNIFICATION OF EGYPT c3118-2181 BC

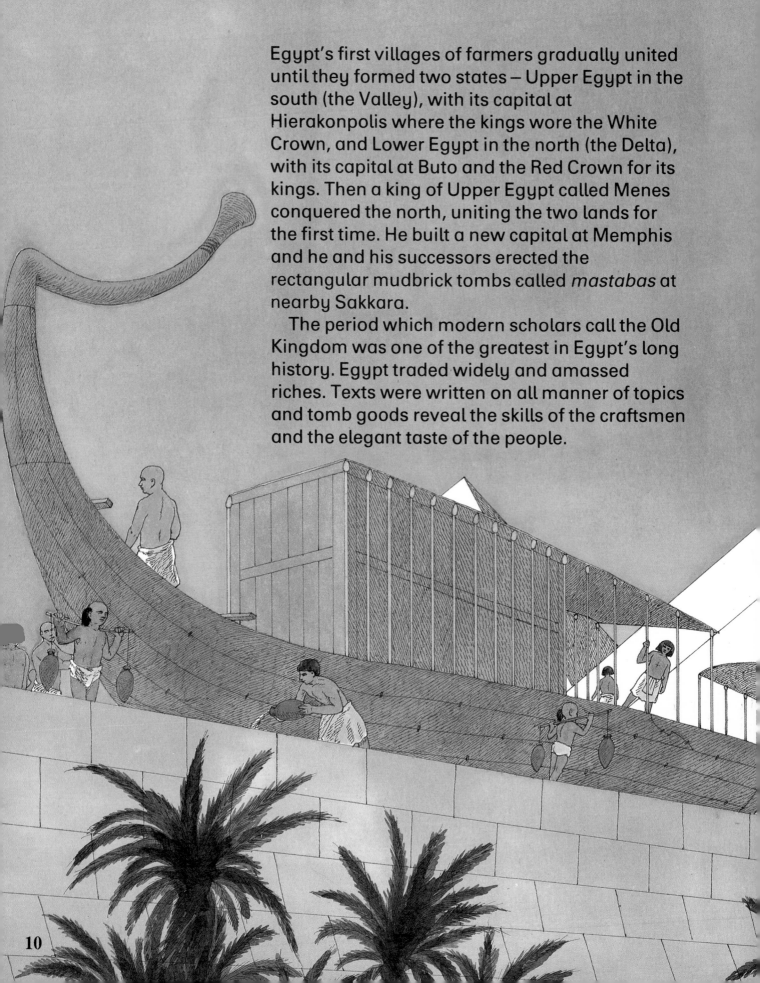

Egypt's first villages of farmers gradually united until they formed two states – Upper Egypt in the south (the Valley), with its capital at Hierakonpolis where the kings wore the White Crown, and Lower Egypt in the north (the Delta), with its capital at Buto and the Red Crown for its kings. Then a king of Upper Egypt called Menes conquered the north, uniting the two lands for the first time. He built a new capital at Memphis and he and his successors erected the rectangular mudbrick tombs called *mastabas* at nearby Sakkara.

The period which modern scholars call the Old Kingdom was one of the greatest in Egypt's long history. Egypt traded widely and amassed riches. Texts were written on all manner of topics and tomb goods reveal the skills of the craftsmen and the elegant taste of the people.

King Khufu of the 4th Dynasty built his pyramid at Giza. It is the largest of all the pyramids. Its temples were to provide all he needed in the next world. Among the things he would need were boats to travel in, so real boats were buried in pits around the pyramid. One has been found and restored to its former glory.

MEDITERRANEAN SEA

Buto

Trade with Middle East

LOWER EGYPT

Giza▲
Sakkara▲   Memphis
The Fayum

RED SEA

Herakleopolis

Nile

Abydos

Hierakonpolis
First cataract

UPPER EGYPT

Aswan
Border of Egypt
in early Dynastic period

Trade
and raiding

NUBIA

Second cataract

Fertile area

Datechart

THE UNIFICATION
c3118 BC Menes, King of Upper Egypt, conquers Lower Egypt and unites the two lands.

THE ARCHAIC PERIOD
c3100-2686 BC 1st and 2nd Dynasties. Monuments are built of mud bricks.

THE OLD KINGDOM
c2686-2613 BC 3rd Dynasty. The architect Imhotep (later worshipped as a god) builds the Step Pyramid at Sakkara for King Zoser. The pyramid of the later King Huni is turned from a step to a straight-sided pyramid.

c2613-2494 BC 4th Dynasty. The famous Giza group of pyramids is built. Mining expeditions to Sinai. Regular trade with Byblos and Nubia.

c2494-2345 BC 5th Dynasty. Kings devoted to the sun god Re and take the title "Son of Re." First known trip to Punt. The pyramids are built at Abusir.

c2345-2181 BC 6th Dynasty. Canal cut in First Cataract (place where rocks fill the river and block it to shipping) to speed journeys to Nubia. More power for district governors called nomarchs, so royal power and prestige are reduced. Pepi II reigns 94 years.

11

The pyramids

In the 3rd Dynasty Egypt was wealthy. As craftsmen were using stone with great skill, it was decided to build the king's tomb in stone so that it would last forever. The architect in charge was called Imhotep. He designed a new style of tomb – a pyramid of steps so the dead king could climb up to the sky to become one of the eternal stars.

Later it was decided to have pyramids with straight sides, but the first one was a failure. The angle of the sides was too steep and had to be altered making the "Bent" pyramid.

To provide the king with all the things he would need in the next world, a great complex of buildings was put up around his pyramid. His courtiers were buried near by in *mastaba* tombs.

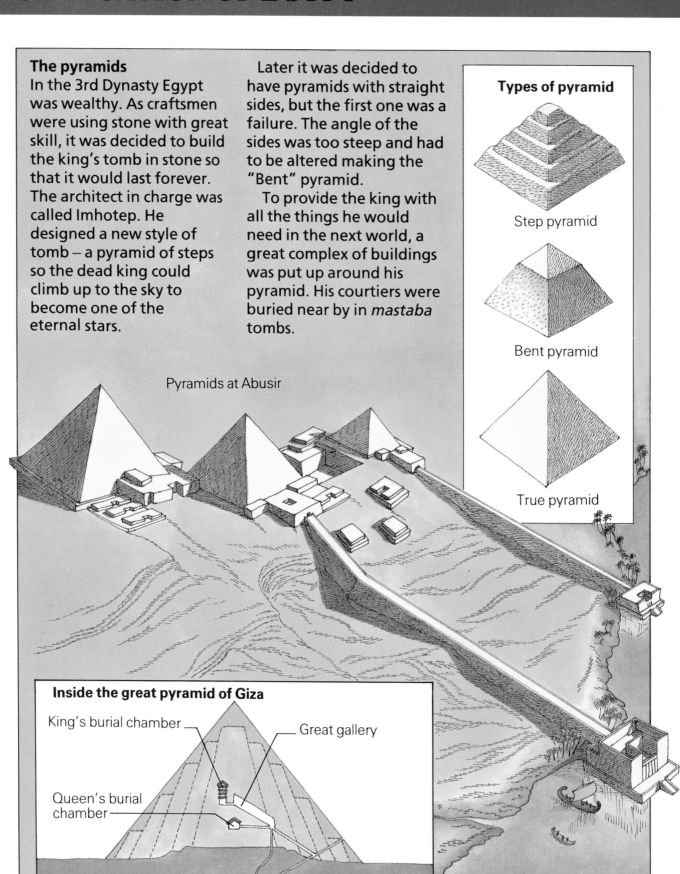

Pyramids at Abusir

Types of pyramid

Step pyramid

Bent pyramid

True pyramid

Inside the great pyramid of Giza

King's burial chamber

Great gallery

Queen's burial chamber

First plan burial chamber

The pharaoh

For the Egyptians, their king the pharaoh was more than just a powerful man. When he was wearing his Double Crown, seated on his throne and carrying his Crook and Flail, the spirit of the god Horus entered him and he became a god. It was also thought that he was descended from the sun god Re. In order to keep this special, divine blood pure, it was the custom for the king to marry his sister.

Many of the pharaohs were warriors. Our illustration shows the first king Menes executing his northern rival.

White crown of Upper Egypt Red crown of Lower Egypt Double crown

Life at the royal court

The king was the source of all power and wealth. Life at court revolved around him, with priests and servants to care for and entertain him.

Being a god set apart from ordinary mortals, the king had a vizier to see that his policies and orders were carried out by the many officials he had appointed to act for him.

Because he was so holy, he was a remote figure, held in great awe. But texts suggest that some kings liked to relax with music and dancing, storytelling and magicians.

A nobleman's estate
Most Egyptians lived in small houses but the rich had large estates like the one in the picture. The villas were set in cool, shady gardens with high walls for privacy.

Behind the villa were the servants' quarters, stables for the horses and stalls for the cattle being fattened for the table. Pigeons and other birds were kept in an aviary and also eaten.

An estate like this would produce most of the things needed by the owner, so there were also workshops where weavers, carpenters, metalworkers and other craftsmen could work.

A farmer's house

This is the home of a peasant farmer. Like the nobleman's house it is made of mud bricks baked hard by the sun. It has only three or four rooms but the cooking and many household tasks are done in the open air. The family can relax on the roof, shaded by the awning and in the breeze.

Granaries and supplies are kept in the courtyard where the farm animals are guarded at night.

The farmer's year

In October when the water of the Inundation went down, farmers plowed their lands with oxen and wooden plows. Others walked behind scattering seed which was trodden in by flocks of sheep. As crops grew, tax men came around and worked out how much should be paid as tax.

Harvest came in March and April. Sickles were used to cut the ears of grain which were loaded into baskets and taken on donkeys to the threshing floor. Here the grain was separated from the ears and winnowed to remove the chaff. It was then taken to be stored in granaries under the watchful eyes of scribes.

Water from the Inundation was stored in canals and guided into the fields through small ditches. In the New Kingdom the *shaduf* was invented to lift water from a canal to a higher one. This simple device is still in use today, as the photograph shows, but it is now being replaced by electrically driven pumps.

MIDDLE KINGDOM AND AFTER

When the Old Kingdom collapsed an unhappy time followed with civil wars, rival claimants to the throne, disorder, foreign invasions and famine. At last the ruler of Thebes, Mentuhotep, swept north and reunited the two lands again.

Under his wise rule Egypt recovered from the recent troubles, but his family was later replaced by that of a high official called Amenemhat. He founded the 12th Dynasty and it was under this that Egypt enjoyed another of the great periods in its history. Egypt was well run. In the Faiyum rich farm land was created by partly draining the large lake there. Trade flourished bringing more wealth. Arts and crafts bloomed and some of Egypt's most famous stories were written. Many of Egypt's eastern neighbors were much influenced by its culture, while its armies marched south and conquered Nubia.

As the king was also a god it was a terrible crime to harm him. But the unfortunate King Amenemhat 1 was attacked and murdered by members of his household. His son and chosen heir Senusret, who had been crowned in his father's lifetime, outwitted the villains and saved his throne.

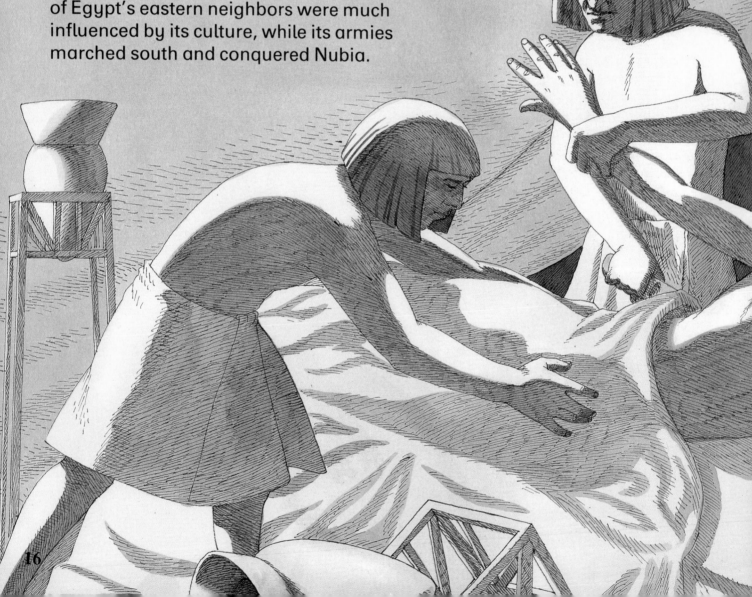

c2181-1567 BC

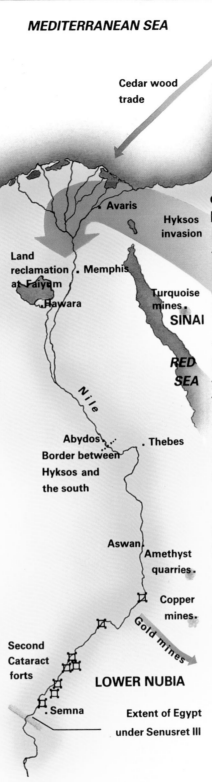

MEDITERRANEAN SEA

Byblos.

Cedar wood trade

Avaris

Hyksos invasion

Land reclamation at Faiyum

. Memphis

Turquoise mines .

SINAI

. Hawara

RED SEA

Nile

Abydos .
Border between
Hyksos and
the south

. Thebes

Aswan.
Amethyst quarries .

Copper mines .

Gold mines

Second Cataract forts

LOWER NUBIA

. Semna

Extent of Egypt under Senusret III

THE MIDDLE KINGDOM

c2133-1991 BC 11th Dynasty. A rival line of kings had ruled in Thebes for several years. In 2040 BC Mentuhotep II overthrows 10th Dynasty kings and unites Egypt.

1991-1786 BC 12th Dynasty. Amenemhat I founds new line of kings. Their pyramids are built around the entrance to the Faiyum. Nubia conquered and forts built on Second Cataract.

1897-1878 BC Senusret II begins work to reclaim land in the Faiyum.

1878-1843 BC Senusret III, great warrior king, crushes Nubian resistance.

1789-1786 BC As there is no male heir, Princess Sobekneferu rules as "king."

1786-1633 BC 13th Dynasty. People from over the Eastern frontier come into Egypt and conquer most of the land.

2ND INTERMEDIATE PERIOD

1633-1567 BC Egypt ruled by the Hyksos.

Datechart

1ST INTERMEDIATE PERIOD

c2181-2160 BC 7th and 8th Dynasties.

c2160-2040 BC 9th and 10th Dynasties set up by princes of Herakleopolis.

Scribes and scrolls

The government of Egypt was based on keeping records. Every order, action, payment and deal had to be recorded. As many Egyptians could not write, scribes often hired out their services to clients. People kept all the family records in case they were ever needed – in a court case, for example.

A scribe might take notes on bits of broken pottery but a finished piece of work was written on a long scroll of papyrus. To work, a scribe sat cross-legged on the floor with his scroll resting on a writing board. He used reed pens dipped in water and he made his own paints from various mineral substances.

Making papyrus

The diagram below shows the different stages involved in making papyrus. (1) Peel off green outer case of the papyrus stem. (2) Split white inner core of stem into thin strips then soak them in clean water. (3) Form a page by overlapping strips of papyrus. (4) Hammer page to get the strips to stick together. (5) Smooth surface.

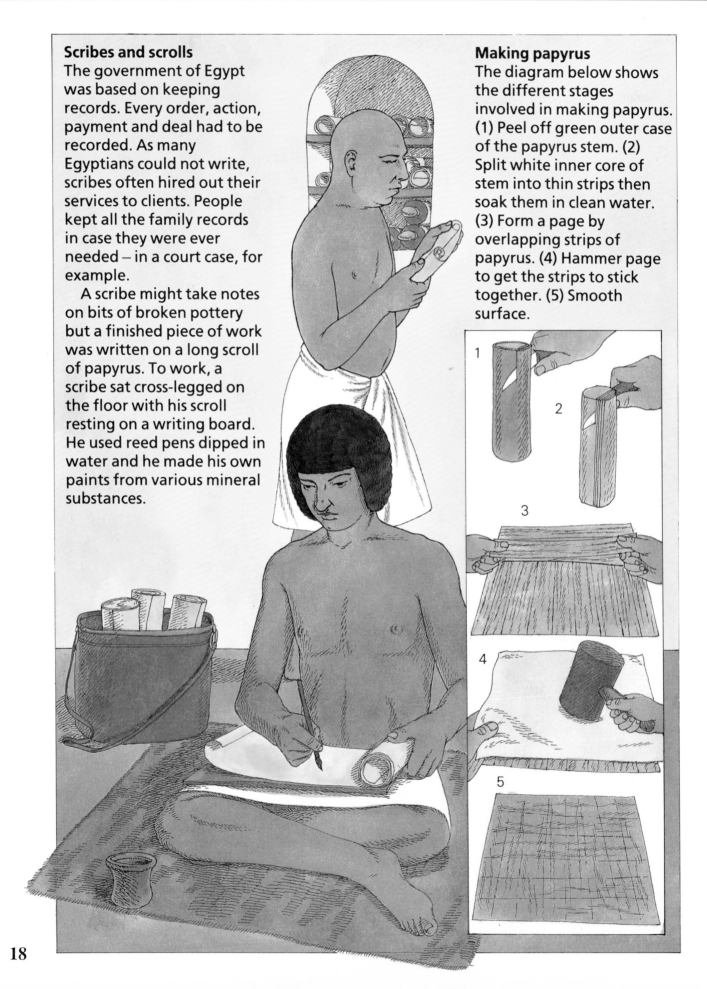

Hieroglyphs

Hieroglyphs, a form of picture writing, appeared in Egypt shortly before the Unification. Some signs represent one letter, some 2,3,4 or 5 letters and yet others actual objects. No punctuation was used. All letters are consonants. The Egyptians did not write down vowels. We have to guess how words sounded with the help of Coptic, ancient Egyptian's descendent, now only used in the Egyptian Christian Church. There were also two scripts for daily use – Hieratic and Demotic.

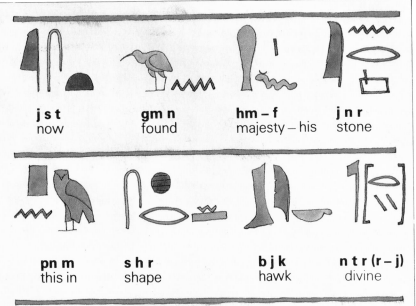

j s t	gm n	hm – f	j n r
now	found	majesty – his	stone

pn m	s h r	b j k	n t r (r – j)
this in	shape	hawk	divine

Translation: His majesty found this stone in the shape of a divine hawk.

Education

Those who could afford it sent their sons to school when the child was about five years old. Girls did not go to school.

First a child had to learn to write. This was done by endlessly copying texts. The more advanced pupils then had to master all the other subjects they would need.

Fun and games

A wide variety of toys like those in the photograph have been found including dolls, tops, balls, models and figures with moving parts. Children and adults enjoyed games played on boards with counters and for the energetic there were many exciting team games.

The army

As in the Old Kingdom, the army of the Middle Kingdom was made up entirely of foot soldiers. They were armed with spears, swords, maces, axes and bows and arrows. As a protection they carried shields but had no armor. The king had a bodyguard and there was a small army of trained, professional soldiers. But when more men were needed for a campaign, officials went out and conscripted men to serve in the army as recruits. It was part of the labor tax all men owed the king.

Egypt's wealth

Papyrus, food, wine, and jewels, like those on the left, were traded for the materials Egypt lacked and for luxuries. Trading was organized by the government.

Byblos (in modern Lebanon) supplied Egypt with timber from its great cedar forests as well as wine, silver, slaves and other goods. Copper and turquoise were mined in Sinai.

Nubia was the source of many of Egypt's slaves and much of its gold, copper and amethyst. Goods from further south — ebony, ivory, ostrich plumes and panther skins — also reached Egypt through Nubia.

In the Middle Kingdom Egypt conquered Nubia. To protect the new frontier, fortresses were built around the Second Cataract. Our picture shows a caravan of trade goods arriving.

The Hyksos invasion

It was the Egyptians' custom to allow nomads from across their eastern frontier to come into the Delta to pasture their flocks. In the 13th Dynasty, Egypt ran into trouble. Disputes over the throne had badly weakened the government. Without strict frontier controls more easterners came in. Finally, using horses and chariots which were not known in Egypt, they conquered most of the land.

These invaders are known as Hyksos, meaning "desert chieftains." At last the princes of Thebes rallied and drove them out.

EMPIRE AT ITS HEIGHT 1567-1085 BC

In the New Kingdom, Egypt was at the height of its power. Having chased the Hyksos out, Egypt went on to conquer a vast empire. The army was enlarged and its soldiers were mostly full-time professionals. Body armor and new weapons were introduced. A chariot squadron was formed which was often led by the king himself.

Egypt's influence was extended from the 4th Cataract of the Nile in the south to the Euphrates River in the east. Nubia and Kush completely adopted Egyptian ways but some of the eastern vassals rebelled against Egyptian rule. In this they were helped by Egypt's great rivals, the Mitanni and the Hittites.

In the reign of Akhenaten the Egyptians lost many of their eastern possessions. Seti I and Ramesses II fought to regain the lost lands but did not succeed in getting them all back.

Incense was vital to the Egyptians. They needed it for temple services and burying their dead. They made long, difficult voyages to Punt (probably in modern Somaliland) to buy incense. In the 18th Dynasty Queen Hatshepsut sent an expedition to buy incense trees so they could be grown in Egypt. The picture shows her officials meeting the Chief of Punt and his wife. They returned home in triumph with incense, trees and other valuable goods.

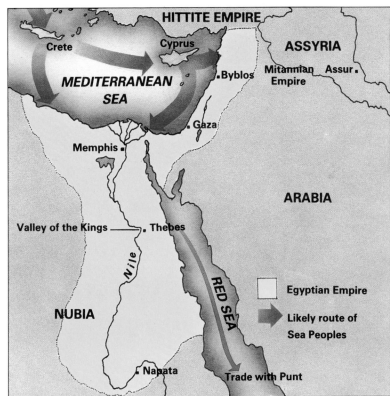

Datechart
NEW KINGDOM

1567-1320 BC 18th Dynasty. Hyksos driven out. Conquest of the empire.

1546-1525 BC The reign of Amenhotep I. He sets up a community of workmen to build the royal tombs.

1526-1512 BC Tuthmosis I has the first tomb cut in the Valley of the Kings.

1503-1482 BC Queen Hatshepsut seizes the throne and rules as king.

1504-1450 BC Tuthmosis III, greatest of Egypt's warrior pharaohs.

1417-1379 BC Empire at its height under King Amenhotep III.

1379-1362 BC Akhenaten – the "heretic" pharaoh. Capital at Amarna where he worships one god but neglects the empire, losing many eastern provinces.

1361-1352 BC Tutankhamun restores old gods.

1348-1320 BC Horemheb reorganizes Egypt.

1320-1200 BC 19th Dynasty. Seti I and Ramesses II win back some of the Eastern empire. Abu Simbel temple built. The Dynasty ends with struggles over the throne.

1200-1085 BC 20th Dynasty. Ramesses III saves Egypt from the Sea Peoples. A period of decline follows.

Egypt at war

When Egypt conquered its empire the fighting was all on land. Ships were used for transport only to speed the army to trouble spots and to spare it tiring marches.

But in the 20th Dynasty Egypt itself was attacked. The enemy was the Sea Peoples. They came from the northeast Mediterranean and were seeking new homes.

They burned many cities and destroyed the Hittite empire. Ramesses III waited at his frontier. He defeated them only after desperate battles on land and sea and so saved Egypt.

Tribute and trade

Once conquered, people had to send tribute to Egypt to prove their loyalty, but they could also continue trading with Egypt. Defeated princes had to send their sons to Egypt as hostages to be brought up as loyal vassals. Foreign princesses were sent to be minor wives of the pharaohs.

The gold mines of Nubia were worked so effectively that one king wrote to the pharaoh asking for gold as in Egypt it was as common as dust! Egyptians became fabulously wealthy. They used their riches to adorn their temples, palaces, houses and bodies and to fill their tombs with treasures.

Gods and temples

The Egyptians worshipped many gods and goddesses, and believed they could visit earth. To persuade them to do so, the Egyptians built elaborate temples decorated with intricate carvings. A splendid example of this can be seen at Abu Simbel (shown right) with huge seated figures guarding the entrance.

Montu Amun   Thoth Khnum Horus Sakhmet   Sobek Anubis   Isis   Osiris   Hathor

Akhenaten and Nefertiti

King Amenhotep IV felt such special devotion to the god Aten (who appeared as the sun's disk) that he changed his name to Akhenaten. He and his wife Nefertiti went to live in a new city, built for Aten's glory. He ordered that no other god was to be worshipped. Akhenaten was so busy with his god that he neglected the empire and so lost many cities to the Hittites. Later generations cursed him as that "heretic" and his god and his city were abandoned.

25

Mummification

The Egyptians believed that if they were going to be able to enjoy the glories of eternal life to the full, their bodies had to be preserved. To achieve this, they invented mummification.

First they removed the internal organs which decay quickly and stored them in jars. The body was then surrounded with a salt which dried it out and so preserved it. Finally the body was wrapped in linen bandages in which jewels and amulets were put. The whole process took up to 70 days and was accompanied by many special prayers. A ceremony called Opening the Mouth gave the dead back all their powers.

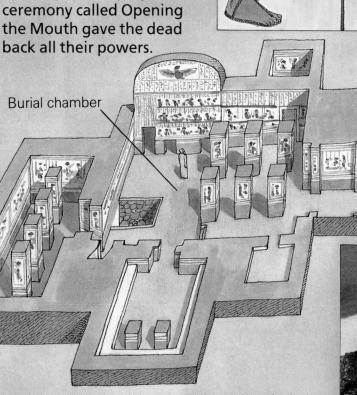

Burial chamber

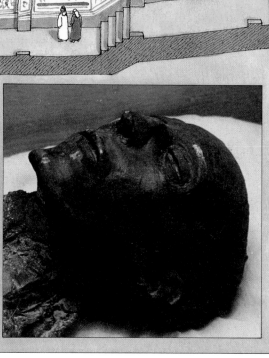

▷ This striking face belongs to Pharaoh Seti I. It is one of the best preserved royal mummies. After the tomb robberies the priests hid the royal mummies together.

The Valley of the Kings

The kings saw that even pyramids provided no real protection against robbers. So in the New Kingdom tombs were cut deep into the sides of a valley on the West Bank at Thebes. This is the famous Valley of the Kings. Members of the royal family also had rock cut tombs in the Valley of the Queens. But the robbers still looted all except Tutan-khamun's tomb.

Tomb of Seti I

The largest tomb in the Valley of the Kings belonged to Seti I. It is decorated with scenes showing how the king would triumph in the Next World.

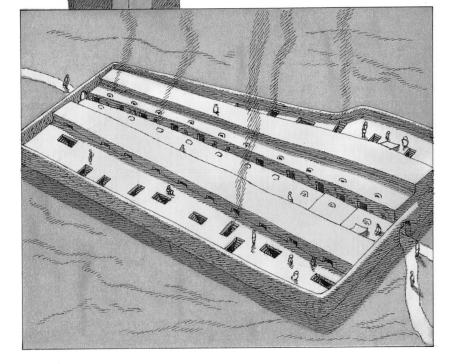

The village of the workmen

The valley now called Deir el Medinah was the home of the workmen who cut and decorated tombs for the royal family and the nobles. A special village, shown in the illustration on the left, was built for them in the desert so they could be near their work. They were well paid by the State for this important work. Other craftsmen who made the objects to go in the tombs, like the goldsmiths above, worked in special workshops attached to the palaces and temples.

27

FOREIGN PHARAOHS 1085 BC-AD 642

One of the worst disasters ever to hit Egypt occurred when it was overrun by the Assyrians, who were cruel and ruthless. When angered by Egypt's Nubian kings and their supporters, the Assyrians sacked Thebes. The city never recovered from its losses despite the loyal efforts of its citizens.

After the triumphs of Ramesses III against the Sea Peoples, Egypt entered into a long period of slow decline. The empire in the east was lost and later Nubia broke away to form a separate kingdom under its own princes. In Egypt officials often became lazy or dishonest and the government was badly run. Robbers looted the royal tombs. Egypt still had wealth, but the power and the glory were gone.

Then rival kings began to struggle for power and, as had happened before under similar circumstances, Egypt fell victim to foreign invaders. First a line of Libyan kings ruled, then Nubians, Assyrians and later Persians. Only during the glorious 26th Dynasty did Egypt have full independence for any length of time and even then several of the kings hired Greek soldiers and allowed Greek merchants to settle.

Ptolemaic Empire at its height

Datechart

3RD INTERMEDIATE PERIOD

1085-945 BC 21st Dynasty. Kings rule from Tanis in the Delta but High Priests of Amun rule the south from Thebes.

945-715 BC 22nd Dynasty. A Libyan family rules from Bubastis.

818-715 BC 23rd and 24th Dynasties overlap with end of 22nd.

728 BC Piankhy, king of Nubia, invades Egypt and founds the 25th Dynasty.

663 BC Sack of Thebes.

LATE PERIOD

664-525 BC 26th Dynasty rules from Saïs.

525-404 BC Rule of Persians as 27th Dynasty.

404-341 BC 28th to 30th Dynasties of native kings.

341-332 BC Return of the Persians.

332 BC Conquest of Egypt by Alexander the Great.

323 BC Death of Alexander.

323-30 BC The Ptolemies rule Egypt.

30 BC Egypt conquered by Rome.

1st century AD Arrival of Christianity in Egypt.

AD 639-642 Conquest by the Arabs. Introduction of Islam.

The royal cities

From 1085 BC the capital was moved as each dynasty rose and fell. First Tanis was favored, then Bubastis and later Saïs. Memphis was also an important center. Even in decline Egypt was still rich and the temples at these cities were magnificent.

Tanis was the capital during the 21st Dynasty. The kings were buried within the Amun temple enclosure with their jewels and vessels of gold and silver. In Thebes the High Priests of Amun ruled and some even took royal titles.

One of the most popular goddesses of the period was Bast. She appeared to her faithful worshippers as a cat (shown in the picture below). She represented the life-giving warmth of the sun but when angered she punished offenders. Her home was in Bubastis.

Magic and medicine

Egyptian doctors were highly respected. A few texts on medicine have survived and we can see that doctors were well-informed and efficient. Because Egyptians were a religious people, every medicine and treatment had to be accompanied by prayers. Doctors realized there were many diseases they could not cure and for those they used magic potions and spells. Magic played an important role in their lives and they used charms to protect and bring good luck.

Mathematics and building

The Rhind Papyrus (photograph right) shows ancient calculations about triangles and pyramids. Such documents indicate that the Egyptians used their mathematical skills in many practical ways.

Mathematics was applied to temple building, for example (shown right). A layer of stone was put in place, the areas between were filled with sand and a short ramp was built. A new layer of stones was dragged into place, and so on until the roof was on.

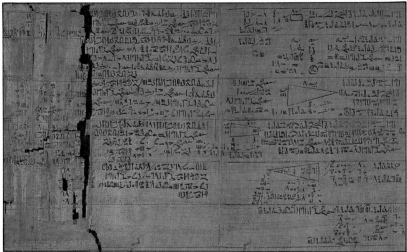

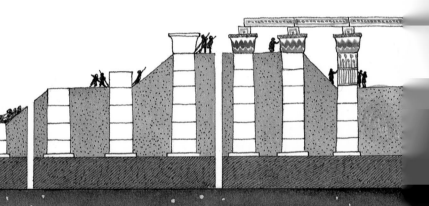

Astronomy

Egyptian priests made a special study of the stars and planets. This enabled them to invent a calendar of 365 days. There were 12 months of 30 days each with five extra days as holy feasts. Each week had 10 days, all with their own star groups. Each day had 24 hours.

The papyrus shown above illustrates one ancient Egyptian story about how the world was made by the creator god, Atum. His two children were Shu (air) and Tefnut (moisture). They too had children – Geb (earth) and Nut (sky). Shu held up Nut so her body arched over Geb her husband. The stars were their children.

FOREIGN PHARAOHS

The Nubian conquerors

The Egyptians and Nubians who ruled Nubia after it had broken away from Egypt held on to their Egyptian ways, particularly their devotion to the god Amun. This picture shows Amun in his ram form with one of the Nubian kings. King Piankhy claimed that Amun had sent him to invade Egypt and restore his worship to its old, pure form.

He and his successors did much to try and revive the greatness of former days. But they angered the Assyrians who took violent revenge. The Nubians fled home once more where they continued to rule.

Alexandria and the Ptolemies

Many Egyptians resented the Persians' rule. Some set themselves up as kings, but the Persians regained control. When Alexander arrived in Egypt during his conquest of the Persian empire, he was hailed as a deliverer and accepted as a true pharaoh. This photograph shows a statue of Alexander as pharaoh.

While in Egypt, Alexander ordered a great city to be built on the coast – Alexandria. The painting shows how it might have looked at this time. It became Egypt's new capital with good harbors and a great lighthouse. It had a theater, a library and a museum. As a center of learning the city was famous throughout the Mediterranean world.

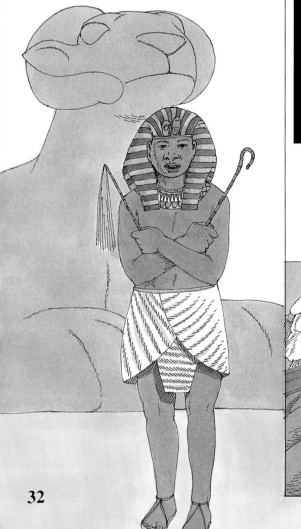

When Alexander died his empire broke up as his generals struggled for power. Ptolemy took over Egypt and founded a new dynasty named after him. In many ways the Ptolemies were a remarkable family and produced some very able rulers. Unfortunately their family feuds were fierce and violent and paved the way for Rome to interfere.

Egypt under Rome

The last ruler of an independent Egypt was Queen Cleopatra. Because of her love for a Roman general, Mark Antony, she became involved in the bitter civil wars which tore Rome apart after the murder of her earlier protector, Julius Caesar. When defeated by Octavian she chose to kill herself. Tradition says she used a venomous snake.

Egypt became just another province of the Roman empire. It was important, however, as its grain was used to feed Rome's hordes of poor citizens. Christianity arrived early in Egypt. It had its saints and martyrs and the first monasteries were set up there. Later when the new Rome was built at Constantinople, Egypt was ruled as part of the Eastern or Byzantine empire until the Arab conquest.

33

LEGACY OF ANCIENT EGYPT

When the Greeks began to visit Egypt they were greatly impressed by its learning, its religion and its monuments. Through the Greeks and the Romans some of Egypt's ancient wisdom has been passed down to us.

The modern world also respects Egypt's ancient culture. Universities study it and archeologists dig there. When the building of the Aswan Dam threatened the monuments in Nubia, countries all over the world helped to mount a massive rescue operation to save them. Thousands of tourists visit Egypt drawn by the grandeur of the ancient civilization. And there is still much to find. New secrets and new objects are being discovered each year.

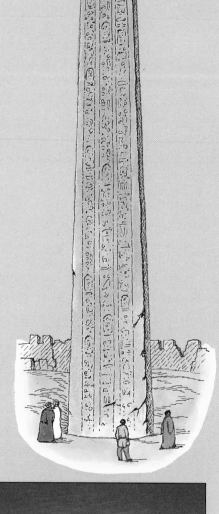

Egyptian treasure

The most famous find of all time was the tomb of the boy king Tutankhamun in 1922. It had been overlooked by the tomb robbers and so still contained his fabulous treasures. The photograph shows the king's death mask.

Egyptian monuments

Obelisks, like the one on the right, were emblems of the sun god and once stood in pairs at temple gates. But few remain in Egypt. They were taken last century to capitals all over the world. But pyramids cannot be moved. They stand like monuments to eternity.

The Nile today
First the British and then the Egyptian governments built dams at Aswan in order to control the waters of the Nile. The modern High Dam at Aswan also provides Egypt with hydro-electric power. But the Nile is still also Egypt's highway. Working barges chug past as tourists drift along and the local ferries pass back and forth as they did in ancient times.

The Rosetta Stone
The meaning of hieroglyphs was lost until the discovery of the Rosetta Stone. It provided the clue that scholars needed to help them decipher the ancient texts. The text of the Rosetta Stone is written three times – in Greek, hieroglyphs and demotic. By using the Greek letters and matching them to the pictures, scholars solved the ancient mystery.

THE
PYRAMIDS

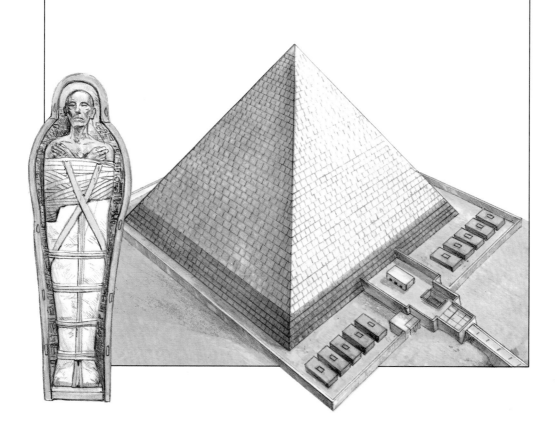

INTRODUCTION

The pyramids, built over 4,500 years ago, were one of the seven wonders of the ancient world. There are more than 70 other pyramids in Egypt and Sudan and the tallest one is 485 feet high. Who built them? How did they organize and pay for such a staggering task? In this *Special Feature* we try to find some of the answers to these questions.

WHY PYRAMIDS?

Pyramids were built to be the permanent tombs of Egypt's kings. Some queens also had pyramids but theirs were very much smaller. Old Kingdom pyramids were built along a stretch of desert, some 29 miles (48 km) long, just west of the city of Memphis. Memphis was Egypt's capital at that time. Now the city has been ruined and buried.

The Egyptians believed pyramids would protect the body of the King and the goods he was taking with him into the next world from robbers. But pyramids had another job to do as well. They were the place from where the soul of the king would go to the sky. Spells written on the walls of later pyramids reveal this. Step pyramids were built as staircases to heaven which the king would climb to reach the stars. In Dynasty IV there was a change in religious beliefs and straight-sided pyramids were built as sunbeams made of stone up which the king would walk to join the sun god.

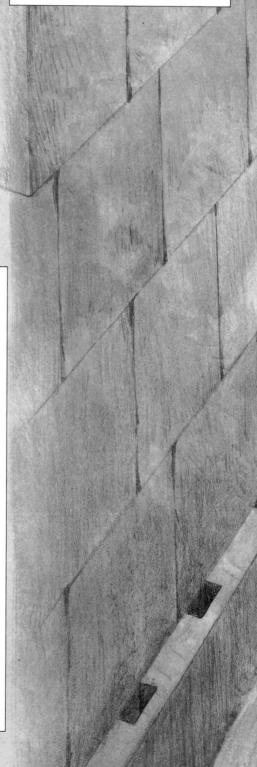

Here the king's body is being taken to its last resting place. The Egyptians did not use wheeled carts so the coffin was dragged on a sled. The coffin was made of stone and cedar wood. The priests chanted prayers because they believed these would help the king up to heaven.

THE GODS

In the Old Kingdom the most important of the gods and goddesses were Re-Harakhte, the sun god, Horus, the sky god, and Hathor, the Great Mother. Ptah was the great craftsman, who created the universe. The common people became very fond of Osiris, their god of the dead, and his wife, Isis. Many of the gods had animal heads and human bodies, like these shown below.

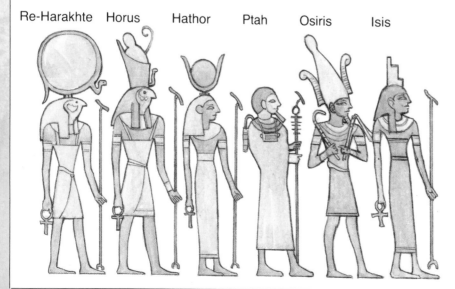

Re-Harakhte Horus Hathor Ptah Osiris Isis

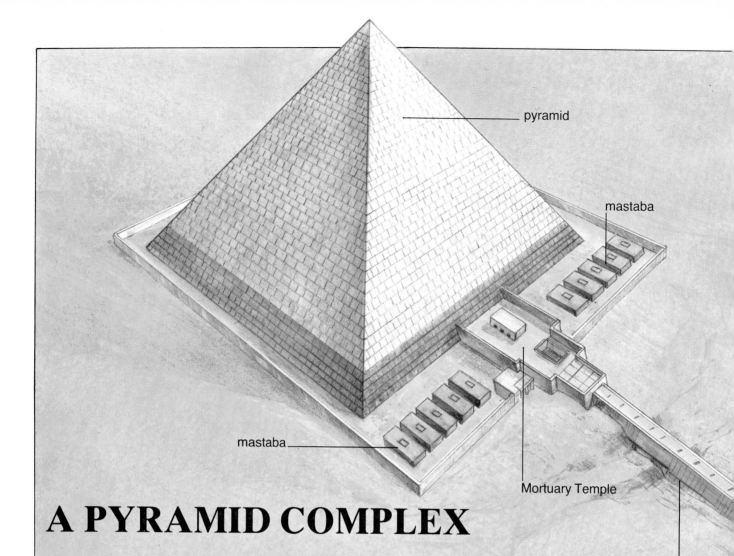

pyramid

mastaba

mastaba

Mortuary Temple

covered causeway

A PYRAMID COMPLEX

Where the desert met the cultivated land of the valley, the Valley Temple was built. There the king's body was prepared for burial and rituals were conducted so his soul could enter his statues and enjoy the offerings placed before them. A causeway (a very long corridor) led up to the Mortuary Temple, built against the east side of the pyramid. There, every day, offerings of food and drink were made for the king's soul. Large estates provided the king with all the provisions he would need for eternity.

The entrance to a pyramid was usually on the north side. From there a passage led down then up to the burial chamber, which was at the center of the base. Apart from one or two side chambers, the rest of the pyramid was solid. A pyramid did not stand alone. Around it were the tombs of the king's family and courtiers. These were smaller rectangular tombs we call mastabas. The queen might have had a small pyramid of her own.

The biggest pyramid of all is at Giza. It belonged to King Khufu of Dynasty IV and it is known as the Great Pyramid. There were several changes of design during its building so it ended up with three chambers, as you can see in the cutaway picture on the right. Only one chamber was used for burial.

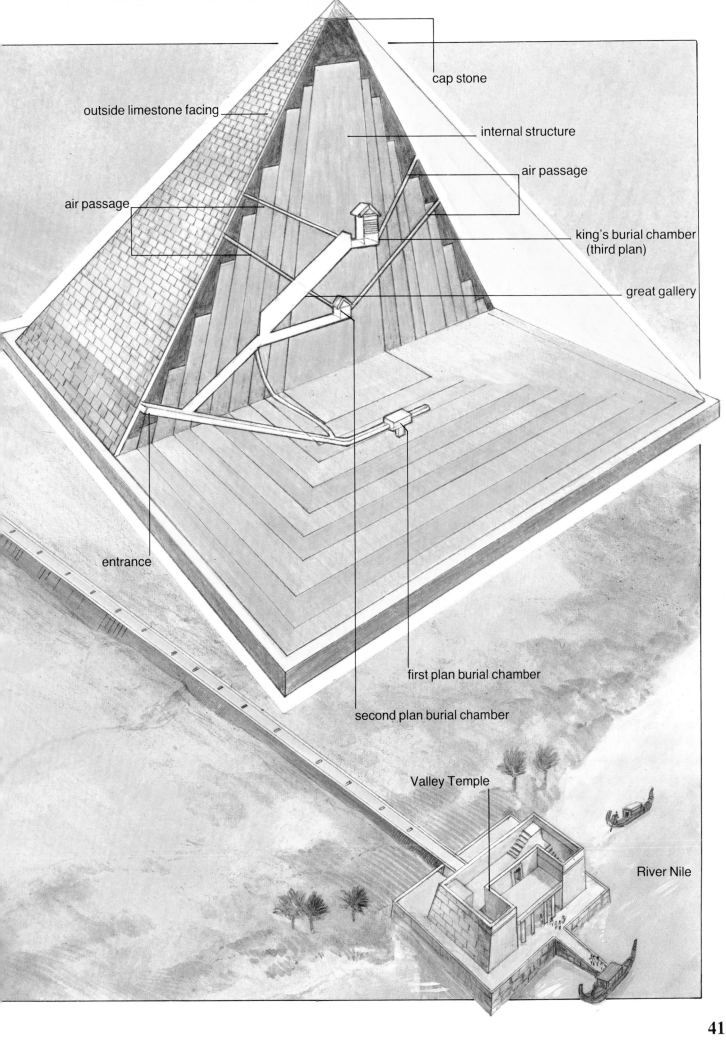

cap stone

outside limestone facing

internal structure

air passage

air passage

king's burial chamber
(third plan)

great gallery

entrance

first plan burial chamber

second plan burial chamber

Valley Temple

River Nile

BUILDING PYRAMIDS

The pyramids were not built by slaves or prisoners of war but by ordinary Egyptians. Because money had not yet been invented, people paid taxes to the king by giving him goods and, at certain times, working for him. When the harvest was safely stored away, thousands of peasant farmers paid their labor tax by helping to build their king's pyramid.

They used sleds and ropes of papyrus (a water plant) to drag the stones into position. Once the bottom layer was in place they built a ramp and brought up the next layer of stone. The ramp was made longer and higher as the pyramid rose. When the top had been reached the whole pyramid was covered with a casing of fine white limestone and the ramp was removed. The masons who cut the casing stones of the Great Pyramid were so skillful that you cannot get a sheet of paper between the stones.

The people worked quite happily because the king fed and clothed them while they labored for him and they knew the work would please the gods. They also believed that, just as the king looked after them in this world, so he would care for them in the next. It was thus very much in the laborers' interests to ensure he got safely into the next world!

THE GIZA PYRAMIDS

Dynasty IV (c2613-2494 BC) kings built the largest pyramids, of which the most famous are the Giza Plateau ones. The kings who built at Giza were:

Khufu (also known by the Greek version of his name, Cheops). His was the first of the Giza pyramids. It is called the Great Pyramid as it is the largest of all. It was finished in about 2565 B.C. It was known as a wonder of the ancient world because of its great size and near perfect pyramid shape. King Khufu had it built to protect his belongings for eternity. However robbers were able to break into it and steal its contents. Later on, in the Middle Ages, people took its outer casing stones away to make buildings in Cairo. Khufu also built some smaller pyramids for his wives. Only the pyramids survive of his pyramid complex – the mastabas, causeway, and temples have all disappeared.

Khafre (the Greek version of his name is Chephren), was the builder of the second pyramid. He was Khufu's son. This pyramid was finished in about 2545 B.C. Although it only slightly smaller than the Great Pyramid, because it was built on higher ground it looks as if it is the same size.

Menkaure (the Greek version of his name is Mykerinus) was the builder of the third pyramid. It had to be finished in a hurry with mud bricks. Its Valley Temple contained a very fine collection of statues.

There are three small queen's pyramids beside Khufu's and three more beside Menkaure's.

CRAFTSMEN

Pictures on the walls of nobles' tombs often show craftsmen making the goods that their masters would need to keep them in comfort throughout eternity. Overseers kept an eye on the work to see it was all up to standard while scribes kept records so no one stole anything!

A small but important group of people in Egypt were the craftsmen. They worked in groups producing the magnificent statues and elegant furniture, the graceful stone vessels and delicate jewelry which were used in the palaces, temples and villas of Egypt. Others built boats, worked in leather, made ropes and bricks.

Stone, semi-precious stones, gold and copper could be found in Egypt. The Giza pyramids were finished with casing stones of limestone from across the Nile. Good timber and silver had to be brought in from foreign lands.

Women were usually in charge of spinning and weaving the flax that made the linen cloth for Egyptian clothes. The best cloth was so fine that it was almost transparent.

The best craftsmen were employed by the king, the temples and the nobles. They were paid for their work in food, beer and wine, linen and oil which they could use or exchange for other goods.

JEWELRY AND TOOLS

This is a falcon made out of gold with obsidian used for eyes. It was probably part of a statue and was found at Hierakonpolis. It shows the art of the goldsmiths.

Iron and bronze were not in use in the Old Kingdom, so craftsmen used tools made of stone, copper and wood. Here are a few of the tools found in tombs.

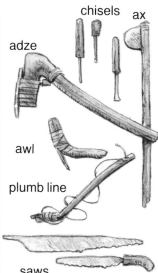

chisels

ax

adze

awl

plumb line

saws

GAMES AND TOYS

This is an Ancient Egyptian board game. It was played with stones and marked sticks. The sticks were like dice. The children threw them to get the number of moves. Children also enjoyed energetic games. Dolls were girls' favorite toys, while boys liked balls and tops. Everyone liked toys with moving parts and ones that could be pulled along. Model animals were also popular.

GROWING UP

Egyptians had to work hard but they knew how to enjoy themselves. Many religious festivals were held. This is the festival known as the "Running of Apis" when the god Ptah sent his spirit into a specially chosen black and white bull. As the bull was led out of the temple the people rejoiced.

Ancient Egyptian parents gave their children plenty of time to play. But even in the rich land of Egypt, farmers had to work hard to survive. This meant that by the age of seven, children were doing simple jobs to help their family.

Unless specially chosen by their lord, children of the Old Kingdom had little chance of going to school. The girls were taught by their mothers how to cook, spin, weave and do other tasks. Cooking consisted of preparing bread, beer, meat, fish and many vegetables. Meanwhile boys were taught by their fathers how to be farmers or craftsmen. Parents chose the husbands and wives of their children. Marriages took place when they were very young – about 15 for a girl and a bit older for a boy. By the standards of the day Egypt had good doctors, but even so life was often short and people wanted to live it to the fullest.

SCRIBES AND SCHOLARS

About the year 3300 B.C. the very first examples of writing appeared in Egypt. The use of writing was a vitally important step in the development of any civilization. It meant people could accurately pass on information and thoughts to future generations without relying on people's imperfect memories. The Egyptian system of running the country involved keeping very detailed written records of everything. The ones who did the writing, the scribes, were very important. In the Old Kingdom, however, a family had to be well off to be able to send a child to school.

Egyptian scholars were famous for their wisdom. They were especially good at medicine, mathematics, engineering and studying the stars. The most famous scholar was Imhotep who designed the first Step Pyramid for King Zoser and was worshipped as a god by later generations.

Scribes and artists cover a tomb wall with texts and pictures. First a grid has been painted on the wall to act as a guide so that every line obeyed the strict Egyptian rules about size and shape. Pictures and hieroglyphs were carved out and painted.

48

HIEROGLYPHS

Hieroglyphs tell us a lot about Egyptian lifestyles. From these symbols archeologists have discovered much about their beliefs, ideas, and everyday concerns. They were recorded on stone, pottery, or papyrus and could be written from left to right, or right to left, or in vertical columns.

49

MUMMIES

△ The picture above shows the wrapped body of a noble found in the tomb of Nefer. It is one of the few Old Kingdom remains to have survived.

▽ The picture below shows the mummy of King Seti I. By the time he was buried, the Egyptians had perfected their skills in preserving bodies. After his tomb had been robbed, the priests secretly reburied his body. The body was not rediscovered until 1871 A.D.

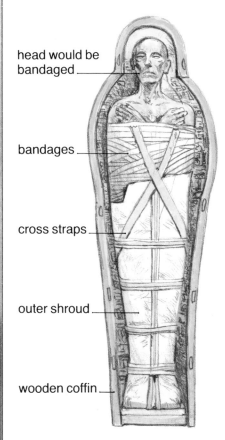

head would be bandaged

bandages

cross straps

outer shroud

wooden coffin

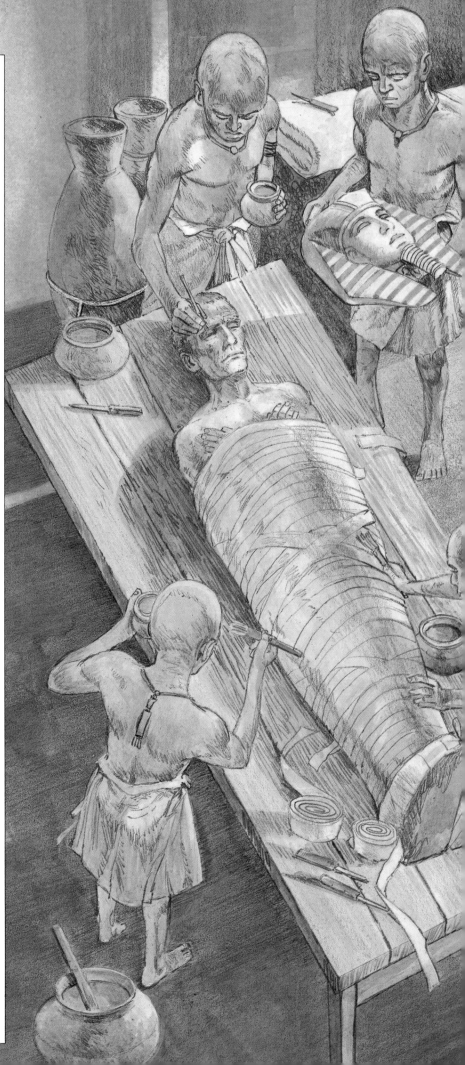

THE NEXT WORLD

Egyptians believed that death was just a gateway to an eternal life in the next world. The kings would join their relatives, the gods, and every day would sail across the sky with the sun god in his sacred boat. The ordinary people would dwell in a land in the West. If they had lived a good life on earth, they would enjoy a happy time in a place that was like Egypt but was without any problems.

Egyptian people believed that after death they would need food and drink and all the other necessities of life. These could be provided either by offerings or by pictures in tombs, which came to life when the right prayers were said. But in order to enjoy all this to the full, they believed that it was necessary for their bodies to survive too and this posed a problem because human bodies naturally decay.

To preserve the body after death, the Egyptians used the process of mummification. Only the bones of the Old Kingdom mummies have survived. First the embalmers removed some of the body's internal organs. Then they washed the body in preserving salts and wrapped it.

51

THE NILE – EGYPT'S LIFELINE

Nobles would go out in their papyrus skiffs with harpoons to catch fish and even hippos and crocodiles for sport. They also used to throw sticks to catch the wild birds that lived in the reeds by the river banks. Those who caught fish and birds for a living used nets – they needed large quantities to sell in the market.

Without the Nile there would be no Egypt but a desert, because it almost never rains there. Only the land which was flooded could be cultivated. Pyramids and graveyards were built on the desert edge so they did not take up any farming land. But the Nile gave Egypt more than just water. It provided fish, reeds and water fowl and was the main route of transportation.

THE NILE TODAY

The Nile is as vital to Egypt today as ever. Now the great Aswan Dam controls the flood waters and makes electricity. The temples at Abu Simbel were threatened by the dam so they were rebuilt on higher ground. The river is still used for carrying heavy loads – machine parts as well as stone – and tourists sail up and down to visit the ancient sites.

Egypt is a long, narrow country with the Nile flowing down the middle. To shift the massive quantities of stone needed to build a pyramid, the Egyptians waited until the flooding so they could float the stones right up to the desert edge and save unnecessary work hauling them across the fields.

Papyrus reeds were useful for making small river boats. Larger ships were built of wood. The best timber was cedar from Lebanon (on the Mediterranean coast). The Egyptians had to import wood regularly.

WHAT HAPPENED TO PYRAMIDS?

Towards the end of the Old Kingdom, pyramids got smaller and were less well made. They had small rough blocks of stone and rubble inside instead of the fine big blocks used at Giza. The Old Kingdom ended in civil war and chaos and, despite all the dangers and difficulties, robbers broke into the pyramids. They stole the treasures and destroyed the kings' bodies.

In the Middle Kingdom order was restored, and in Dynasty XII a new line of powerful kings built themselves pyramids. They were made of mud bricks with a casing of stone. The builders used many tricks to hide the burial chambers from robbers, but none worked and later kings gave up building pyramids.

Some New Kingdom nobles and even middle class craftsmen began to build tiny pyramids over their tombs, but it was not a style that lasted long. Then, far to the South, in what is now the Sudan, the local kings, heavily influenced by Egypt, began building brick pyramids as their tombs.

Thieves break into the tomb of a long-dead king. When the kings' rule was weak, men began robbing tombs. It was a crime punishable by death. But the treasure in the royal tombs and even in nobles' tombs was so rich that the robbers could not resist.

54

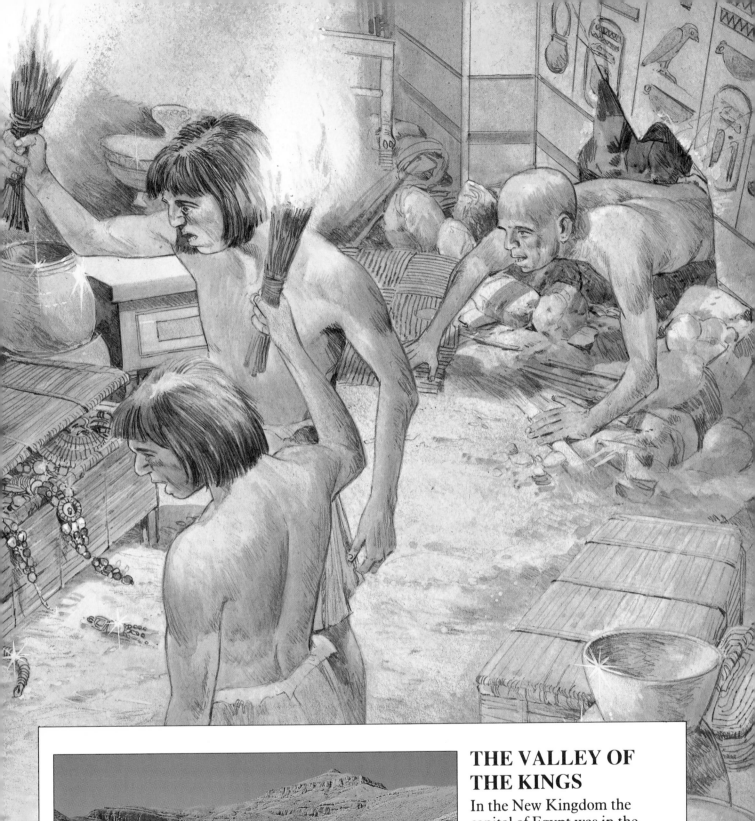

THE VALLEY OF THE KINGS

In the New Kingdom the capital of Egypt was in the southern city of Thebes (modern Luxor). The kings were buried there in rock-cut tombs in the Valley of the Kings. They may have chosen this place because the mountain that towers above is pyramid shaped. The Kings probably wanted to be buried beneath this sacred symbol.

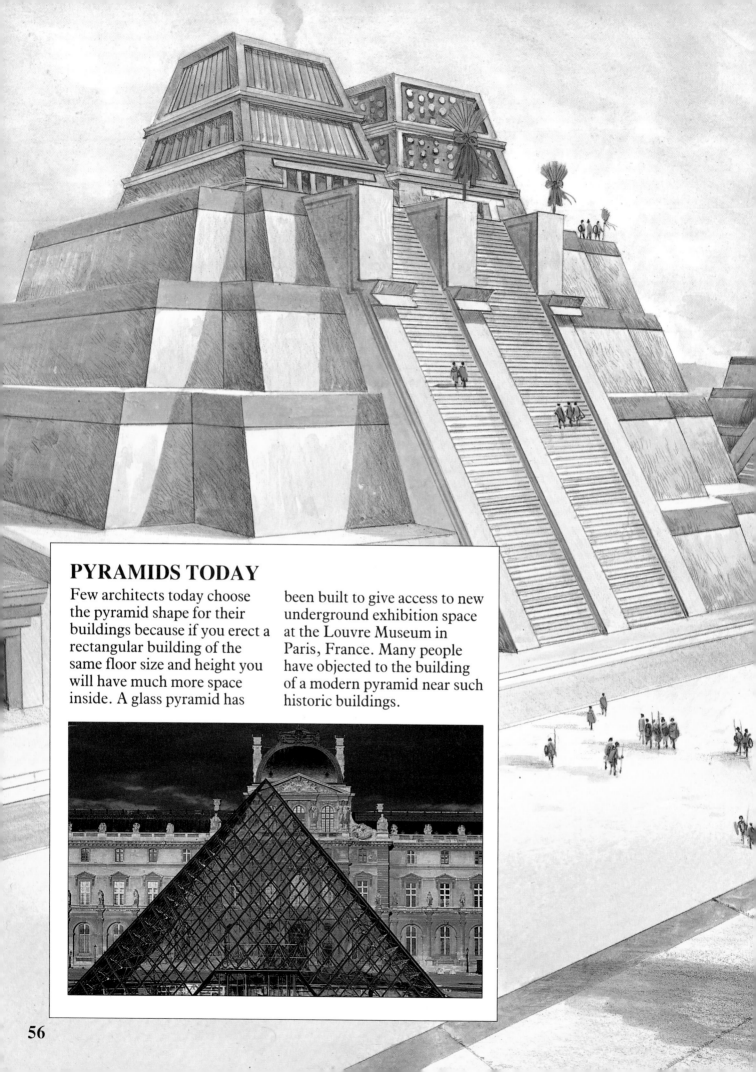

PYRAMIDS TODAY

Few architects today choose the pyramid shape for their buildings because if you erect a rectangular building of the same floor size and height you will have much more space inside. A glass pyramid has been built to give access to new underground exhibition space at the Louvre Museum in Paris, France. Many people have objected to the building of a modern pyramid near such historic buildings.

PYRAMIDS WORLDWIDE

The peoples of South America offered their gods human sacrifices. In the Aztec capital Tenochtitlàn hundreds of victims were killed on the temple altars.

Apart from the Sudanese, who were influenced by Egyptian culture, none of the Egyptians' contemporaries built pyramids, so they remain a uniquely Egyptian symbol. Many hundreds of years after the Egyptians had finished with pyramid building entirely, halfway round the world, the people of South America started building a kind of pyramid of their own without ever having heard of Egypt!

The great stone pyramids of the Incas of Peru and the Aztecs of Mexico had flattened tops, not points as in true pyramids. They had steps that led to the flat tops where they built temples to their gods. South American pyramids therefore look completely different from Egyptian ones and were built for a different purpose. The Incas and Aztecs were at the height of their power toward the end of the period which we call the Middle Ages in Europe.

DATE CHARTS

All dates for the Old Kingdom are approximate.

c. 5000-3100 B.C. Predynastic Period. Small communities of farmers gradually united to form two kingdoms – Upper and Lower Egypt. The King of Upper Egypt wore the White Crown and his capital was Hierakonpolis. The king of Lower Egypt wore the Red Crown and his capital was at Buto.

c. 3100-2686 Archaic Period (Dynasties I-II). Menes, King of Upper Egypt, conquered Lower Egypt and united the two lands. He built a new capital at Memphis. Royal tombs of mud brick mastabas built at Abydos and Sakkara.

c. 2558-2533 Khafre rules Egypt.

c. 2533-2505 Menkaure is Pharaoh.

c. 2181-2040 First Intermediate Period (Dynasties VII-X) Collapse of kings' rule; wars and famine.

c. 2040-1684 The Middle Kingdom (Dynasties XI-XIII) Egypt reunited by a Prince of Thebes (modern Luxor).

c. 1684-1567 Second Intermediate Period (Dynasties XIV-XVII). Another period of chaos. Invasion by foreigners we call Hyksos, who ruled northern Egypt.

Sais
Alexandria
Buto
Tanis
The Delta
LOWER EGYPT
(CAIRO)
Red Crown
GIZA ▲
Memphis
SAKKARA ▲
Faiyum
River Nile
RED SEA
White Crown
▲ **Pyramids**
Abydos
Thebes (Luxor)
Valley of the Kings
UPPER EGYPT
Hierakonpolis
Aswan
Ist Cataract

EUROPE
▲ Paris (Louvre)
ASIA
AMERICAS
AFRICA
▲ Aztecs
▲ Incas

c. 2686-2181 The Old Kingdom (Dynasties III-VI). One of the greatest period's of Egypt's long history.

c. 2686-2613 King Zoser

c. 2613-2589 Sneferu ruled Egypt.

c. 2589-2566 Khufu becomes Pharaoh.

c. 1567-1085 The New Kingdom (Dynasties XVIII-XX). Hyksos driven out by the Princes of Thebes, who then ruled a united Egypt from Thebes. Kings buried in rock-cut tombs in the Valley of the Kings at Thebes.

c. 1318-1304 Seti I is Pharaoh.

NUBIA
N
SUDAN

AFRICA	ASIA	AMERICAS	EUROPE
3000 B.C. Egypt already a united nation. Metal and writing both in use.	**3000 B.C.** City states in Mesopotamia, using metal and writing. Farming in China.	**3000 B.C.** Corn cultivated by South American farmers.	**3000 B.C.** People of France and British Isles building stone circles. Development of metal industry in Greece and Crete.
2700 Beginning of Egyptian Old Kingdom. Step pyramids built.	**2700** Silk weaving and bronze work in China. Indus Valley culture in India develops.		
2600 Straight-sided pyramids built.		**2600** Temple mounds on coasts of Peru.	
2500 Increasing drying up of Sahara.	**2500** Growth of cities in Indus Valley. Use of writing. Cotton cloth made there. Royal Graves of Ur.	**2500** Improved farming and weaving techniques. Use of irrigation.	**2500** Bell beaker culture.
	2300 Sargon of Akkad unites southern Mesopotamian cities into an empire.	**2300** Pottery in Mesoamerica. In Mexico farming people build permanent villages.	**2300** Bronze Age.
	2230 Akkad invaded by Gutians.		
2150 End of Old Kingdom			
2000 Beginning of Dynasty XII		**2000** Early Eskimo culture stretches from Greenland to Siberia.	**2000** Main building phase of Stonehenge.
			1900 Construction of great palaces on Crete. Use of writing.
	1800 On the Steppes, horses first used to pull carts, then used in Near East to pull chariots. Rise of Babylon. Hsia dynasty rules in China.		
1700 Middle Kingdom collapses. Hyksos invade.			
	1600 Hittites settled in Anatolia. They form an empire from the Mediterranean to the Persian Gulf.		**1600** Rise of Mycenae (Greece).
1550 New Kingdom established.		**1550** First metal working in Peru.	* Note: all dates are approximate.

59

CONTENTS
CHINA

INTRODUCTION 62
THE AGE OF CONFLICT 1400-221 BC 64
Confucius – Laozi and Taoism – Writing – Bronze Casting
Burials – The Family – Ancestor Worship
THE FIRST EMPIRE 221 BC-AD 618 70
Qin Shihuang – The Great Wall – Life at Court – The Jade Prince
Medicine – Papermaking – Science and Technology
THE GOLDEN AGE AD 618-1368 76
Town life – Theater – The Life of Women – Justice
Buddhism – Trade Routes – Poetry
IMPERIAL SPLENDOR AD 1368-1911 82
The Emperor and the People – Agriculture – Porcelain
Exploration – The Jesuits – Opium – The Boxer Rebellion
"LET THE PAST SERVE THE PRESENT" 88

ENCYCLOPEDIA OF GREAT CIVILIZATIONS

CHINA

INTRODUCTION

China is the world's most populous country. Its written history dates back over more than 3,000 years, and the Chinese people today are the proud inheritors of a civilization which produced some of the world's finest works of literature and art.

Society in ancient China was divided into aristocrats and common people. Emperors had absolute power over their subjects. Farmers and town dwellers paid taxes of grain and goods to support the government and army. For over 2,000 years, the ideas of Confucius, a philosopher of the sixth century BC, shaped Chinese life. Confucius taught that subjects must obey their rulers and sons must obey their fathers.

The story of China's past starts with myths about the earliest kings. Their heroic and virtuous lives provided an important role-model for later emperors. Until comparatively recently, Chinese government was more concerned to imitate the sages of antiquity than to deal with the world beyond the middle kingdom, as China's name, *Zhong guo*, means.

This book describes important scenes in China's past. It is divided into four periods: from the earliest historical times until China was united under one ruler in 221 BC; the first empires; China's golden age, leading into the time of Mongol domination; and the late imperial period, the Ming and Qing dynasties.

Peking man

The most famous forebears of the Chinese nation were a hunting nomadic group who lived over 500,000 years ago – Peking man. Their remains were discovered by archeologists in 1927. Before then, nothing was known about hunters like the one in the picture, who ate fish and meat and used tools of bone and stone. Peking man was followed by the first farmers, who learned to grow millet and rice and lived in settled communities.

THE AGE OF CONFLICT 1400-221 BC

The earliest historical evidence of Chinese civilization points to the lavish life of the nobility in about 1500 BC. Excavations show that when powerful men died, their servants and belongings were buried with them. Rival kingdoms controlled large parts of the country and wars constantly broke out between them. By the fourth century BC, some smaller states were being defeated and absorbed by their stronger neighbors. Finally in the third century BC, the Qin dynasty imposed control over all China.

A writing system was developed at this time which is clearly related to the way Chinese is written today. Impressive bronze vessels were cast, and iron farm tools were used from the 7th century onwards. Scientific achievements of the time included large-scale irrigation works and astronomical observations.

Weapons, armor and chariot fittings of bronze were used in fierce inter-state battles after Zhou toppled Shang. Known to Chinese historians as the "Warring States" era, this was a time when commoners were conscripted into state armies. Many stories are told of the cunning strategies used by contenders for power against their rivals.

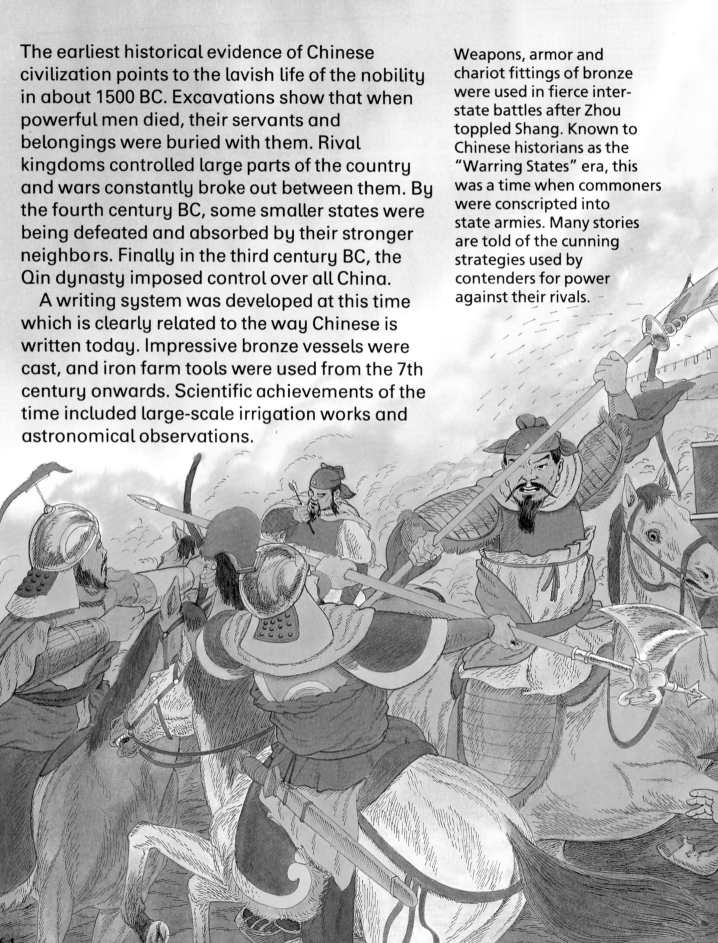

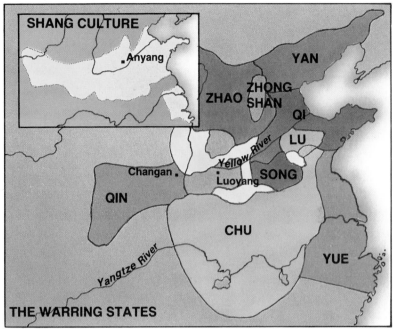

SHANG CULTURE

·Anyang

YAN

ZHONG
SHAN

ZHAO

QI

LU

Yellow River

Changan ·

·
Luoyang

SONG

QIN

CHU

YUE

Yangtze River

THE WARRING STATES

DATECHART

c5000-2000 BC Neolithic period. Agricultural communities with domesticated animals grew up, using decorated baked earthenware pots. No written records survive.

c1500 BC Priests use cracks in heated animal bones to predict the future, writing with symbols related to today's Chinese characters.

c1500-1100 BC The heartland of early Chinese civilization, the Yellow River valley of northwest China, sees the rise of China's first historically recorded rulers, the Shang.

c1400 BC Shang moves its capital to Anyang, a symmetrical city of square buildings where bronze-casting is developed into a highly refined art.

1027 BC King Wu of Zhou overthrows the Shang and founds the Zhou dynasty.

770 BC After invasions by western barbarians, Zhou moves the capital east to Luoyang.

c700 BC Iron is used to make farm tools for the first time.

551 BC Confucius, China's most influential philosopher, is born.

403-221 BC Rival kingdoms fight for control of China, giving rise to the name "Warring States" for this period.

4th and 3rd centuries BC In the west of the country, the state of Qin grows in power and after absorbing Han, Zhao, Wei, Chu and Yan, Qin unifies China in 221 BC.

THE AGE OF CONFLICT

Confucius

Kong Fu zi (Master Kong, or Confucius in Latin) was a traveling philosopher who gave advice to the lords of the warring kingdoms. He taught that kings of past times had ruled by setting a good example to the common people. His book, the *Analects*, influenced politicians and scholars for centuries after his death. His disciples included Mencius, who taught that human nature was basically virtuous.

Laozi and Taoism

In contrast to the followers of Confucius, Laozi believed that politics was a futile activity. Laozi taught that the *Tao*, or "Way," reflected the patterns of nature. Taoists (followers of the Way) said that inactivity and contemplation were the only possible course of action for a wise man. Laozi, shown here contemplating nature, wrote a treatise on the Way and thought that people who bustle about trying to improve the world are fools. His philosophy advocated doing nothing ("wu wei") and achieving harmony with nature.

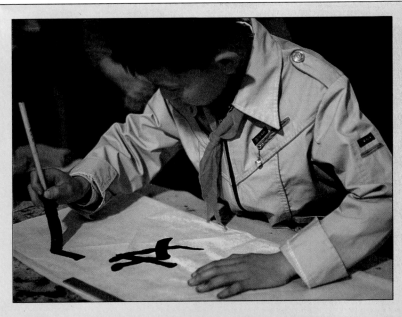

Writing

Chinese writing today is closely based on the pictorial characters of Shang times. Beginning by portraying objects (as in the characters for water and field) the writing system built up the ability to convey complicated and abstract ideas. Chinese people have always admired fine calligraphy. The photograph shows a child practicing calligraphy in the traditional way.

	Ancestor	Then (Man and bowl)	Prayer	Earth	Field	Water	Pot
Ancient							
Modern	祖	就	祝	土	田	水	鼎

Bronze casting

From Shang times, bronze vessels were cast in a marvelous variety of shapes and guises. No one knows how the Chinese first learned to make elaborate bronze vessels over 3,000 years ago. But we do know that beautiful, complicated pots, decorated with animal faces and abstract designs, were used for the ceremonies which dominated court life. They were used in sacrifices to the gods, for example. Ordinary people never used bronzes. The picture shows craftsmen preparing molten bronze, ready to mold the hot liquid metal into utensils for ritual use.

THE AGE OF CONFLICT

Burials

The early Chinese believed that after death, spirits pass into an afterlife. The spirit had to be in a place with good omens, protected from evil spirits. It was also important for the dead to have their belongings buried alongside them. They needed to be cared for after death in a way which reflected their status in life. Rich people had food and wine vessels and weapons buried with them. This picture shows a nobleman's tomb with horses and servants. A dissatisfied spirit would bring unhappiness to his family. In the case of a king, his subjects would suffer if the tomb was not fine enough.

The family

Confucius' teaching lies at the root of China's traditional family structure. He taught that women had to obey men, and the young must obey the old. Brides always went to live with their husband's family.

Ancestor worship

Because the Chinese believe that ancestors watch over the family from beyond the grave, they have always made offerings to dead relatives to ensure that their souls are at peace. In ancient times, even the poorest households kept a shrine like the one in the picture. At New Year, the Chinese family still gathers around and bows deeply in a *kowtow*, to show respect for the ancestors. Since people believed that emperors were like fathers to their subjects, sacrifices to the royal ancestors were especially important. They affected both the emperor's family and the whole country.

Confucius taught that children must be devoted to their parents. Widows were supposed to be eternally chaste, never remarrying. The Chinese family in the photograph still expects the father to be head of the household.

THE FIRST EMPIRE 221 BC-AD 618

Although China was often divided after the first unification in 221 BC, the ideal of one nation ruled by an emperor who was "son of heaven" was never forgotten. The harsh policies of Qin did not last long. Soon the Han took power and ruled with one short interruption for almost 400 years. Envoys were sent to the barbarian kingdoms in the west and pacified the border areas. Philosophers and politicians set up a system of government which lasted for centuries. Taxes were imposed on the whole country and goods were sent from the rich lands of the south to the court, which moved east from Changan to Luoyang in 25 AD.

When the Han collapsed, 300 years of division and civil war followed. The second emperor of the dynasty which reunited the country, the Sui, was Yangdi. He left a permanent legacy to future governments in the shape of a waterway linking the Yangtze delta to the north – the Grand Canal.

Believing that the dead required protection as much as the living, the first emperor of China, Qin Shihuang, made elaborate preparations for building his own tomb. His actual burial chamber has not yet been uncovered, but several enormous pits containing life-size terracotta warriors have been excavated by archeologists. The warriors were lined up to defend the emperor from hostile forces. The picture shows one of several enormous antechambers with thousands of warriors and horses. A huge pottery produced the tomb figures, no two of which are identical.

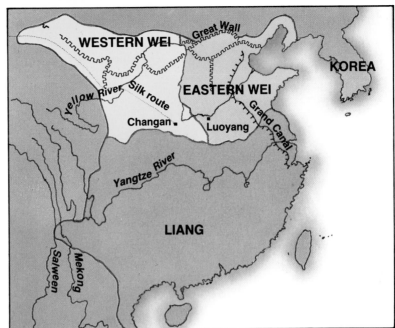

DATECHART

221-211 BC Qin rules China, unifying weights and measures and building roads.

214 BC Sections of defensive walls in north and northwest China are joined to form the Great Wall. It acts as a protection against invaders known as Huns (Chinese *Xiongnu*).

210 BC After the death of the first emperor of Qin, uprisings spread throughout the country.

202 BC The Han, a new ruling house, is founded, proclaiming a return to the ways of the earliest kings.

138-115 BC Zhang Qian, a Han minister, makes two journeys to the far west as part of a determined attempt to quell the *Xiongnu* invaders.

c120-90 BC Sima Qian writes the first official history, the *Records of the Historian*.

AD 25 The later or western Han regime is founded after a period of civil war.

AD 105 Paper is invented by Cai Lun.

AD 220 Cao Cao, a powerful general, defeats the Han and China splits into three kingdoms.

cAD 375-406 Gu Kaizhu lived, China's earliest known great painter.

AD 420-581 The country is divided into rival kingdoms in the north and south.

AD 581 After over 300 years, China is reunified.

AD 605-610 The Grand Canal is built.

THE FIRST EMPIRE

Qin Shihuang

The first unifier of China (Qin Shihuang means "first emperor of the Qin") was a ruthless leader who was both cruel and talented. He believed that the emperor should rule by force, and punished anyone who displeased him. At the same time, his tough government made useful changes, like standardizing the writing system. He is condemned in China for the episode in the picture. He buried scholars alive and burned ancient books. He was particularly scornful of Confucians, thinking them weak and unrealistic. He favored a philosophy called "Legalism," which rewarded and punished different kinds of behavior.

The Great Wall

Qin Shihuang also left a legacy of achievement. He joined up fortifications in the north to make the Great Wall.

The Wall was designed to protect China from the raids of the *Xiongnu*. The picture shows laborers at work beating the earth to make the wall's base.

Life at court

The emperor ruled with the assistance of ministers and officials. He had absolute power, and was surrounded by feuding factions hoping to increase their wealth and influence; intrigue at court was a recurring problem. But nobles and courtiers enjoyed a brilliant and lively way of life. Jugglers and acrobats like the one in our picture performed at sumptuous banquets. They were accompanied by musicians playing flutes and drums. From models found in tombs, we know that singers and dancers often performed at feasts for the rich. Upper-class families owned large estates and loved hunting and falconry. They wore fine robes of embroidered silks and women had jewelry of gold and precious stones.

The jade prince

The suit in the picture is made of jade, a beautiful green stone which the Chinese believed acted as a preservative. It was made for the burial of a Han prince and shows how the luxury which aristocrats enjoyed in life went with them to the grave.

THE FIRST EMPIRE

Medicine

Texts from 2,000 years ago show that Chinese doctors had found paths in the body which responded to stimulation by needles. Acupuncture, the science of healing by applying needles, has been used by the Chinese ever since. The picture shows an acupuncture path in the arm. Chinese doctors thought illness could result from too much fire or sluggishness in the body. Heat and cold were part of the patterns of *yang* (male) and *yin* (female), the basic forces running through the universe.

Science and technology

China is the home of many important scientific advances. Enormous engineering feats like the Great Wall and the Grand Canal (shown in the photograph being used today) are well known. But the inventive Chinese also used magnetic compasses and wheelbarrows as early as the Han dynasty. The abacus, a kind of early calculator, was in use in the second century. Astronomers noted comets and eclipses, and engineers built roads and bridges, spurred on by the court's need for efficient communications with all corners of the empire. The illustration shows an impressive system of salt-mining used in the southwest.

Papermaking

Ancient tradition says that Cai Lun invented paper in the first century. Before then, wood and silk were used for writing on. Paper-making, a complicated process illustrated in these scenes from a technical manual, later spread to the west. Printing from wooden blocks is also a Chinese invention. It allowed books to reach large numbers of people because printing is cheaper than writing by hand. The earliest printed book in the world was produced in China.

Cutting and soaking bamboo

Cooking the mixture

Dipping mold into pulp

Pressing wet paper

Drying on hot wall

THE GOLDEN AGE AD 618-1368

The Tang and Song periods saw Chinese culture assuming many of the features it was to retain for the rest of the imperial era. Officials were selected through stiff competitive examinations on Confucian texts. Literary forms – poems, ballads and essays – became fixed. Painters produced fine scrolls. Most of the population lived on the land, but cities also grew up with lively pleasure quarters. There were often rebellions, especially when court life became so lavish that high taxes were needed to support it! This was also the age when courtiers and commoners were devout followers of the Buddhist religion, and when monasteries and temples amassed great wealth. Civil wars broke out in the 10th and 13th centuries. The court had to abandon north China when Mongol power grew in China and throughout the world.

Wen Tianxiang
Many Chinese were devastated when the Song court moved south. A courageous soldier, Wen Tianxiang, fought against the Mongols. But the Song were no match for the Mongol horsemen. Wen was captured, imprisoned and executed. Here he refuses to bow to the Mongols.

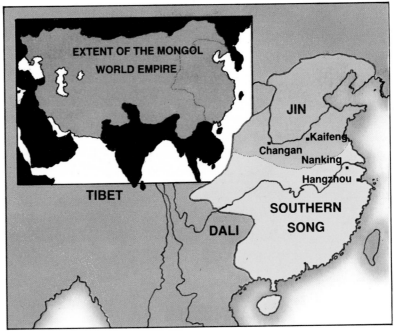

EXTENT OF THE MONGOL WORLD EMPIRE

JIN

Kaifeng

Changan
Nanking

Hangzhou

TIBET

DALI

SOUTHERN SONG

DATECHART

618 The second emperor of the Sui, Yangdi, is assassinated and a new dynasty, the Tang, is founded.

621 A system of competitive civil service examinations is founded. It lasted, with modifications, until the end of imperial times.

755 After a period when culture and the economy flourished to an unprecedented degree, the Tang regime is rocked by the rebellion of An Lushan.

907-960 The Tang finally collapses. A period of civil war follows.

960 Zhao Kuangyin founds the Song dynasty, with its capital at Kaifeng on the Yellow River.

1138 A long period of trouble on the northern borders leads to the capture of north China by the Jurched, a nation of horse-riding warriors. The Song court is forced to flee south to Hangzhou.

1279 After years of war, remnant Song forces surrender to the Mongols under Kubilai Khan, who founds the Yuan dynasty. Gradually the Mongols fall under Chinese influence, and adopt Chinese ways of life.

1275-1292 Marco Polo visits China in the service of Kubilai Khan. His account of the fabulous riches of Cathay enthralled Europeans.

1368 The peasant rebel Zhu Yuanzhang founds the Ming dynasty and drives the Mongols out of China. He establishes the new dynastic capital at Nanking.

THE GOLDEN AGE

Town life

In Tang and especially Song times, cities had grown to an enormous size. Musicians and singers entertained crowds at market places. Peddlers called out their wares, and visitors from all over the country bought fine foods, fabrics and pots at busy market stalls. The city of Changan was the capital of the Tang court. It had a million people and was built on a grid plan on a north-south axis. The palace, facing south, was seen as the symbolic and actual center of the Chinese empire and of the world itself. The luxurious life of the court went on alongside the humble existence of innkeepers, carters and tradesmen. Craftsmen like silk weavers and silversmiths produced goods for the wealthy consumers of the time. Rich men amused themselves with wine and dancing girls.

Theater

Entertainment flourished in the towns. Markets attracted ballad singers and storytellers. At inns and taverns, working men and soldiers gathered to relax. Opera troupes, like the one in the illustration, would travel from city to city. Performances were brilliant spectacles, with gorgeous costumes and loud music. In Yuan times, rules for opera dress, movement and make-up were formal. The actor in the photograph is applying make-up in the traditional way, using bright colors that help the audience to identify her character.

The life of women

In classical China, women lived to serve and obey their husbands. Women had to cook and look after children, and were not expected to learn to read and write. Court ladies were restricted to their quarters. Many rich men had more than one wife. It was common from Song times onwards for women to bind their feet small, making walking painful. This cruel practice persisted until the early 20th century.

Justice

Ordinary citizens were terrified of the power of government officials. Many stories and operas describe how a suspect could be cruelly punished at the command of a magistrate. Our picture shows prisoners locked into a "cangue" (the Chinese equivalent of the stocks in Europe).

THE GOLDEN AGE

Buddhism
Buddhism is a major world religion. It originated in India in the sixth century BC, and entered China from the west around the first century AD. Buddhists believe that life is an illusion and that we are all born and die many times, in different incarnations. Chinese from all walks of life became Buddhists. Artists made wonderful paintings and carved monumental images of the Buddha on cliff faces to prove their devotion and piety. Our picture shows a massive sculpture of the Buddha in Sichuan, south-west China.

Trade routes
For centuries, caravans laden with fine silks and other desirable goods made dangerous journeys.

Poetry

Our picture shows the Song emperor Huizong, who reigned 1101-1126, and the photograph is of one of his paintings. Like most Chinese aristocrats, the emperor composed poetry and practiced calligraphy. The Tang and Song periods produced some of China's most famous writers. Their poems describe the beauty of nature and the hardships endured by the common people, contrasted with the corruption and greed of some officials. These poems are still read and loved by Chinese people today.

They traveled overland from metropolitan China through central Asia to the middle east. The caravans took camels to survive the arid conditions on the way. Ideas and cultural influences were exchanged along the trade routes. Marco Polo traveled overland to China from Italy in the 13th century in the service of the Mongols.

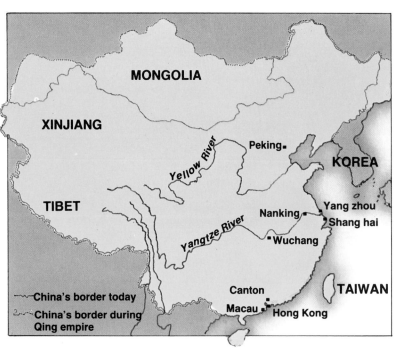

MONGOLIA

XINJIANG

Yellow River

Peking

KOREA

TIBET

Yangtze River

Nanking

Yang zhou

Shang hai

Wuchang

Canton

TAIWAN

Macau

Hong Kong

~~~ China's border today

~~~ China's border during Qing empire

DATECHART

1368-1398 After chasing the Mongols from China, the founder of the Ming dynasty, Zhu Yuanzhang, consolidates his control over the entire country.

1405 The great navigator Zheng He leads voyages of exploration.

1408 The Yongle emperor sponsors the great *Yongle dadian*, an encyclopedia having over 22,000 volumes.

1421 The capital is moved from Nanking to Peking and the court takes up residence in the Forbidden City.

1644 After growing in strength for decades, Manchu forces from the northeast take Peking and found the Qing dynasty. Nurhaci, their leader, becomes the first emperor of the Qing.

1715-1763 Cao Xueqin, author of China's best-loved novel, *Dream of the Red Chamber*, lives in an impoverished aristocratic family.

1755-59 The Qing empire's borders expand westward. China absorbs Xinjiang province.

1839-1842 China is humiliated by the western powers in the Opium Wars. Many coastal cities later come under foreign control.

1850-64 Taiping rebellion: south China undergoes upheaval and carnage as rebels try to defeat the Manchus.

1900 Anti-foreign sentiment erupts in north China.

1911 Fall of the Manchu dynasty; founding of the Republic of China.

IMPERIAL SPLENDOR AD 1368-1911

For over 150 years, China was the eastern flank of the great Mongol world empire. Then the country was reclaimed for the native Han Chinese by a dynasty which took the name Ming, meaning "bright." China entered a period of stability. With its own traditions of medicine, warfare, transportation and the arts, China felt little desire for contact with the outside world.

In 1421 the Yongle emperor moved the court north to Peking, which has been the seat of most Chinese governments ever since. The early 17th century saw the rise of a new power, the Manchus. After defeating the Ming, the Manchus abandoned their nomadic lifestyle and became absorbed into Chinese traditions. Their Qing dynasty ruled China well for 200 years. When western powers demanded to expand trade in the 19th century, the Qing could not resist.

The imperial palace in Peking is known as the Forbidden City because commoners were not allowed to enter. It was first built in the 15th century. In the picture, the emperor walks past his courtiers.

83

IMPERIAL SPLENDOR

The emperor and the people
Every Chinese owed absolute obedience to the emperor. As "son of heaven," the emperor's life was attended by elaborate pomp and many ceremonies.

On the rare occasions the emperor left the palace, courtiers would ensure that ordinary people kept their distance. His procession would include rare and exotic animals. Special

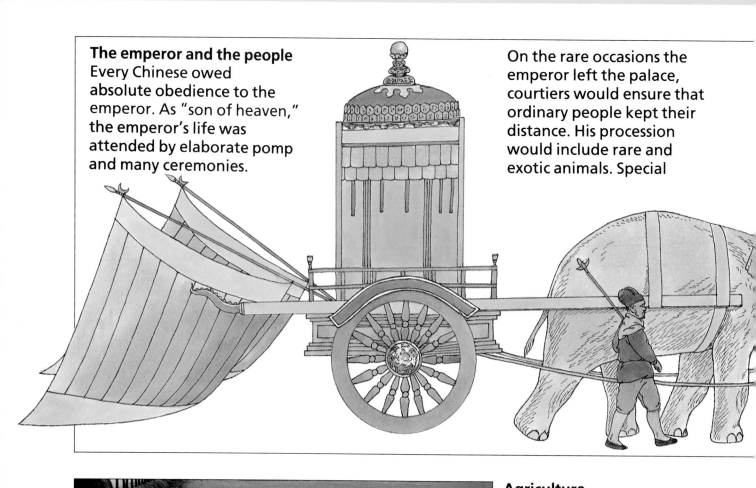

Agriculture
To feed his family and pay the high taxes which supported court life, the Chinese farmer grew grain. The picture shows how rice (which is the staple crop of south China) was planted in paddy fields. Methods of growing rice have changed relatively little.

palaces were built for him, even in places he might visit only briefly. The ordinary people thought the emperor was a kind of god, and the magnificence of his train reflected his power.

He alone could select officials. He ruled by a system of "memorials." These were reports sent by the magistrates and governors who looked after day-to-day government.

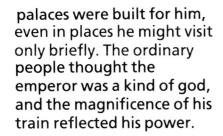

The photograph shows modern Chinese farmers planting rice in south China. In north China, where the weather is colder and drier, wheat has traditionally been grown. Northern Chinese people still like eating noodles and bread, whereas southern Chinese would rather eat rice.

Porcelain
Craftsmen in different parts of the country made bowls and pots of various colors and styles. Chinese porcelain became so famous around the world that today we often call our crockery "china." The picture shows an artist painting a pot. The artists who decorated porcelain continually experimented with new colors and firing techniques.

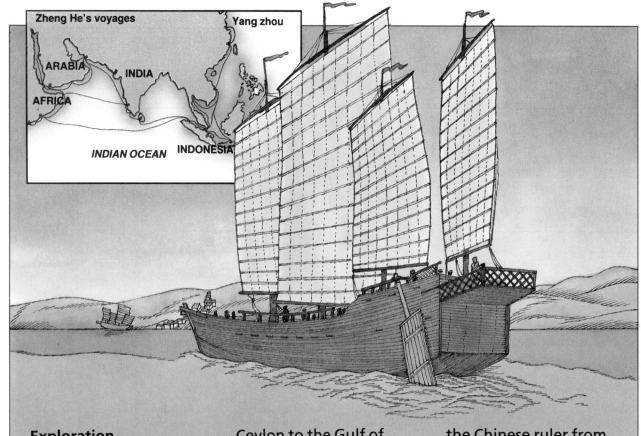

Zheng He's voyages
Yang zhou
ARABIA
INDIA
AFRICA
INDIAN OCEAN
INDONESIA

Exploration

Setting out from southeast China in an enormous wooden ship, Zheng He led a flotilla on seven expeditions. He journeyed through southeast Asia, India and Ceylon to the Gulf of Persia and the east coast of Africa. These journeys of exploration brought back treasure (and also unusual animals like giraffes for the emperor's menagerie) as tribute to the Chinese ruler from distant countries. Zheng He used a maritime compass perfected by Chinese scientists to guide him. His journeys taught the Chinese about distant lands.

Jesuits

China's civilization and culture have long intrigued people in other lands. In the 16th century Jesuit Catholic priests, like the one in our illustration, made the dangerous journey across the world from Europe to China. They hoped to convert the people and rulers of China to Christianity. Their knowledge of astronomy and mathematics impressed Chinese scholars, but few Chinese were persuaded to become Christians.

Opium

In the 19th century, the habit of opium smoking became widespread. Traders sold Chinese teas, silks and ceramics to the west in exchange for opium. Lin Zexu, the political leader in the picture, became so enraged at the harm opium did to the Chinese people that he publicly burned a huge consignment of the drug. The European powers reacted to this act of defiance by sending gunships to China to fight what became known as the "Opium Wars."

The Boxer Rebellion

Several massive social upheavals shook China in the closing years of the Qing dynasty. The government had lost control of large parts of the country. The picture shows an episode in the war of 1900, when patriotic Chinese soldiers known as "Boxers" attacked British, French, Russian and Japanese forces in China. The Boxers had no modern weapons and were soon defeated. Like many Chinese of the time, they could not understand how their once strong country could be invaded by foreign armies. Soon after the defeat of the Boxers, the Qing dynasty fell, and with it ended a tradition of imperial rule stretching back 2,000 years.

87

"LET THE PAST SERVE THE PRESENT"

In the early 20th century, China changed from an empire ruled by a god-king to a socialist state governed by political leaders. It was a turbulent period in which civil war and invasion by the Japanese caused millions of deaths. Between 1911 and 1949 the country was split up, with foreign rule in many cities and warlords controlling vast areas. Famines and epidemics occurred regularly. Gradually, a group of revolutionaries under Mao Zedong (later the leader of the People's Republic of China) became the strongest force. Mao's slogan "let the past serve the present" sums up his philosophy: keep the things which make China strong and throw out backward customs which hold up the drive towards modernization.

China today

China is the world's largest nation, with over a billion people. Most of them still live on the land, but huge cities like Peking and Shanghai are growing. Feeding, clothing and educating the enormous population is the government's biggest headache. Couples are encouraged to have only one child (like the parents on the government poster in the photograph). Over China's enormous area people live and speak in many different ways, but they are united by a common past and by their written language.

Mao Zedong

The man who led China out of the tumultous first half of the 20th century was Mao Zedong. He defeated the Nationalists in 1949 after years of civil war. The Long March, shown in the photograph, was an incredible journey by Mao's army. Mao built China into an independent country. He had bitter memories of China's humiliation by foreign powers, and when he gained power he turned China's back on the outside world. His first priority was to free the peasantry from famine and debt. Since Mao's death in 1976 China has opened up to foreign trade, but many Chinese still admire Mao and his vision of a strong China, proud of her past and confident of her future.

Chinatowns

All over the world, communities of Chinese people are known for their hard-working way of life. Many cities have a Chinatown. The photograph shows the lion dance in London's Chinese area. In Chinese communities all over the world, just as in China itself, thousands of people join in noisy celebrations at Chinese New Year, and watch the lion chase off evil spirits and bring good luck.

Tourism

A few years ago, China was completely isolated from the rest of the world. Now visitors go to China in their millions to see famous sights like the Great Wall and the terracotta warriors. China is repairing old sites and buildings, hoping to attract foreign tourists and the money they bring.

89

CONTENTS
JAPAN

INTRODUCTION 92
THE MAKING OF JAPAN 5000 BC-AD 1192 94
The Early Settlements – Shinto Religion – Burials
Chinese Influences – Writing – The Nobility – The End of the Heian Period
THE AGE OF STRIFE 1192-1603 100
The Shoguns – The Common People – Samurai – Fishing – Swordmakers
Castles – Life in the Towns – Christianity and Guns
ISOLATION AND PEACE 1603-1853 106
The Four Classes – The Rise of the Merchants – Arts and Craftspeople – Buildings
Poetry and Cherry Blossom – Education – Entertainment
OPEN TO THE WORLD 1853-1980s 112
The Black Ships – Learning from the West – War and Peace
The Economy – New Technology – Family and Home
ANCIENT AND MODERN 118

THE SAMURAI WARRIORS

INTRODUCTION 121
WHO WERE THE SAMURAI? 122
ARMS AND ARMOR 124
KAMIKAZE 126
SAMURAI RELIGION 128
THE ARTS 130
SAMURAI WOMEN 132
SHOGUNS AND DAIMYOS 134
SAMURAI BATTLES 136
WHAT HAPPENED TO THE SAMURAI? 138
SAMURAI TODAY 140
DATE CHARTS 142

ENCYCLOPEDIA OF GREAT CIVILIZATIONS

JAPAN

Including a special feature on
The Samurai Warriors

INTRODUCTION

A Japanese myth tells how Amaterasu, the Sun Goddess, was angry with her brother the Storm God. She hid in a cave. Darkness fell. The other gods gathered outside the cave and hung a jewel and a mirror in the sacred tree. A goddess did a funny dance to make them all laugh. Amaterasu heard, peeped out and saw her bright face in the mirror. She came out further to have a closer look. A god quickly closed up the mouth of the cave and the sun shone again.

Japan is a small but rich island country in the Far East of Asia. It is a varied, living civilization that has ancient roots. Its written history dates back to Chinese historians writing in the first century AD. Almost throughout its history Japan has been independent of other countries. But the people of Japan have always been curious about the outside world. For almost 2,000 years they have borrowed ideas from China and Korea, Europe and the United States. However, they always change things to suit their tastes, so their way of life and arts have a strong Japanese flavor. The people have a keen sense of order and a love of nature, beauty and perfection, shown in the way they live and work.

Ancient myths tell of the founding of Japan and its imperial family. Over the centuries there have been many power struggles but the original imperial family still survives. It is a link with the past in this modern industrialized country.

This book divides Japan's history into four parts. First Japan changes slowly from a country of scattered tribes to a nation ruled by an emperor. Next comes a period of civil wars during which the Europeans arrive. Then Japan shuts out the outside world and peacefully develops its own arts and society. Lastly Japan changes to a country committed to a policy of modernization and becomes a strong and prosperous world power.

THE MAKING OF JAPAN

Japanese civilization began to develop very slowly from about 5,000 BC when people started to make pottery. Around 300 BC new ideas came from the Asian mainland about rice-growing and how to make metal tools and swords. Chinese writers of the time described how the many small clans in Japan were fighting for power. Eventually, one strong Japanese leader took control in about AD 400. The emperors are his descendants. The capital was set up in Yamato province in the west. Then more settlers began to move slowly to the east.

Life became peaceful. Japan learned many things from China about government, Buddhist religion and the arts. The emperors built fine capital cities, temples and palaces. Gradually, however, the emperors became weak and real power fell into the hands of warrior leaders.

94

5000 BC-AD 1192

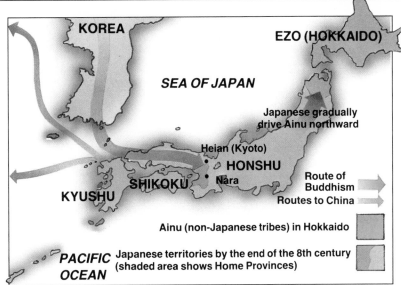

In the Heian period, from AD 794 to 1192, the imperial court was one of the most elegant in Japanese history. An aristocratic family named Fujiwara advized the emperor and arranged his entertainments. At New Year there was the annual archery contest.

DATECHART

c10,000 BC-300 BC People live by hunting and fishing. Primitive pottery becomes more sophisticated and people begin to live in huts.

c300 BC-AD 300 A different style of pottery appears. There are bronze and iron objects and rice-growing.

AD 57 Japanese messengers visit China, beginning 800 years of Chinese influence.

cAD 300-552 The Japanese imperial family becomes established in Yamato. Emperors and empresses are buried in tombs covered by huge mounds.

cAD 450 Introduction of Chinese writing.

AD 594 Buddhism becomes the state religion supported by Shotoku Taishi.

AD 645 A new Chinese-style central government is set up.

AD 710 New capital at Nara.

AD 752 The Todaiji Buddha is made.

AD 794 New capital at Heian.

cAD 894 End of first period of Chinese influence.

AD 858 The Fujiwara family starts to gain power.

cAD 1010 Murasaki Shikibu writes *The Tale of Genji*.

AD 1160 The kidnapping of Goshirakawa.

AD 1180-1185 The Gempei War: the Taira family are defeated by Minamoto Yoritomo and his clan. He starts an age of military rule.

The early settlements

The early Japanese lived by hunting and fishing. Rice-growing started about 300 BC. It was very hard work. The rice had to be planted in flooded fields with banks around them to keep the water in. At harvest time whole villages would work together in a group.

For a long time taxes were paid in rice instead of money. One *koku* of rice was the amount eaten by one man in a year. A man's wealth was measured by the number of *koku* he could grow on his land.

Japanese people still eat rice every day. They also like to work in groups, just as their ancestors did when cutting rice. In modern times machines have made rice-growing much easier.

Early potters made cooking pots, storage jars, funeral urns and clay objects for religious rites. The pots were probably coil pots like those in the picture. At first pots were decorated with curved lines and rope patterns. Simpler forms came in after 300 BC.

Shinto religion

The oldest religion in Japan is called Shinto, which means "The Way of the Gods." The Japanese used to believe that every natural thing – tree, river or mountain – was the home of a god. They built holy places for them called shrines. Today Japanese people still visit shrines, especially at New Year, to pray for good fortune and health. Most people have a Shinto wedding and enjoy festivals for the gods.

The first emperor, Jimmu, was said to be descended from the Sun Goddess, who gave him Three Sacred Treasures: a Mirror, a Sword and a Jewel. They are kept in the Ise Shrine, shown in the picture. This shrine is rebuilt every 20 years. The priestesses' costumes have not changed for 1200 years.

Burials

The power and wealth of the early emperors was shown by the enormous burial mounds called *Kofun* which covered their tombs. The tomb of Emperor Nintoku in the photograph is 1,600 feet long and is shaped like a giant keyhole. Around the mounds were rows of *haniwa*. *Haniwa* were clay models of warriors, horsemen, courtiers and court ladies. They acted as guards and servants for the dead man. Stately dances were performed at the funerals.

THE MAKING OF JAPAN

Chinese influences

In AD 57 Japanese messengers were sent to China. For the next 800 years the Japanese borrowed many Chinese ideas. A Chinese-style government and tax system were set up. Capital cities were planned like the Chinese city Changan. Chinese learning and arts also came to Japan.

The religion of Buddhism started in India and came to Japan through China and Korea in the 6th century. A powerful statesman called Shotoku Taishi welcomed Buddhist monks to the court. Many temples were built and most people belonged to both Shinto and Buddhism. Todaiji temple in Nara contains a bronze statue of Buddha 53 feet high (right).

Writing

The Japanese started using the Chinese writing system in the 5th century. They added two sets of new letters so that they could write down the Japanese language. The writing was done with a brush and ink on fine paper. It became very important for people to have good handwriting.

Around AD 1010 a court lady called Murasaki Shikibu wrote a famous story called *The Tale of Genji*. It tells of the life and loves of a handsome, clever Heian nobleman called Genji, "The Shining Prince."

源氏

Gen – ji

Warrior monk   Buddhist Prince   Nobleman   Nobleman's wife   Children of noble family

The nobility

The nobility of the Heian period were descendants of clan chieftains of earlier times. They worked as officials in the emperor's court. The Fujiwara became the most powerful by marrying their daughters to different emperors.

Heian, later called Kyoto, was in one of the five Home Provinces. The nobles all wanted to live in or near Heian. They thought that people who lived outside this area were barbarians who only existed to grow rice and pay taxes.

Court life was very formal. Children rarely saw their parents. But the nobility loved beautiful things, elegant clothes and nature. In this narrow world a very special Japanese culture grew up.

The end of the Heian period

In the 12th century some emperors gave up ruling and became priests, or "cloistered emperors." They tried to control the new young emperor from behind the scenes.

Two big warrior families, the Minamoto and the Taira, began to compete for power. At the same time the emperors began to quarrel with the Fujiwara courtiers who advized them.

A cloistered emperor called Goshirakawa was captured by the Minamoto and Fujiwara. There was war between the Minamoto and the Taira and the Minamoto won.

THE AGE OF STRIFE 1192-1603

In 1192 Minamoto Yoritomo became military ruler, or Shogun. He set up his military government, the Shogunate, in Kamakura. For the next seven centuries the shoguns were the real rulers of Japan. The emperors remained in Kyoto, powerless. But later shoguns were not so strong. Local lords called *daimyo* set themselves up in authority in each district. Every *daimyo* had a private army of *samurai* warriors. This led to the Age of Strife with everyone fighting for survival, and central government lost control.

Even so, arts and religion flourished. Zen Buddhism, which taught a simple way of life, was introduced from China. Trade and industry also increased. Eventually three great leaders came forward one after the other: Oda Nobunaga, Toyotomi Hideyoshi and Tokugawa Ieyasu. They succeeded in unifying Japan.

Fierce invaders from China called Mongols attacked Japan in 1274. The *samurai* warriors fought them off and built great walls for defense. The Mongols came again but a great storm wrecked their ships.

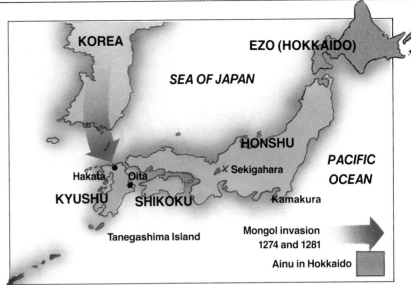

KOREA

EZO (HOKKAIDO)

SEA OF JAPAN

HONSHU

PACIFIC OCEAN

x Sekigahara

Hakata Oita

Kamakura

KYUSHU SHIKOKU

Tanegashima Island

Mongol invasion
1274 and 1281

Ainu in Hokkaido

DATECHART

1192 The Kamakura Shogunate is established by Minamoto Yoritomo. He appoints provincial officials.

1190s The monk Eisai brings Zen Buddhism from China. The Zen arts of tea ceremony, flower arrangement and ink-painting grow in Japan.

1274 and 1281 Mongol invasions.

1338 Ashikaga family establishes Shogunate headquarters in Kyoto.

1401 New government contacts and trade with China.

1467 A series of wars leads to the Age of Strife.

1543 Arrival of first Portuguese at Tanegashima. Introduction of guns.

1549 St Francis Xavier preaches Christianity.

1568-1576 The first great leader and general, Oda Nobunaga, overthrows the Shogunate and wins the Battle of Nagashino. For thirty years there is no Shogun as the fight for leadership continues.

1570s The Portuguese move to Nagasaki port.

1576 Nobunaga builds Azuchi castle.

1582 Nobunaga is murdered by a traitor.

1590 The second leader, the general Toyotomi Hideyoshi, unifies Japan.

1592 and 1597 Invasions of Korea end in failure.

1600 William Adams, first Englishman in Japan, is shipwrecked at Oita.

1600 The third leader, Tokugawa Ieyasu, establishes his power at the Battle of Sekigahara.

THE AGE OF STRIFE

The shoguns

Early shoguns guarded Japan's frontiers from the Ainu, non-Japanese people living in the north. But with the arrival of Minamoto Yoritomo, shoguns became military dictators. This meant they controlled the emperors and ruled the whole country through their officials.

Minamoto Yoritomo had fought in his first battle at the age of thirteen. His headquarters were at Kamakura. In the picture, the Shogun is receiving some visitors very formally. His sword-bearer sits to his left. Guards hide behind sliding doors to leap out at the first sign of trouble.

The common people

The lives of the farmers and other workers were ruled by the *daimyo*. Forestry, mining for gold and local industries such as papermaking became important at this time.

Life was hard. Sometimes farmers rebelled and tried to run away, especially if there was a poor harvest. However, farming people enjoyed dancing and drinking *sake* (rice wine) at festival time.

Taxes were paid in *koku* of rice. The *koku* were taken on horseback to the *daimyo*'s steward. The steward made calculations of what was owed on his abacus and a scribe wrote down the accounts.

Swordmakers

Swordmakers were the top craftsmen. They used their secret skills to beat the finest steel into the sharpest blades. A *samurai* always carried two swords. They were his most precious possessions.

Samurai

The *samurai* were warriors who served the shogun or *daimyo*. They swore loyalty to their masters and would gladly die for them. It is said they never complained about hardships and never broke a promise.

Martial arts such as *judo* and *kendo* (fencing) began as *samurai* fighting skills. Although they were fierce warriors the *samurai* led simple lives. They followed a new kind of Buddhism called Zen. They often sat cross-legged in meditation.

Fishing

Fishing became important at this time and fish has been a popular food in Japan ever since. In the photograph below, modern fishermen sort through the night's catch.

A *samurai* warrior

103

THE AGE OF STRIFE

Castles

As the *daimyo* grew more powerful, many of them built castles to show their strength. The castles were built on mounds faced with stone and they had wooden towers. There were narrow slits for windows through which defenders shot arrows or bullets when they were under attack.

Castle towns grew up around the castles. Many of these towns, such as Osaka, are now important centers. The photograph shows Osaka castle. Many of the castles today are modern concrete copies of originals.

Some towns had weekly markets, or, if they were on the coast, they developed into ports. Ships sailed between the ports or went overseas for trade. As the towns became important cities, the influence of the central government was forgotten.

Christianity and guns

In the 16th century Portuguese, Spanish, Dutch and English traders sailed far and wide to find wealth. The Portuguese were the first to arrive in Japan. The Japanese were fascinated by these tall men with long noses and baggy pants, who spoke an unknown language and came from an unknown land.

The Portuguese are remembered for two things. First they brought guns which the Japanese soon learned to make and use. And they also brought Christianity. At first the religion was quite popular. By 1581 there were about 150,000 Japanese Christians, including several *daimyo* in the western island of Kyushu.

Osaka castle

Life in the towns

From their open-fronted shops the shopkeepers watched the world go by. There would be quarreling *samurai*, pilgrims on their way to a shrine and farmers with bales of rice. Passersby would sit for a while on the edge of the raised shop-floor to talk and look at the goods inside. Serious customers left their shoes outside and stepped up into the shop to buy silk or *sake*, ricebowls or fans.

ISOLATION AND PEACE 1603-1853

The Tokugawa were the shoguns for the next 250 years. Tokugawa Ieyasu moved his capital to Edo (modern-day Tokyo) and made strict rules to keep the peace. He made his 250 *daimyo* spend half the year in Edo. When they returned home they had to leave their wives behind as hostages. This was done to guarantee their loyalty. Ieyasu also gave favors to his most faithful *daimyo*.

A later shogun became suspicious of the many Europeans who were now in Japan. He was afraid of their power, so he made them all leave and banned Christianity. For over 200 years Japan cut herself off from the rest of the world. A few Dutch, Chinese and Korean merchants were allowed at Nagasaki. Some Japanese scholars read Dutch books to keep in touch with new ideas. Then in 1853 four American ships arrived demanding supplies and trade agreements. Another big change was on the way for Japan.

The busy main road from Edo to Kyoto was called the Tokaido. Today this journey takes 3½ hours by Bullet Train. In the Edo period it could take up to 30 days. There were few bridges and many checkpoints. This made it impossible for *daimyo* armies to move in secret to attack the shogun.

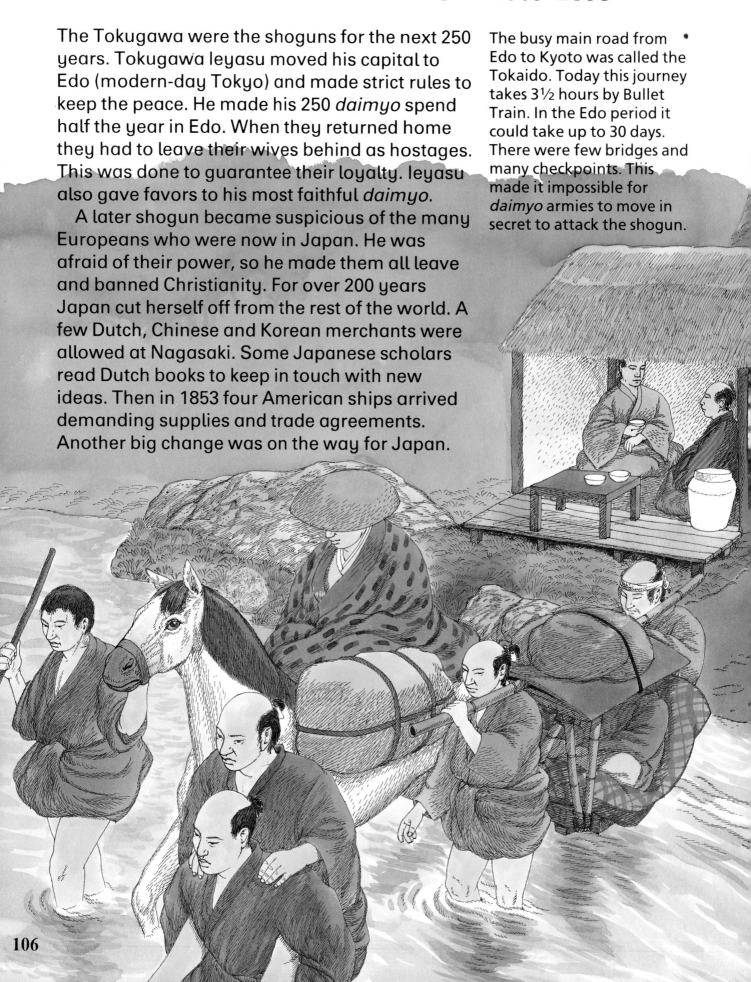

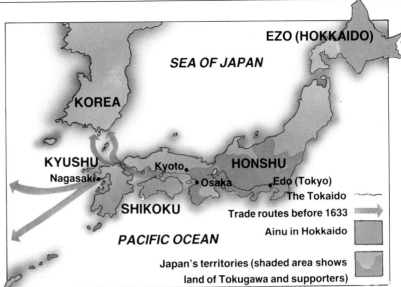

DATECHART

1603 Tokugawa Ieyasu becomes Shogun. He makes his headquarters at Edo. He also builds Nijo Castle in Kyoto to show his power to the Emperor.

c1603 *Kabuki* theater develops. At first the plays are performed by women, but later men take over.

1609 The Dutch establish a trading post at Hirado.

1616 Ieyasu dies. He is buried in the famous Shinto shrine at Nikko.

1635-1639 Laws are made to stop Japanese from traveling abroad and foreigners from landing in Japan. Christianity is abolished.

1641 The Dutch traders are moved to Deshima Island near Nagasaki. Raw silk, sugar and medicines are imported.

c1635 The rise of big merchant families, such as Mitsui which now owns many banks and department stores.

1657 Edo is destroyed by fire.

1687 The Genroku Period begins. It is a time when town life flourishes and the *Kabuki* and *bunraku* puppet plays become more and more popular.

1694 The poet Basho dies.

c1720 The Japanese begin to import Dutch books.

1774 First translation of a Dutch book and growth of 'Dutch Learning'.

c1794-1840 Flourishing of famous wood-block artists.

1853 Arrival of American ships – the first "Black Ships". Their commander Commodore Perry demands trade with Japan.

The four classes

Everyone knew their place in Edo society. Below the emperor and shogun there were four classes. At the top were the *samurai*, their swords ready to cut down anyone who disobeyed.

Next came the farmers who grew rice for everyone to eat. The craftspeople made various kinds of goods to sell in the markets. The merchants came at the bottom because they did not grow or make anything.

The rise of the merchants

Merchants slowly became more important because of their wealth. They traded in rice and luxury goods. The huge drapery stores which opened in Edo times (see picture) are now big department stores. Osaka was, and still is, the main center for merchants.

Merchants were a pleasure-loving class, often seen in theaters and restaurants. They competed with the *samurai*. They bought the most expensive silk kimonos for their wives and daughters, although this was against the law.

Arts and craftspeople

Many beautiful articles made by Edo craftspeople still survive today. Apprentices learnt their crafts from masters who belonged to guilds. Each guild had a rich patron, for example, a rich priest who looked after it.

There were craftspeople who made swords, pottery, *tatami* floormats, fans and lacquerware – wooden articles with a hard, shiny surface made of resin.

Making cloth was a long and difficult process. The raw materials had to be spun, woven and dyed. Silk was worn only by the rich. Common people wore cotton dyed with patterns in indigo, a blue dye.

Buildings

All Japanese buildings used to be made of wood. Fire was a big danger. Houses had shutters to keep off the rain and snow. People changed from their outdoor shoes before stepping inside. Floors were covered with *tatami* mats made of rice straw for sitting and sleeping on. Houses, like the one in the photograph, were cold because of sliding doors and poor heating.

Today Japanese people still change their shoes when going indoors and modern houses keep many of the traditional features.

ISOLATION AND PEACE

Poetry and cherry blossom
A poet called Basho developed *haiku* – poems with seventeen syllables about nature. Poets wrote about frogs, rain, the moon, mountains, the seasons and particularly cherry blossoms.

Japan has rugged mountains, volcanoes and earthquakes. Life was sometimes hard and even dangerous. Life could also end unexpectedly. The beauty of the cherry blossom, which came and went so quickly, reminded people of the uncertainty of life. They went for picnics under the cherry trees to enjoy their brief beauty.

Education

There were a few schools in the 16th century. But during the peaceful Edo period, many more children went to school.

The *daimyo* set up new schools for the sons of *samurai*. The main subject for study was Chinese texts. Long hours were spend practicing calligraphy (brush-writing). Chinese ideas of loyalty, martial arts and good manners were also taught. *Samurai* girls learned the arts of flower arrangement and the tea ceremony from their mothers. This would help them find good husbands.

Many commoners' children in villages and towns also went to school to learn reading and writing. Craftspeople's sons learned from their fathers or masters.

Entertainment

We can learn about leisure in the Edo period by looking at the many wood-block prints and paintings which still survive. They are called *ukiyoe*, or floating world pictures.

Some of these show scenes from the popular *kabuki* plays about revenge and love. The female parts were all played by men. Modern performances in Tokyo (photograph right) have not changed much since Edo times.

Other pictures show the ancient sport of *sumo* wrestling (right). There are also pictures of beautiful women from the pleasure quarters of Edo and Kyoto. This was the "floating world" where rich men went to forget their problems. They ate, drank and talked with the women called *geisha*.

OPEN TO THE WORLD 1853-1980s

The Americans and other foreign arrivals forced Japan to open her ports which had been closed for over 200 years. Japan felt weak compared with Western nations. The emperor was given back his power in order to modernize the country and build up its strength. Japan learned from Western countries and introduced modern reforms. *Samurai* and the class system were abolished. An industrial revolution took place. Many people left their farms to work in factories.

As Japan modernized, it also strengthened its armed forces. Like Western countries it used them to build up an empire. But it lost this empire when it was defeated in World War II. Since the war Japan has made friends with former enemies and has worked hard on economic recovery and growth. Now it is a leading world power and one of the world's most technologically advanced nations.

In 1964 Japan hosted the Olympic Games in Tokyo. Over 90 nations took part and for the first time modern Japan was on show to the whole world. At the opening ceremony a Japanese athlete carried the Olympic Torch.

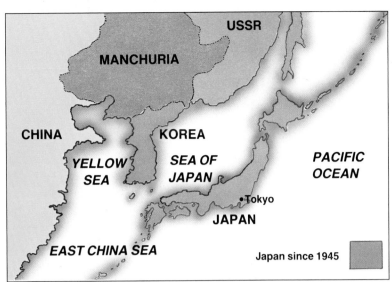

Japan since 1945

DATECHART

1854-1858 Japan makes treaties of Trade and Friendship with the United States, Britain, Russia, France and Holland.

1862-1868 A period of unrest with some violence between Japanese and foreigners. Armed Japanese rebellion against the treaties.

1868 Restoration of the Emperor Meiji. End of Shogun rule.

1870s Japanese study foreign ideas and advanced engineering. Education for all.

1889 The Emperor Meiji grants New Constitution.

1890 The first parliament meets. It is called the Diet.

1894-1895 War with China.

1904-1905 War with Russia.

1910 Japan colonizes Korea.

1931-1945 Japan invades Manchuria and China and fights the United States and her allies in World War II.

1945 Japan surrenders after atomic bombs are dropped on Hiroshima and Nagasaki.

1945-1952 Occupation of Japan by Allied Forces.

1946 The New Constitution gives new laws and rights.

1946-1964 Economic recovery and rapid growth of incomes.

1956 Japan enters the United Nations.

1964 Tokyo Olympics

1979 Tokyo Economic Summit attended by leading world powers.

1985 Expo '85 in Tsukuba.

113

OPEN TO THE WORLD

The Black Ships

In 1853 the sight of four strange American ships – the first "Black Ships" – was a big shock to the Japanese. Soon more ships arrived from other countries, such as Britain and Russia. These countries demanded the right to trade with Japan. The Shogun signed treaties with each of them giving them special favors. Foreign officials arrived to live and work in Japan. Strangely-dressed foreigners were often seen in Yokohama. The Japanese watched them carefully. Some even began to try out Western clothes.

Learning from the West

Emperor Meiji left Kyoto and traveled with great ceremony (illustrated right) to Edo which he renamed Tokyo, meaning eastern capital. He promised to make Japan a strong modern nation by learning from other countries.

Japanese people went to the United States and Europe to study. Foreign engineers and teachers were welcomed in Japan. Using Western models, the Japanese set up new systems of government and education. The photograph (right) shows an early meeting of parliament. Western clothes, food and arts also became popular.

Many Japanese feared these foreigners. They criticized the shogun for giving in to them. Finally the Shogunate was abolished and in 1868 the emperor regained his power.

War and peace

Japan won wars against China in 1895 and Russia (below) in 1905. It supported Britain and its allies in World War I.

In the late 1920s, army leaders took control of the government. They planned to extend Japan's empire all over east Asia and drive out the Westerners. Japanese armies invaded Manchuria in 1931 and China in 1937. In 1941 Japan entered World War II with an attack on the United States. Defeat finally came when the Americans destroyed Hiroshima and Nagasaki with atomic bombs. Over 150,000 people were killed. Now thousands of people visit memorials like the Peace Dome in Hiroshima (bottom). Since the war Japan has armed forces for defense only.

The economy

By 1930 Japan was a fully industrialized country producing chemicals, machinery, silk and cotton. But during World War II all the factories were destroyed.

Japan recovered very quickly. In 1970, millions of people visited the world industrial exhibition, Expo '70 at Osaka, when Japan's progress was at its height.

Japan's main problem today is lack of raw materials, so it imports oil for energy and iron ore. It is a leading producer of cars, ships, iron, steel and TVs and trades all over the world. The old silk mills look very different from modern factories where robots do the dangerous work.

New technology

Japan is now moving away from heavy industry and into high-technology — products which rely on compact precision engineering. The Japanese are considered to be world leaders in "hi-tech." Big developments have been made in robotics, advanced computers, energy, space research, electronics and medicine.

In Japan's space program three astronauts, including a woman, are being trained for the first Japanese manned space flight. Japan often does research with other countries. For example, Britain and Japan produced the space satellite which was lauched from Kagoshima in 1987 (right).

Family and home

Japanese houses today are quite small because building land is scarce. However, they have many labor-saving machines and nearly everyone has color TV. Homes are a mixture of Japanese and western styles. Japanese food is beautifully served in small bowls and eaten with chopsticks.

In Japanese families the wife is generally in charge of the children and their education while the husband goes out to work. However, things are changing slowly as more mothers go out to work.

Many workers are employed by big Japanese companies which are themselves like families. These companies take great care of their workers. In return, the workers usually stay with that one company until they retire.

In the past old people were looked after by their eldest son and his wife. Now, because houses are so small, many old people live in a separate house nearby. But they still meet their families very often. Our picture shows a family outing on a very special occasion. The women and older children are wearing their kimonos.

ANCIENT AND MODERN

In many ways modern Japan looks like any other thriving Western country. It has huge cities with skyscrapers and department stores. Most Japanese wear Western clothes. They like hamburgers and coca cola. They watch videos and play golf.

However, traditions are still very much alive in Japan. Craftspeople work with clay and bamboo, wood and paper. On special occasions women put on their traditional kimonos to visit shrines. Rice and fish are important foods. There are *samurai* dramas, *sumo* and *kabuki* on TV. Many people practice martial arts or calligraphy as hobbies. Japan belongs to both East and West.

Tokyo

Tokyo has over eight million inhabitants. During the week many more people travel in to work. Most of Tokyo was rebuilt after World War II. It has several skyscrapers. The main shopping street, called the *Ginza*, (shown right), is closed to traffic on Sundays. People in holiday mood stroll up and down window-shopping.

International finance

Japan plays an important part in trade and financial organizations worldwide. Its currency (money called *yen*) is accepted everywhere. Now, because of its economic success, many foreigners deal on Japan's stock markets.

Enjoying the past

The top photograph (right) shows one of Japan's most famous festivals, the Gion Festival in Kyoto. It dates back to the 9th century. Crowds of visitors come every July to watch the splendid procession.

Japanese schoolchildren often visit famous places. These children (right) are visiting a Buddhist temple to learn about their country's history and culture.

The Shinkansen, or Bullet Train, is the world's second fastest train (130 mph).

THE SAMURAI WARRIORS

INTRODUCTION

The *samurai* were Japanese knights, rather like the knights of the Middle Ages in Europe. Today Japan is a rich, powerful, and highly industrialized country. However at the time of the *samurai* it was a collection of islands off China's coast, whose people lived by fishing and farming. Japan was greatly influenced by China, whose civilization from the 7th to the 14th century was very advanced. In this *Special Feature*, we take a closer look at the world of the *samurai warrior* and his place in Japanese culture.

WHO WERE THE *SAMURAI* ?

The *samurai* were the warriors of Japan from the 12th century until the founding of modern Japan in the mid-19th century. In the same way as medieval knights of Europe valued their honor above all things, so too did the *samurai*. They called their code of honor *bushido* which means "the way of the warrior." The *samurai* believed that they had to obey their master; this allegiance came before anything else like friendship or family ties.

A *samurai* was supposed to be always alert and ready to do battle on his lord's behalf. He was prepared to give his life in his master's service. A *samurai* would always rush into the fiercest fighting, eager for glory. He would not retreat unless ordered to do so, and would never allow himself to be taken prisoner.

The way of the *samurai* demanded perfection in matters of honor, both on the battlefield and in daily life. A *samurai* was also expected to be able to write, understand poetry and perform traditional dances.

RITUAL SWORDS

Sometimes a *samurai* would take his own life if he felt he had behaved dishonorably. This was done by cutting his own stomach open in a ritual known as *seppuku*; this is often (and incorrectly) known as *hara-kiri*. When this was done, a friend would quickly cut off his head with a specially sharpened sword. A *samurai* would also commit suicide if he was in danger of being captured or if his master had given him an order that went against his conscience.

Seppuku swords were very beautifully made and the swordmakers were highly regarded. The Tachi sword (shown below) is another example of their great skill and was decorated with precious metals, jewels, and laquer.

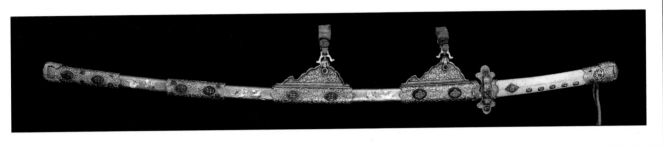

All *samurai* were trained in archery and sword-fighting. They were brilliant horsemen and took good care of their horses. The *samurai* were also expert at unarmed fighting like *jujutsu*.

ARMS AND ARMOR

Samurai swords were the finest ever made anywhere in the world. The *samurai* usually had both a long and a short sword. The *wakizashi* was a short sword and was worn at the waist. A longer curved sword called the *katana* was thrust through the belt. As well as these, a samurai often carried a *naginata* which is a long pole with a curved blade at the end.

The *samurai* wore special suits of armor made by craftsmen. These craftsmen also made the swords and were greatly respected by the *samurai*. The quality of the work was very high. Not only were the arms and armor of the *samurai* skilfully made, they were also extremely decorative. Swords were thought to be so important that special mystic rituals were performed while they were being made.

Early *samurai* warriors were mounted archers and carried longbows and arrows into battle. No armor was worn on the right arm to allow the warrior to draw his bowstring back.

A *samurai* would have a metal helmet with special flaps to protect the neck. Warriors often wore beautifully decorated helmets and fierce-looking face masks to frighten their enemies.

Samurai armor was constructed from separate plates bound together with silk or leather thongs. It was all in one piece like a box, and fastened around the waist. Only the section under the right arm was separate. This was known as a *yoroi*.

KAMIKAZE

In 1274 Japan was threatened with invasion by the Mongol forces of China under the emperor Kublai Khan. He had already conquered most of Eastern Europe and Asia. The Mongols had prepared a large fleet of ships and at first they seemed to be winning as they were better organized. But when night fell there was an enormous storm which forced the Mongol troops away from Japan and back out to sea. Eventually, with 13,000 men drowned, the Mongols retreated to China.

In 1281 the Mongols again prepared to invade Japan, with an even larger force. This time the *samurai* were better prepared and had a fleet of their own. They fought with the Mongols in the Bay of Hakata. After two months a typhoon again helped to defeat the Mongols with even greater losses than before.

After this the Japanese believed that the strong winds which had twice saved them from the Mongols were sent from the gods. They were called *kamikaze* which means "divine winds."

Despite being unprepared for an invasion, the *samurai* were able to fight off the Mongols in 1274. After the first invasion, the Japanese built great walls to defend themselves from future attacks. Kublai Khan went on planning to conquer Japan until his death in 1294.

Kamikaze pilots

In World War II, many young Japanese pilots were taught to believe they were the "divine winds." The *kamikaze* pilots would die crashing their aircraft into American warships. They would sometimes whiten their faces as the *samurai* had done. They often wore red headbands and white clothes as a sign of ritual purification. The aircraft were packed with explosives. As the young pilots climbed aboard they would say "see you at Yasukini," meaning that their spirits would meet again at this famous Shinto shrine. Their sacrifice was a useless gesture and made no difference to the war's outcome.

SAMURAI RELIGION

Shinto was the first religion of the Japanese people. Followers of Shinto believe that all natural objects contain a god. They also believe that the first emperor of Japan was a descendant of the Sun Goddess, so they think of their emperor as a god.

The followers of Shinto built many shrines because they thought that the spirits of the dead used them as gathering places. At certain times in the year, people light lanterns and float them on the water to light the path for the spirits as they return to their home in the mountains.

Buddhism was introduced to Japan from China. The *samurai* believed in a kind of Buddhism known as Zen. The word Zen means meditation or focusing the mind on a single object or idea. Believers in Zen think that they can find truth and knowledge through meditation and self-control. The *samurai* thought that Zen would help them act without hesitation, especially in battle, and develop inner peace.

The most famous statue of Buddha is at Kamakura. It is made of bronze and was created in 1252. Originally it was surrounded by a wooden temple, but this was swept away by a giant tidal wave in 1495.

THE ISE SHRINE

The most holy Shinto shrine in Japan is the Ise shrine. It is rebuilt every 20 years. Two sacred treasures – a jewel and a mirror – are kept there. The Sun Goddess is believed to have given these things to the first Japanese emperor, Jimmu. The shrine is based on the design of a prehistoric grindstone. It was last rebuilt in 1973.

THE ARTS

Samurai were not just skilful warriors. They were expected to understand and appreciate all forms of art. The *samurai* enjoyed reciting and composing poetry. In the middle of the 17th century the poet Matsuo Basho developed the *haiku*, a 17-syllable poem in praise of nature. The *samurai* would have written these and read them to one another.

The *samurai* also learned the traditional forms of dancing. The fierce General Oda Nobunaga is said to have danced gracefully with a fan in front of his troops before leading them into battle.

The *samurai* enjoyed theater. In the 12th century they attended popular plays known as *kabuki*. Toward the end of the *samurai* period, the classical Japanese theater of *Noh* was considered more suitable. In both kinds of theater, the women's parts were played by boys. "Practice the arts of peace on the left hand, and the arts of war on the right" was a popular *samurai* saying of the time.

The *samurai* appreciated calligraphy, which is the art of writing with brush and ink on paper. Each "character" has to be painted gracefully and accurately, without hesitation.

SASHIMONO

Many *Samurai* warriors had a *sashimono*, or personal flag, which was worn on the back in a special carrier. These identified the wearer and often had a poem written on them. In the case of one clan, the *sashimono* of the whole army would spell out a longer poem when everyone was together. It said: "Colors are fragrant, but they fade away. In this world of ours none lasts forever. Today cross the high mountains of life's illusion, and there will be no more dreaming, no more drunkenness."

SAMURAI WOMEN

Samurai women followed the same code of honor as the men. They were expected to show the same obedience to their fathers and husbands as a *samurai* would to his master. Women were often forced into arranged marriages in order to increase the power of their families.

It was considered very important that a *samurai* had a son to inherit his possessions. Sometimes the *samurai* would take another wife if the first one did not give birth to a boy.

One *samurai* woman, Tomoe Gozen, fought alongside her husband, Yoshinaka, in all his battles. Her story is told in the long poem *Heike Monogotari*.

Some *samurai* women learned to fight and they defended their homes against enemies; in defeat, they also committed *seppuku*. One *kabuki* play tells of two sisters, Miyagino and Shinobu, whose father was murdered by a *samurai* called Shiga. They swore to avenge their father's death. In secret they trained themselves to fight, then they went to the local *daimyo* and asked permission to challenge Shiga to a duel. In the fight that followed, Shiga was killed and family honor was satisfied. The story of Miyagino and Shinobu is still performed on the Japanese stage to this day. It shows the courage of *samurai* women.

SAMURAI CHILDREN

In the Edo period, schools were set up for the sons of *samurai*. Calligraphy and Chinese writings were the main subjects taught, as well as the *samurai* codes. Girls learned *ikebana*, the art of flower arranging, and the tea ceremony from their mothers. At the age of 13, boys had the front part of their heads shaved. This was a sign that they had become men.

Girls wore their hair parted in the middle and falling over their shoulders. By the time they grew up, it touched the ground. Boys liked to catch dragonflies and make them fight each other. Girls caught fireflies and kept them in jars to use as lanterns.

13 year-old boy

Young boy

Young girl

SHOGUNS AND DAIMYOS

In the 12th century two powerful clans, the Minamoto and the Taira, declared war on each other. Minamoto Yoritomo won and he forced the emperor to give him the title of *shogun*, which means "commander-in-chief for the suppression of barbarians." He ruled Japan through his officials called *shugos*. Their job was to collect taxes and keep order. Taxes were paid in *koku* of rice. One *koku* was equal to the amount of rice that one man would eat in a year. The more land a *samurai* had, the more *koku* of rice he had to pay.

DAIMYOS AND CULTURE

This print shows a *daimyo* sitting on a battlefield. To show their importance, *daimyos* liked to surround themselves with beautiful things. They often commissioned hand-painted screens and ceramics for their castles. A *daimyo* thought that performing the tea ceremony or looking at a landscaped garden were just as important as making war. When they went into battle, the *daimyos* took pride in the beauty of their intricate armor.

A *daimyo* visits a fellow *daimyo*. Before setting out for battle, the *daimyo* would eat a ritual meal of dried chestnuts, seaweed and abalone. He would drink rice wine served within three cups, one inside the other. These things were thought to bring good luck.

With time, nobles began to resent the *shogun*. They wanted more power in their own regions. Rich people built castles and called themselves *daimyo*, which means "big name." The *daimyos* recruited many loyal *samurai* and fought with other *daimyos*. They did not always obey the *shogun*. In 1603 a *shogun* called Tokugawa Ieyasu found a way of controlling the *daimyos*. He forced the *daimyo* wives and children to live at Edo, now known as Tokyo. The *daimyos* were only allowed to live there every other year. The rest of the time they lived at their castles. The *shogun* could hold a *daimyo* family as hostages if the *daimyo* rebelled.

SAMURAI BATTLES

Before a battle could begin, messengers were sent from each side to decide when and where the battle would take place. When this was agreed, the two armies would draw up facing each other. One *samurai* from each side would step forward and would shout out the reason they were fighting. Then two "humming" arrows were fired in the air, which was a signal for the fighting to start. Mounted *samurai* on each side would fire their arrows into the enemy, then they would charge and begin their attack.

It was important to find someone of the same rank to fight. The *samurai* would try to knock each other from their horses. Then they would fight hand to hand on the ground until one of them was dead.

The *samurai* were rewarded by their masters if they fought well. They were given land and money. The *samurai* would cut the heads off their victims, and a servant would collect them up and bring them home. The *samurai* were rewarded according to how important their opponents had been.

Armies were controlled on the battlefield by big war-drums called *taiko* and by blowing conch shells known as *horagai*. An expert could blow the *horagai* loud enough to be heard six miles away. *Horagai* were also used to tell the soldiers what time it was.

CASTLES

Daimyos often built fortresses to defend themselves from their enemies. These would be built wherever there were natural defenses like hilltops, and were made of wood. Later castles were built of stone on an earth mound; they were solidly built to withstand earthquakes. The most beautiful example of these is Inuyama castle.

137

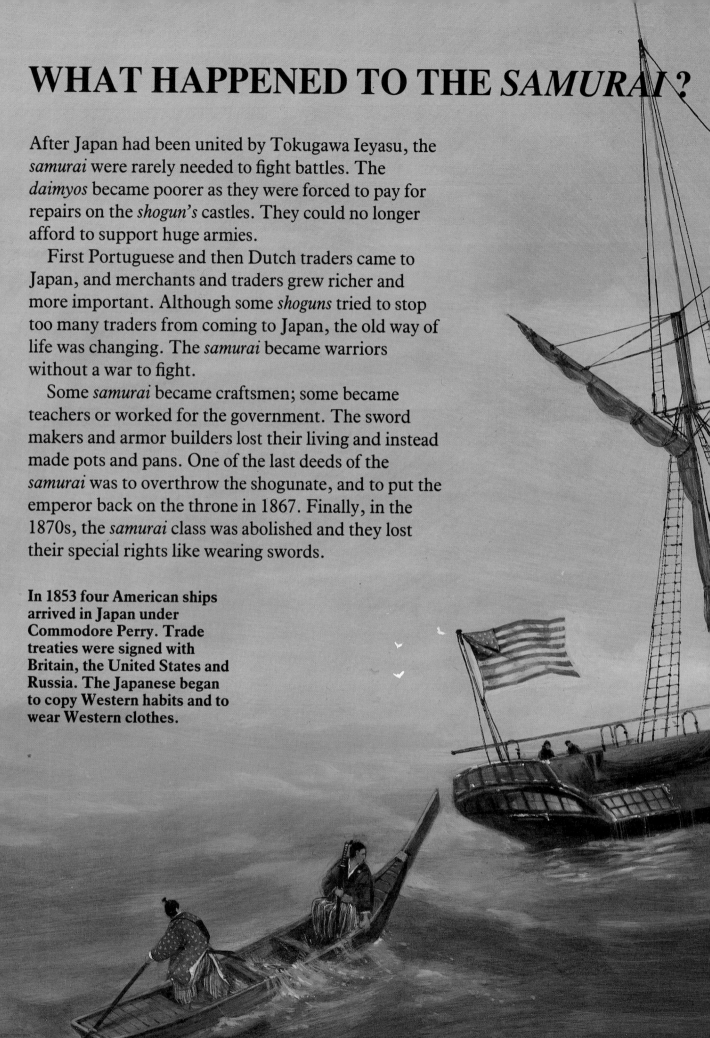

WHAT HAPPENED TO THE *SAMURAI*?

After Japan had been united by Tokugawa Ieyasu, the *samurai* were rarely needed to fight battles. The *daimyos* became poorer as they were forced to pay for repairs on the *shogun's* castles. They could no longer afford to support huge armies.

First Portuguese and then Dutch traders came to Japan, and merchants and traders grew richer and more important. Although some *shoguns* tried to stop too many traders from coming to Japan, the old way of life was changing. The *samurai* became warriors without a war to fight.

Some *samurai* became craftsmen; some became teachers or worked for the government. The sword makers and armor builders lost their living and instead made pots and pans. One of the last deeds of the *samurai* was to overthrow the shogunate, and to put the emperor back on the throne in 1867. Finally, in the 1870s, the *samurai* class was abolished and they lost their special rights like wearing swords.

In 1853 four American ships arrived in Japan under Commodore Perry. Trade treaties were signed with Britain, the United States and Russia. The Japanese began to copy Western habits and to wear Western clothes.

THE FORTY-SEVEN RONIN

In 1701 a *daimyo* called Asano was executed and his land confiscated. His *samurai* became *ronin*, meaning they had no master. Some 47 of these *ronin* killed the man responsible for Asano's death. Such acts of revenge were by then illegal, so they were forced to commit suicide.

SAMURAI TODAY

Today Japan is a rich and modern country. Japan exports goods like cars, electronics and machinery all over the world.

However, there are many aspects of Japanese life that remind us of the age of the *samurai*. The arts are still considered to be very important. Examples of calligraphy, ceramics and paintings are found in most Japanese homes. Women still perform the tea ceremony at home or in special tea houses where businessmen come to relax after a busy day.

Although many people still enjoy Western entertainment, the traditional sports of kendo, judo and karate are still very popular. On television people still watch *kabuki* plays and *Noh* dramas.

Many customs still reflect the ways of *samurai*. Japanese children obey their parents and work hard at school. Japanese workers are very loyal to the company that employs them; in return the company looks after the work force and provides training and cheap housing. This loyalty to the company is rather like the loyalty that a *samurai* would have shown to his lord.

The tea ceremony is a traditional ritual for sharing tea with friends. Tea is served in delicate china bowls and there is always a graceful flower arrangement in a special vase. Japanese people appreciate the harmony and tranquillity of this simple act and it is an important part of Japanese culture.

THE SEVEN *SAMURAI*

Many writers and film directors have been inspired by the *samurai* legends. In 1956 the Japanese film director Akira Kurosawa made a film called *The Seven Samurai*. It won international awards and is still a great favorite with Japanese and Western audiences. It is the story of seven *ronin*, who band together to defend a village against bandits. Each *samurai* is master of a different combat skill, and they drive off the bandits with brilliant fighting and clever strategy. In 1960 John Sturges remade the film as a Western, called *The Magnificent Seven*.

DATE CHARTS

AD 794 Heian period begins

858 Fujiwara family gains power

1010 Lady Murasaki writes *The Tale of Genji*

1180-85 The Gempei war between the Minamoto and the Taira clan; the Minamoto win

1183 Tomoe Gozen fights in battle of Kurikara alongside her husband Minamoto Yoshinaka

1191 The monk Eisai visits China and brings back Zen Buddhism

1192 Kamakura Shogunate established by Minamoto Yoritomo

1240 First great war epic: *Heike Monogotari*

1274 The First Mongol Invasion

1281 The Second Mongol Invasion

1338 Ashikaga Shogunate established

1467-1603 The age of strife; many small wars fought before unification

1543 The Portuguese arrive in Japan, bringing guns

1549 St Francis Xavier spreads Christianity in Japan

1568 Oda Nobunaga takes power from shogunate; begins to unify Japan

1584 Toyotomi Hideyoshi controls Japan

1592 Hideyoshi fails to invade Korea

1597 Second invasion of Korea

1603 Tokugawa Ieyasu becomes *shogun*. He establishes new capital at Edo

1616 Christianity abolished. Japan tries to discourage foreign influence

1702 The 47 *Ronin* are punished for avenging their master's death in traditional *samurai* style

1774 First translation of foreign books into Japanese

1853 Commodore Perry arrives in Japan from America

1868 Shogunate rule abolished. Emperor Meiji restored to power

1870 Special rights of *samurai* abolished

1876 Swords banned

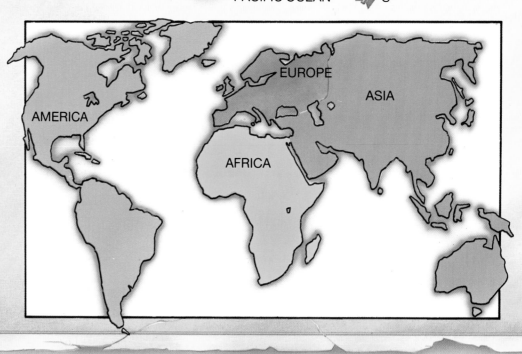

HOKKAIDO

SEA OF JAPAN

KOREA

HONSHU

Kamakura

Tokyo (Edo)

Kyoto

Osaka

Tokyo Bay

Hiroshima

SHIKOKU

Nagasaki

KYUSHU

N

S

PACIFIC OCEAN

EUROPE

ASIA

AMERICA

AFRICA

AFRICA	ASIA	AMERICA	EUROPE
	c1010 AD Lady Murasaki writes *Tale of Genji* **1031** Jain Temple built on Mount Abu, India		**1016 AD** Canute ascends English throne
1070 AD Constantine the African translates Greek medical texts into Latin, bringing medicine to West			**1066** William of Normandy invades Britain
			1086 Domesday book finished in England
1173 Saladin assumes power in Egypt			**1170** Death of Thomas à Becket
	1180 Gempei war in Japan		
	1192 Kamakura Shogunate in Japan	**1200 AD** Inca rule established in Peru	
	1271 Marco Polo reached China		**1215** King John signs the Magna Carta
	1338 Ashikaga Shogunate in Japan		**1340** Black Death reaches Europe
1352 Ib Battuta crosses Sahara Desert			**1381** Peasants' revolt in England
	1421 Beijing established as capital of China	**1492** Christopher Columbus sails to America	
1505 Mozambique founded		**1519** Cortes defeats Aztecs	
	1526 Mogul Empire of India founded **1545** Portuguese arrive in Japan		
	1603 Tokugawa Shogunate in Japan		**1558** Queen Elizabeth I ascends English throne
1652 Capetown founded in South Africa			
		1776 American Declaration of Independence	**1789** French Revolution
		1789 George Washington elected President	**1804** Napoleon Bonaparte declared Emperor of France
			1837 Queen Victoria ascends English throne
	1868 Emperor Meiji restored to power in Japan **1870** *Samurai* privileges abolished	**1853** Commodore Perry arrives in Japan	**1870** Franco-Prussian War

CONTENTS

GREECE

INTRODUCTION 146

THE MYCENAEANS c1600-1150 BC 148

Mycenaean Treasure – Hunting Boars – Tombs – Linear B

Poems about the Mycenaeans – The Storytellers – The Trojan War – Odysseus

AGE OF EXPANSION c1000-479 BC 154

The Polis – Country Life – The Immortals

The Life of Women – The Persian Wars

THE GOLDEN AGE 478-405 BC 160

Life in Athens – Greek Ideas – Life in Sparta – Schools and Education

Decisions at Athens – Land Warfare – The Peloponnesian War– Sea Warfare

THE HELLENISTIC AGE 336-30 BC 166

Alexandria, City of Learning – The New Learning – Mathematics – Inventions

Alexander in the East – The Range of the Empire – Greek Influence on Rome

THE LEGACY OF ANCIENT GREECE 172

ENCYCLOPEDIA OF GREAT CIVILIZATIONS

GREECE

INTRODUCTION

The ancient Greeks were among the liveliest and most creative people ever to have lived. Their towns and villages were the scene of colorful festivals, noisy parties – and savage warfare. Storytellers told tales of love, war and adventure, sometimes passing on with wonderful accuracy details from prehistoric times. Critical thinkers developed ideas about religion and the human mind which are still found useful today.

The Greeks learned to use a form of writing which is the ancestor of our alphabet. Drama was a Greek invention. So was the idea of democracy, organized politics which allowed ordinary men to control their own towns.

Ancient Greece was made up of hundreds of independent towns. Greeks probably could have conquered huge areas of Europe and Asia, but these little towns loved their independence and they never united to form an unbeatable force.

Eventually a ruler from the fringe of the Greek world, Alexander, came to control Greece. Adapting Greek methods of fighting, he quickly conquered almost the whole of the Middle East spreading Greek language and customs.

This book looks at Greek civilization from about 1600 BC to the last century BC. There are four main periods: the age of the Mycenaeans; the era of expansion; the golden age of Athens; and the Hellenistic period.

The Greeks made progress as thinkers partly because they could criticize and laugh at themselves. Here is the festival of Dionysus, god of wine. Part of the festival, at Athens, was comic drama in which even the great were teased. For example, the wise politician Pericles was known to keep Athens safe from its grim enemy, Sparta. Pericles was much admired, but at the festival people called him "onion-head" and said he was as pompous as the god Zeus!

THE MYCENAEANS c1600-1150 BC

The first great civilization of the Greek mainland is named after the town of Mycenae. We know of this civilization from archaeological excavations, and from the poetry of the Greeks themselves. The language of the Mycenaeans was Greek. Their style of metalwork, painting and palace-building was largely borrowed from an older civilization, the Minoan, on the island of Crete.

The Mycenaean world probably consisted of many rich little kingdoms. Archaeologists have found palaces in several parts of southern Greece, some with enormous royal tombs nearby. To build these must have meant much hard work for ordinary Mycenaeans. It is clear that their rulers had great power over the people.

The Mycenaean civilization was overthrown violently around 1200 BC by invaders from the north known as Dorians.

Our picture shows the main entrance to Mycenae – the Lion Gate. Laborers struggle to take in a bull for slaughter, while two ladies of the royal family drive out their chariot. Guards on the ramparts wear helmets made with wild boars' tusks.

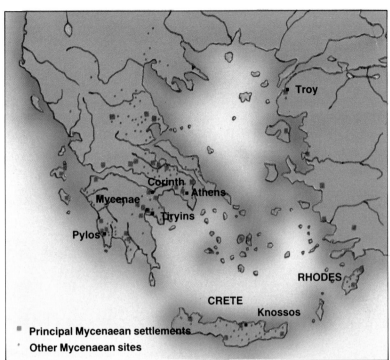

Principal Mycenaean settlements
· **Other Mycenaean sites**

DATECHART

1500s BC The metalwork placed in graves at Mycenae shows that there were fine local craftsmen and rich rulers.

1400s BC Mycenaean Greeks rule the great palace at Knossos on Crete. Mycenaeans had learned much from the Cretans, but now they dominated them.

1400 BC Destruction of Knossos.

1400s-1200s BC The great age of Mycenae. Trade with eastern Mediterranean lands and with Egypt.

1200s BC Huge "beehive tombs" are built at Mycenae, and elsewhere in Greece. The Mycenaean world is threatened. Fortifications are built around its palaces. The Lion Gate is built.

Late 1200s BC The Mycenaeans may have raided the town of Troy in northwest Asia Minor – a raid later remembered as the great Trojan war.

1200 BC The palace at Pylos is captured and burned.

1150 BC Mycenae suffers the same fate. We do not know who the enemy was. It may even have been part of the local population. But more likely the destroyers came from northern Greece. Their fires accidentally baked, and so preserved for us, the many tablets of clay on which palace records were kept.

149

THE MYCENAEANS

Mycenaean treasure

Greeks down the centuries remembered that Mycenae had been "rich in gold." A German excavator, Heinrich Schliemann, dug at Mycenae in the 19th century (illustrated). He found golden death masks, representing the faces of Mycenae's dead rulers. The most famous is shown on the right. Skilled metalworkers of the period also made ornamental daggers, with different colored metals representing figures in hunting scenes. Copper and gold were imported from abroad.

Hunting boars

Hunting was a favorite pursuit of the Mycenaean aristocracy. Hunting wild boars was exciting and dangerous. Their tusks gave serious wounds, which could easily be fatal. A wall-painting from Tiryns shows that aristocrats of both sexes hunted boars. Afterward, the flesh was eaten and the boar's tusks were sliced lengthwise to form the covering of helmets. Mycenaean figure-of-eight shields were also used in hunting lions.

Tombs

Mycenaean rulers were given high honors even when dead. It was hoped that there was life after death. Several rulers were buried in "beehive tombs." They were magnificent chambers of carefully shaped stone covered with earth. Great wooden platforms were probably used to raise the biggest stones. The lintel over the door of the tomb shown here weighs about 100 tons.

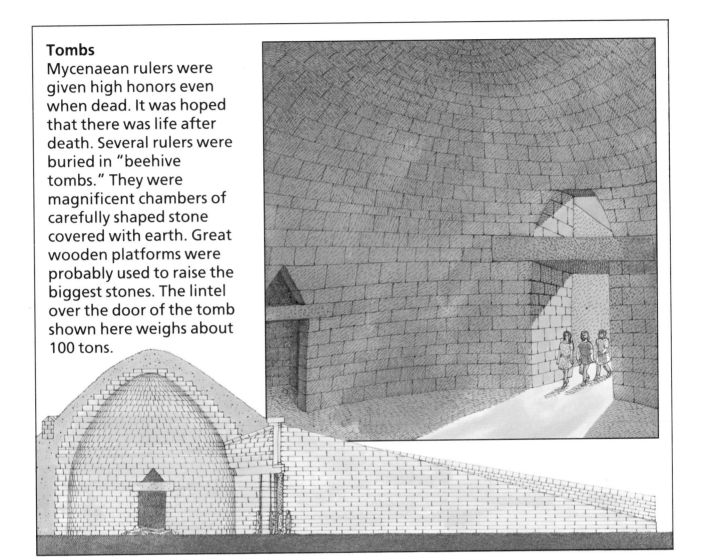

Linear B

Palace scribes wrote on tablets of clay, with signs quite different from the Greek script used in later times. In the 1950s, this early script – "Linear B" – was deciphered and shown to be Greek. The tablets record life just before the Mycenaeans were conquered. They record presents given to the gods – honey and perfumes, for instance. They also show what was in the palace storage rooms, down to broken chariots.

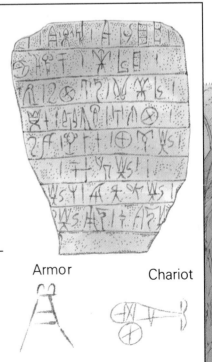

Armor   Chariot

THE MYCENAEANS

Poems about the Mycenaeans

Two great poems, each as long as a modern novel, have been enjoyed by Greeks through the ages – the *Iliad* and the *Odyssey*. They told of warriors who, led by a king of Mycenae, attacked the fortress city of Troy (shown in the illustration as it was, and in the photograph as it is today). Afterwards the warriors faced terrible dangers returning home.

The storytellers

Greeks thought that the *Iliad* and the *Odyssey* were the work of one poet, Homer. But it is now known that many poets, or "bards," shared in making the poems. They composed orally and learned lines from earlier poets by heart. Bards also added ideas and verses of their own. They recited to music, often to audiences of peaceful country people who loved to hear of adventures and violent deaths.

The Trojan War

The *Iliad* tells of an episode in King Agamemnon's war against the Trojans. The king had been publicly shamed. Queen Helen, wife of his brother, had run away to live with a man in Troy. People had to be reminded of the king's power: Troy had to be beaten.

Characters in the *Iliad* are realistic; they are not just good or bad. Agamemnon himself makes a mistake. He insults his best warrior, Achilles, by taking away his girlfriend. Achilles withdraws, leaving the Trojans free to go on a rampage. The violence is honestly described. Men scream in agony.

Achilles returns when his friend is killed by Prince Hector of Troy. Achilles kills Hector, and drags his corpse around the walls of Troy — watched by Hector's horrified parents.

Odysseus

The hero of the *Odyssey*, Odysseus, is a man of strength and cunning. But he has to fight against the supernatural, and his journey home from Troy takes many years. Some of his men are eaten by a one-eyed monster, the Cyclops. Odysseus escapes by blinding the Cyclops with a wooden stake. Odysseus's boat gets caught in a whirlpool. The hero hangs above the water "like a bat" until the boat reappears.

153

AGE OF EXPANSION c1000-479 BC

After the fall of the rich Mycenaean towns, Greece entered a period of which little is now known – a dark age. Farmers, fishermen and craftworkers struggled for a living; there was not enough food or land. Many chose, or were forced, to emigrate. They founded colonies on foreign coasts, first in western Asia Minor, then on the Black Sea and the western Mediterranean.

Greek settlements abroad were originally farming communities. But once the settlers were organized, they could trade their extra grain with other cities. This brought some of them great wealth and Greeks in the old homeland joked that some colonists could afford to sleep all day and drink all night!

During this period the Mycenaean form of writing was lost. But after several centuries of illiteracy, Greeks adapted a script from the Phoenicians. Its first letters were alpha and beta; it is the ancestor of our alphabet.

Thera, a small island in the Aegean Sea, sent away some of its people. They sailed to the coast of North Africa and tried to found a colony – without success. Then they returned to Thera. But the people at home were furious. They would not let the men land, but threw things at their boats and forced them to return to Africa. There the colonists succeeded at last in founding the city of Cyrene.

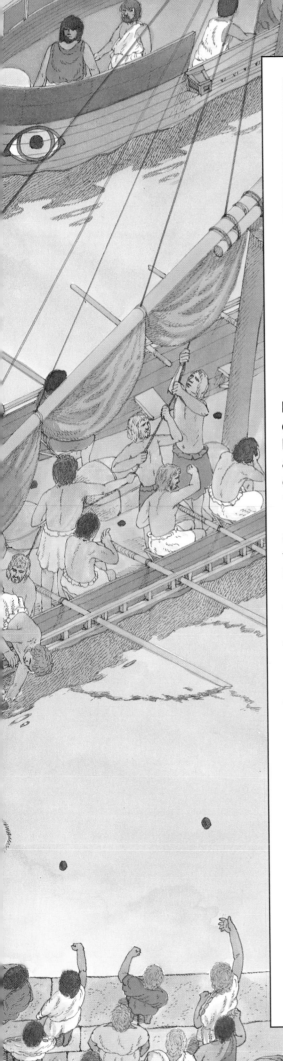

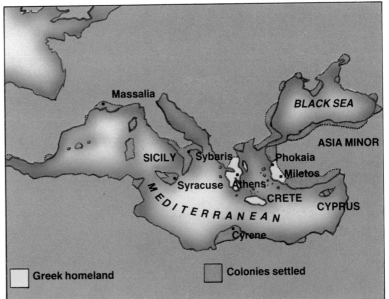

Map labels:
- Massalia
- BLACK SEA
- ASIA MINOR
- SICILY
- Sybaris
- Phokaia
- Miletos
- Syracuse
- Athens
- CRETE
- CYPRUS
- MEDITERRANEAN
- Cyrene

☐ Greek homeland ☐ Colonies settled

DATE CHART

c1150 BC The fall of Mycenae. Palace-building and fine metalworking cease. This is the start of "the dark age."

c1000 BC Greeks colonize the western coasts of Asia Minor.

700s BC Homeric poems reach their final form. The arrival of writing. The Olympic Games begin. Men from Corinth create the colony of Syracuse in Sicily.

c700 BC Invention of fighting in a "phalanx," a close formation of heavily armed foot soldiers, known as "hoplites." The power of these soldiers brings to an end many aristocratic governments in Greek cities. New rulers called "tyrants," champions of the hoplites, rule many cities in the 600s and 500s BC.

c600 BC Greeks first use coinage, an invention of (non-Greek) Lydians in Asia Minor.

Early 500s BC Fine poetry, which we can still read today, is written by Sappho, a woman of Lesbos.

500s BC Philosophy is invented. Pythagoras explores mathematics. The first Greek maps are drawn. There is intelligent speculation about astronomy, physics and the gods.

490s BC Athens helps the vain attempt of Asia Minor Greeks to throw off Persian rule.

490 BC Persia raids Athens in revenge, but is defeated at Marathon.

480-479 BC The great Persian invasion of Greece. It is crushed on sea at Salamis and on land at Plataea.

The polis

Ancient Greece, after Mycenaean times, was made up of hundreds of little states. Some were no bigger than villages. Each was known as a *polis*, and had its own government. In some states "oligarchs" ruled – a few rich men who announced their decisions to the people. Others were ruled by a "tyrant," a dictator above the law. From the late 500s BC some Greeks had democracy. Under this system, male citizens held meetings with much laughing and shouting to decide how the polis should be run.

Country life

Most Greeks made their living in the countryside. Here a poor family works on the estate of a wealthy man. His house is in the background, with a tall tower in which his wife and daughters lived a secure and sheltered life. The man plowing uses a plowshare of iron – a metal which came into widespread use after the Mycenaean period. In the background the wife of the plowman collects honey, while his daughter harvests olives with a long stick. His son has hares from a hunt. Much work, indoors and out, was also done by slaves.

One farmer and poet wrote: "Get a woman to follow the plow. But don't marry one – buy one."

The immortals

Most Greeks believed that gods and goddesses controlled events on earth. If lightning struck someone's house, that might be Zeus's anger at work. When a woman died in childbirth, it was the work of Artemis and her "gentle arrows." To attract a boyfriend or girlfriend a person prayed to Aphrodite. Before a sea voyage, a sacrifice of wine was poured to Poseidon, so that he would not cause a shipwreck. Anxious people asked the gods for advice. And to please the gods, temples for them to occupy were built in the loveliest places, on hilltops and headlands with fine views.

1. Artemis (hunting)
2. Asclepius (medicine)
3. Dionysus (wine)
4. Athena (wisdom)
5. Pan (shepherds)
6. Zeus (lord of heaven)
7. Hera (wife of Zeus)
8. Apollo (music and arts)
9. Ares (war)
10. Demeter (corn and earth)
11. Aphrodite (love)
12. Poseidon (sea)

Many farming methods from ancient times are used in Greece today, and women still do much of the work on the land.

Farm produce is often transported by donkeys. The photograph shows a donkey threshing corn in the traditional way.

157

The life of women

Few women in ancient Greece got an education. Sappho was one. She wrote poems about her girlfriends and about her lovely daughter Cleis.

Women of wealthy families were meant to stay at home. Their main task was to have children – and especially sons – to support the parents later in their old age. A childless woman could be divorced and abandoned. Some women were so afraid of this that they pretended to be pregnant, then smuggled in other women's babies.

Women also prepared raw wool and made clothes from it, as in the picture below. (The photograph shows a Greek woman today weaving in the traditional way.) To have a suntan suggested that a woman worked outdoors because she was poor. So rich, fashionable women were proud to be pale.

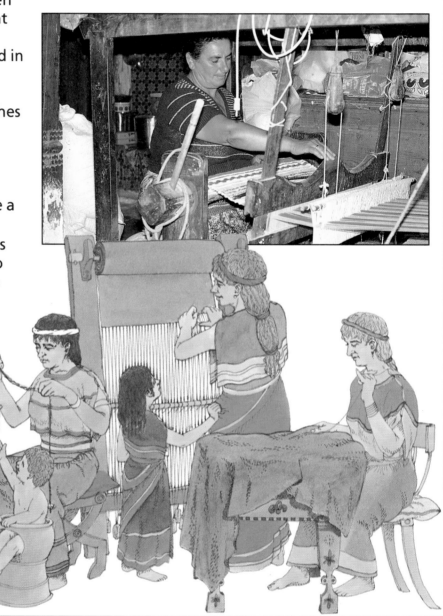

The Persian Wars
Stretching away to the east of Greece was the vast Persian Empire. It included most of the Middle East, and had far greater resources than Greece. In 490 BC King Darius of Persia sent a fairly small force to attack Athens, which the Athenians defeated at Marathon. According to legend a messenger ran with news of victory to Athens – the original Marathon run!

Persia had to gain revenge, otherwise her subjects might think her weak and revolt. So in 480 BC Persia sent an enormous invasion force, hundreds of thousands of men by land and sea, under King Xerxes. The Greeks were terrified,

but did not panic. Three hundred Spartan hoplites went bravely to their deaths, trying to block the pass of Thermopylae against the Persians.

At the battle of Salamis (illustrated) the Persian fleet was tricked into fighting in a narrow space. The slower, heavier, Greek ships crashed triumphantly into the crowded enemy. Xerxes fled. The full Greek land army, led by Sparta, crushed his remaining troops on land at Plataea.

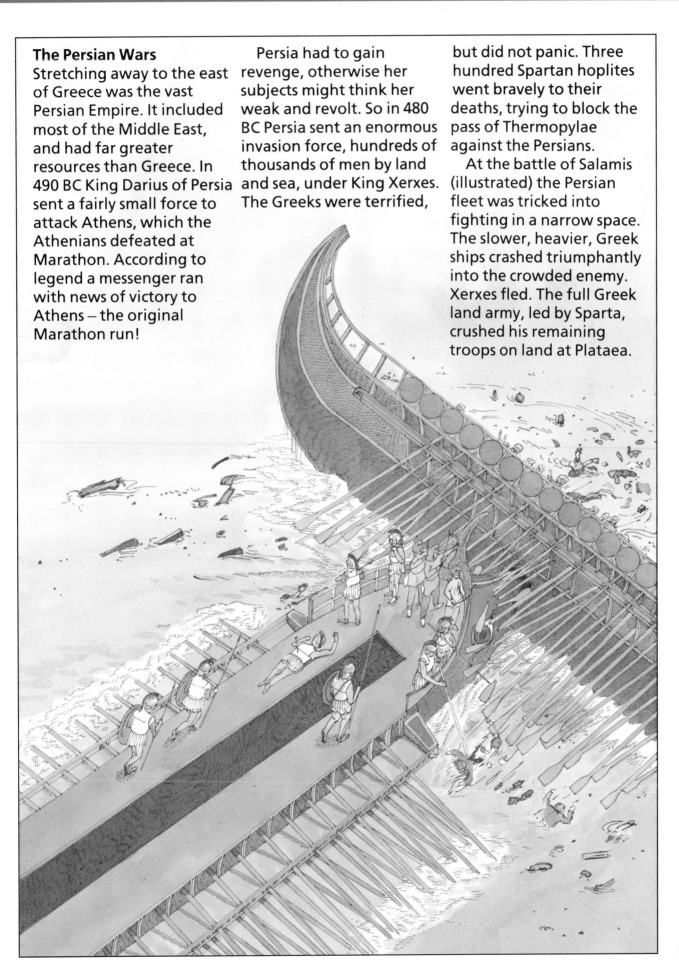

THE GOLDEN AGE 478-405 BC

After Salamis, Athens' ships dominated the Aegean Sea. Other Greek states allied with Athens, and paid her to organize naval raids on Persian territory. By degrees this alliance became an Athenian empire. Athenian warships protected traders and captured pirates. They forced other Greeks to adopt democracy, as Athens had, and made them pay tax to Athens.

With this new income, Athens entered a "golden age." Superb temples were built which still stand today. The most important was the Parthenon. There was also wealth to produce drama, and new and shocking ideas were expressed about society and the gods. But Athens' rise was watched with dread by her rivals – the Spartans. Cunning, brave and savage, the Spartans crushed Athens after long years of war.

A scene from the 440s BC. On the acropolis ("high city") of Athens, the Parthenon, Athena's great temple, is being built. Some Greeks called it Athens' "pretty face." Behind wooden scaffolding, columns rise, made of stone drums. Citizens admire the sculpture to be placed above the columns.

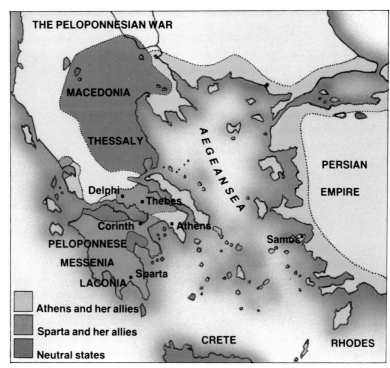

THE PELOPONNESIAN WAR

MACEDONIA

THESSALY

AEGEAN SEA

PERSIAN EMPIRE

Delphi
Thebes
Corinth
Athens
PELOPONNESE
Samos
MESSENIA
Sparta
LACONIA

CRETE

RHODES

Athens and her allies

Sparta and her allies

Neutral states

DATECHART

477 BC Athens leads a new alliance against Persia.

469 BC Her admiral Cimon crushes the Persian fleet in the eastern Mediterranean.

c460-455 BC An Athenian fleet tries to dominate Egypt. However, it is stranded and captured when the Persians cunningly drain the water from under it.

c460-446 BC The first Peloponnesian War – Sparta and her allies against Athens and hers – ends in a draw.

Mid and late 400s BC Age of great Athenian dramatists. Athens encourages – or forces – many allies to adopt democracy.

447 BC Athens begins building the Parthenon. Soon after comes the complex gateway building, the *Propylaea*. This is even more impressive to Greeks.

431 BC Sparta, seeing an Athenian weakness, begins the great Peloponnesian War.

421 BC The first stage of the war ends, with Athens slightly ahead.

415 BC Athens invades Sicily, and seeks to become queen of the Mediterranean.

413 BC Athens loses her great invasion force at Syracuse in Sicily.

404 BC Sparta and allies starve Athens into surrender.

THE GOLDEN AGE

Life in Athens

The Athenian democracy was famous for free speech. Ordinary men were not afraid of the authorities, because in many ways they *were* the authorities. Rich men complained that the poor and even the donkeys wouldn't get out of their way in the street!

Athens was an open city. Foreigners brought new ideas. There were many festivals, with free food. Money was given to the poor to buy theater tickets. Actors wore masks, but still they made the audience feel terror and sympathy during a tragedy. Comedy was more relaxed. The audience was merry from drinking. The actors made rude jokes and criticized politicians.

Greek ideas

Athens became the center of Greek ideas. Athenians practiced philosophy – a Greek invention. Wise men like Socrates asked intelligent questions, which revealed that ordinary ideas about knowledge and justice were too shallow. At drinking parties men would learn by discussing and criticizing each others' ideas.

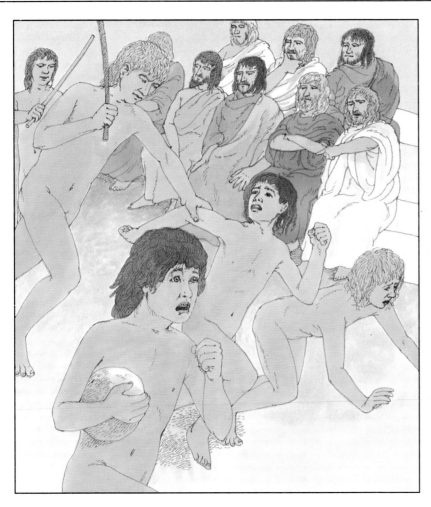

Life in Sparta

At Sparta there was less fun and freedom than at Athens. The city was like an army camp. Spartans feared that their unfree workers, the *helots*, would attack. So they trained to become good soldiers. Cowards were hit and insulted. This was to teach Spartans to face death bravely on the battlefield. They called themselves "the similars." Anyone who was a bit different was unpopular. Books and new ideas were not welcome.

Boys were taught to steal and lie, to make them cunning warriors. The cheese-stealing contest, shown here, taught them to be brave but also how to avoid being hit.

Schools and education

Athenian boys went to school, but girls did not. Girls were meant to learn from their mothers at home. The boys were taught to read and write and also to respect the wisdom in the old poems of Homer.

Probably the teaching of boys was rather relaxed, without written examinations. This may be one reason why Greeks in adult life still found learning to be fun. Greek men were said to be like children, because they kept on asking intelligent questions.

THE GOLDEN AGE

Decisions at Athens

Big decisions, such as whether to go to war, were made by mass meetings of Athenian male citizens. These ordinary men had much more power than in most countries today.

Election was used to choose generals, such as the aristocrat Pericles (far right). But most official jobs were awarded by lot, so that ordinary people would get them. A man who was too powerful could be "ostracized" – sent away for 10 years. Voters, like those shown here, wrote his name on *ostraka*, bits of broken pot.

Hoplite

Helmet

Cuirass

Sword

Spear

Shield

Greaves

Land warfare

The main force in most land battles was the phalanx, formed of heavily armed hoplites in lines. They had large shields, and fought shoulder to shoulder, moving slowly. Archers could damage them and so cavalry was used to chase these opponents away. A hoplite killed by thrusting a spear at an enemy's neck. Below, a hoplite arms while his wife and father look on.

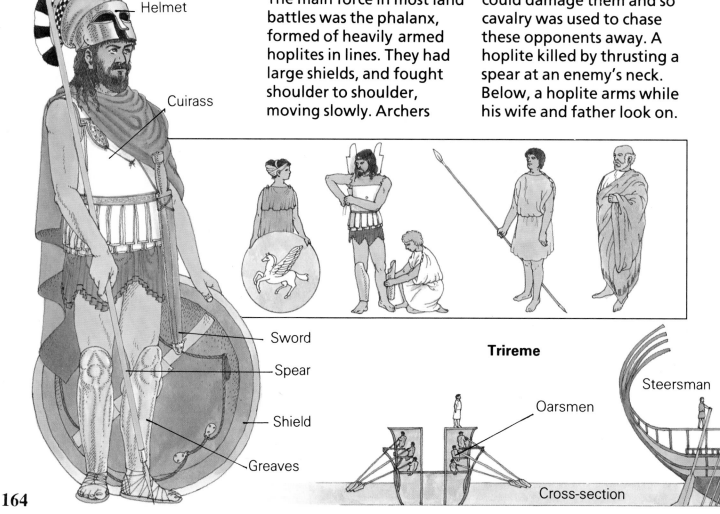

Trireme

Steersman

Oarsmen

Cross-section

The Peloponnesian War

Spartans dreaded that Athens would one day dominate the area of southern Greece which Sparta controlled, the Peloponnese. So Sparta's policy was to wait for a moment of Athenian weakness, then to attack.

In 431 BC Spartans and their allies burned the farms and homes around Athens (shown here), challenging the Athenians to come out and fight. Advised by Pericles, the Athenians sensibly refused to fight. Instead, Athens' city walls kept the Spartans out, while her fleet brought in food and money. After 413 BC, Sparta built a fleet of her own and cut off Athens' corn supply. Hunger forced Athens to surrender in 404 BC and Sparta took over her empire.

Sea warfare

For a long time Athens dominated at sea. Her fleet at one point had 300 "triremes," ships in which the rowers were arranged on three levels. Each trireme had a crew of about 200. A pipe-player helped the rowers to move their oars in time.

A trireme's crew aimed to maneuver until the ram at the front of their ship could crash into the weakest part of an enemy ship – its side section. The enemy ship would then break and sink. Its sailors drowned or were speared in the water.

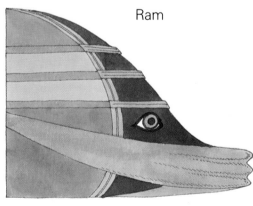

Ram

Marines

Archers

THE HELLENISTIC AGE 336-30 BC

After the fall of Athens, Greece was dominated first by Sparta, then by Thebes. But both were poor cities, and growing in strength on the northern border of Greece was an enemy who owned a gold mine – Philip of Macedon.

Philip's gold bought him allies in Greece, and a professional army, fighting winter and summer. Philip and his experienced men proved too much for the Greek hoplites, most of whom fought seldom and spent winter on their farms. By 338 BC the Macedonians had control of Greece.

In 336 BC Philip was murdered. His son and heir, Alexander, was 20 and less than 5ft tall. "Just a boy," sneered his enemies. But the boy did what Greek men had often dreamed of: he conquered the Persian empire. Alexander and later rulers spread Greek – Hellenic – language and customs from Egypt to northwest India.

For long the Persian empire had been protected by its sheer size. But Alexander's troops were unusually obedient, and marched vast distances at his command. He won his men's respect partly by his courage. The picture shows the battle of Issus in Syria, where Alexander (left) met the inexperienced King Darius III of Persia (right).

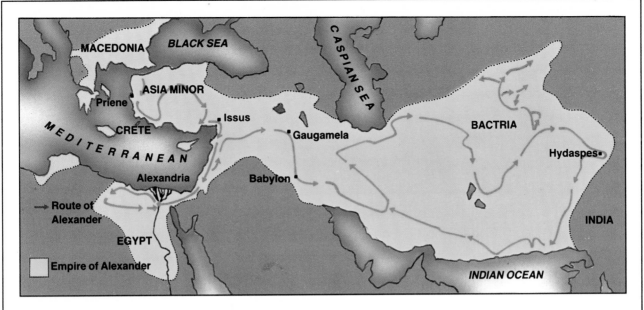

DATECHART

336 BC Alexander inherits Macedonia and Greece.

334 BC Alexander invades the Persian empire and wins Asia Minor.

333-1 BC Alexander crushes King Darius III at Issus and at Gaugamela

and takes over the Persian Empire. He founds Alexandria in Egypt.

326 BC Alexander's conquests in Punjab, northwest India.

323 BC Alexander dies at Babylon. His generals

divide his empire. Seleucos and his descendants got Asia; Ptolemy and his family got Egypt and Alexandria.

40s-30s BC The last Ptolemy, Cleopatra VII, loses her kingdom to Rome.

THE HELLENISTIC AGE

Alexandria, city of learning

Alexander founded many cities called Alexandria. The greatest was on the northern coast of Egypt. It became the leading center of learning. Scholars from abroad received generous salaries at the *Mouseion* (the original Museum).

The great lighthouse of Alexandria, the Pharos (right), was used by the merchants who sailed to India and the east.

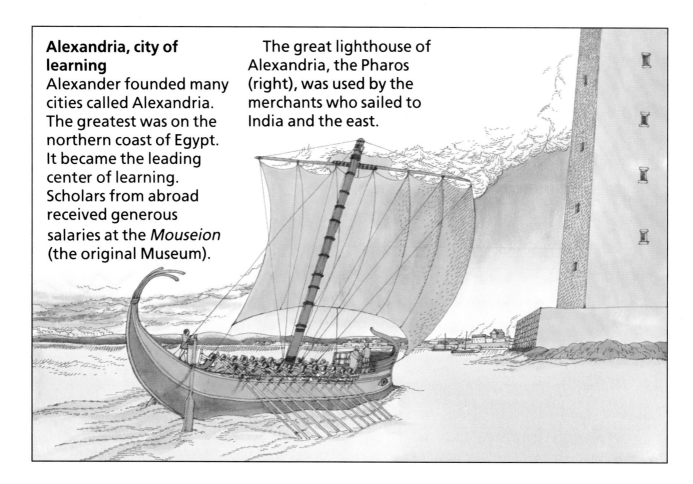

The new learning

Hellenistic rulers had great power over their subjects, and were often worshipped as gods. Writers who criticized or offended them were punished. So the Hellenistic world produced romantic poetry and science. These subjects were relatively safe!

The science of medicine flourished at Alexandria. Herophilos was the first to study anatomy by cutting up human bodies. Much was learned about the parts of the body, and also about the causes of illnesses and deaths. Another doctor, Erasistratos, made important discoveries about the circulation of the blood.

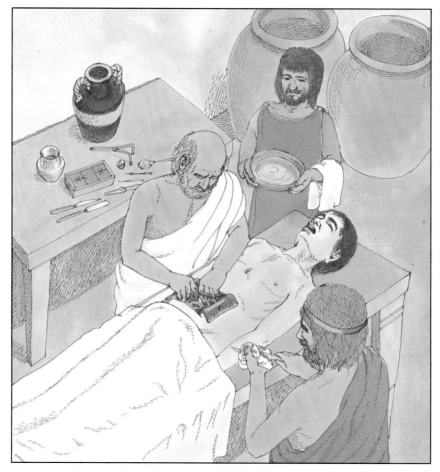

Mathematics

The scientists of Alexandria worked out the size of the earth using geometry. Eratosthenes saw that in southern Egypt a vertical sundial cast no shadow at the summer solstice; the sun was directly overhead. But at the same moment, sundials *did* cast shadow in Alexandria, in the north of Egypt. By measuring the angle of that shadow, and the distance between the northern and southern sundials, he worked out with 90% accuracy the circumference of the earth.

Inventions

Many things were invented at this time. Archimedes invented machines of war.

These included a crane to grab and upset enemy ships. It was also said he invented a device using mirrors to burn ships. Heron of Alexandria built a steam engine.

Industrial production was despised as slaves' work. The picture shows Archimedes at a forge. Blacksmiths are fitting iron bands to a device now known as Archimedes' screw. This is a machine for raising water from one level to another. The photograph above shows the screw still in use in Egypt.

Alexander in the east

Alexander was not content with conquering the Persian Empire. He tried to reach the end of the world. This was thought to be the east coast of India. In the way stood the army of an Indian king, Porus, with terrifying war elephants. Alexander won the battle of Hydaspes and marched on into India (326 BC). But at last his tired soldiers said "No more." They were afraid they would never get home. Alexander pretended to sulk, saying that he would go on alone. But the troops stood firm. At last it was announced, to a great cheer, that they could turn back. The soldiers had done what the enemies could not: they had stopped Alexander.

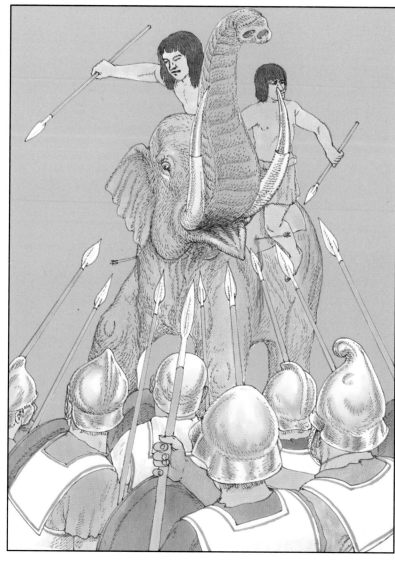

About 200 trained war-elephants stood at the front of King Porus' army in the battle of the Hydaspes. The king himself commanded from the back of one. When the animals charged they served as weapons. At other times they were like a wall for soldiers to shelter behind. After Alexander's death, the Greeks got 500 trained war-elephants of their own, like the one shown here. In exchange they had to give up land in India.

The range of the empire

Alexander's empire was enormous. The coins shown below were from just three of its many parts: Crete, Egypt and Persia. They all carry Alexander's head.

To guard the far-away east of his empire, Alexander left soldiers to colonize Bactria and north-west India. When Alexander died, they tried to march west again. But they were forced back with the help of Persian cavalry. Alexander's generosity to the Persians worked: they were now defending their dead conqueror's empire. Some Greeks in India and Bactria formed lively independent kingdoms. We show the remains at Priene, a Hellenistic city in Asia Minor.

Greek influence on Rome

The Romans eventually conquered the main Hellenistic kingdoms. But Greek ideas lived on. Most Roman writers modeled their work on Greek literature. Greek slaves and ex-slaves acquired great power. The picture shows one of them advising a Roman emperor. In the early AD 300s the capital of the Roman empire was moved from Rome to a Greek city – Constantinople. The people of the new capital were proud to call themselves "the Romans" – in Greek!

171

THE LEGACY OF ANCIENT GREECE

Many of the ideas of Ancient Greece were so intelligent or entertaining that they have attracted people from many times. During the Middle Ages, the long centuries in which Christianity dominated Europe, most Greek literature was lost forever. But from the fifteenth century people rediscovered how interesting the Greeks had been.

From that time until the present day, some schools have taught ancient Greek. Greek writings on politics and religion are still read with respect by many people. And modern scientists, when they want new words for new notions, often make them up — like "catalyst" and "electron" — from the language of the Greeks.

The Olympic Games

Today's Olympic Games are not very old. They began in 1896. They are modeled on the ancient Greek games, which were held every four years at Olympia. Like the modern Olympics (right), the ancient games were the supreme contest for athletes. Ancient Greek states, like nations today, used athletes for propaganda. They fixed races and bribed umpires!

The theater
Drama seems to have originally grown from a simple chorus, which sang in honor of the god Dionysus. The illustration shows a famous playwright of Ancient Greece – Aeschylus – with his players. Plays were presented in theaters specially built into a hillside so that as many people as possible could see. Some of these theaters are still used today (above), and their design has been copied in many modern theaters.

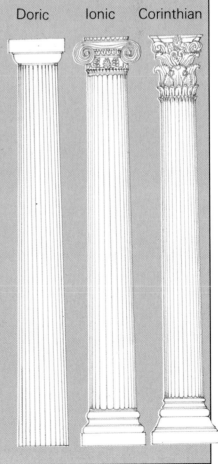

Doric   Ionic   Corinthian

Architecture
Greek architecture is famous for its tall columns. They decorated important buildings, such as the Parthenon (above) in ancient times. Today, many towns have buildings in the Greek style, especially buildings where people go to think, like libraries and museums.

CONTENTS

ROME

INTRODUCTION 176

CITY TO SUPERPOWER c750-40 BC 178

Myth and Reality – The Republican Army – The Senate and the People

Elephants and Warships – Power Brings Riches – Civil War and Murder

THE EARLY EMPIRE c40 BC-cAD 120 184

The First Emperor – A Day at the Games – The Life of the Rich

The Bustling Towns – Roman Children – The Public Baths

THE ROMAN PEACE cAD 120-c230 190

A Mosaic of Peoples – The Rich Become Romans – Building-Large and Small

Arteries of the Empire – Ships and Cargoes – Camels and Cults – A World of Many Gods

FIGHTING FOR SURVIVAL AD 230-527 196

Desperate Times – Rough Justice – Brother Emperors – The Christian Empire

Collapse of the West – Survival of the East – The New Rome – The Roman World in AD 525

THE LEGACY OF ROME 202

THE ROMAN FORTS

INTRODUCTION 205

THE ROMAN ARMY 206

THE ROMAN SOLDIER 208

CAMPS AND FORTS 210

INSIDE A ROMAN FORT 212

DEFENDING A ROMAN FORT 214

OUTSIDE A ROMAN FORT 216

CITIZENS AND SLAVES 218

WHAT BECAME OF ROMAN FORTS? 220

THE ROMAN EMPIRE TODAY 222

DATE CHARTS 224

ENCYCLOPEDIA OF GREAT CIVILIZATIONS

ROME

Including a special feature on
The Roman Forts

INTRODUCTION

The Roman Empire was the greatest in the history of the ancient Mediterranean world. At its height, it enclosed the entire Mediterranean Sea, and stretched from Scotland to the Sahara desert, and from Spain to Syria.

Rome united all these lands for the only time in history. It ruled an area that is today divided up among about thirty countries. This vast territory included a bewildering variety of peoples and cultures. The warlike Celts of France and Britain, the beautiful Greek cities of the Aegean, the ancient civilization of Egypt and the tribesmen of the Syrian desert were all governed by one man: the Emperor of Rome.

This book divides the story of Rome into four main periods. First, there is the rise of Rome from her obscure origins in the eighth century BC to mistress of the Mediterranean in about 40 BC. The second period, from 40 BC to AD 117, saw the Mediterranean united under Roman rule. The third period, from AD 117 to 230, was the climax of the Empire, a time of peace and prosperity which turned to chaos with civil war and foreign invasions. The last period, from AD 230 to 525, saw a new sort of Empire, struggling to survive against its foes. The story ends with the collapse of the Western Empire, and the evolution of the Eastern Empire into Byzantium.

Legionaries on the march
The soldiers who conquered Britain in AD 43 were heavily armed infantrymen. They had to be trained not only to fight, but also to build the forts and roads needed to hold conquered lands. Legionaries were Roman citizens who served as soldiers for twenty years or more.

CITY TO SUPERPOWER c750-40 BC

Rome began as an insignificant town in central Italy in the eighth century BC. For the first three hundred years, there seemed nothing special about her. Like most towns, Rome was a city state that fought with her neighbors. But, gradually, Rome beat all the other powers of Italy, from the strong Etruscan states to the north, to the rich Greek colonies in the south. In the third century BC she clashed for the first time with overseas powers, especially Carthage in North Africa. The terrible wars that followed almost destroyed Rome, but left her tougher and able to defeat anyone else in the Mediterranean.

By 40 BC, much of the known world had been turned into Roman provinces. But the generals of the conquering armies were thirsty for power, and began to fight for it. Rome, the superpower, became wracked by civil war.

Roman versus Roman
During the civil wars, Rome's oldest ally, the Greek city of Massilia (Marseilles) supported General Pompey. She chose the losing side. Below, Pompey's enemy, Julius Caesar, besieges Massilia.

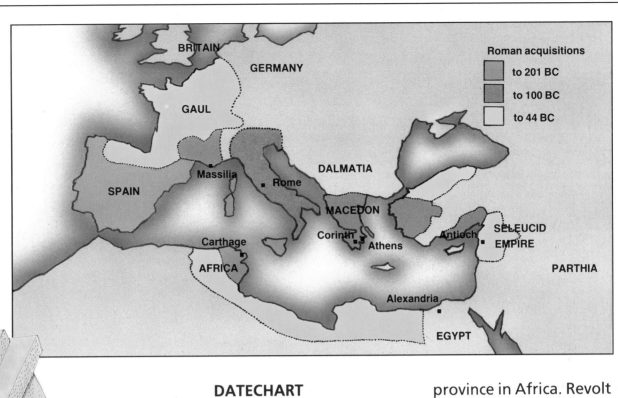

Roman acquisitions
- to 201 BC
- to 100 BC
- to 44 BC

DATECHART

753 BC Foundation of Rome.

510 BC Last king expelled. Rome becomes a republic.

4th to early 3rd century BC Rome becomes supreme in Italy.

264-146 BC Punic Wars.

218 BC Hannibal crosses the Alps.

197 BC Rome sets up provinces in Spain.

196 BC Defeat of Macedon. Rome controls Greece.

192-189 BC War with the Seleucid Empire. Victory brings Roman power into Turkey.

146 BC Destruction of Carthage; Roman province in Africa. Revolt in Greece. Destruction of Corinth.

129 BC Province of Asia set up in western Turkey.

90-88 BC War between Rome and her Italian allies. Rome forced to increase their rights.

63 BC Pompey destroys Seleucid kingdom. Syria becomes a province.

60 BC Pompey, Caesar and Crassus jointly rule the Empire.

58-54 BC Caesar conquers Gaul and raids Britain.

49-46 BC Civil war among Pompey, Caesar and others.

48 BC Pompey murdered.

44 BC Caesar murdered. New civil wars.

Myth and reality

According to legend, Rome was founded in 753 BC by Romulus, one of the twin sons of the war-god Mars. Abandoned near the Tiber River, the new-born twins, Romulus and Remus, were saved by a she-wolf (depicted in the statue of the Capitoline Wolf in Rome, shown in the photograph). When they grew up, the twins decided to create a city at the spot where the wolf had found them. But they quarreled and Remus was killed. Romulus became the first king of Rome.

The Republican army

Rome gradually became the most powerful of the many states in Italy, largely due to the organization and tactics of her army. The army was made up of Roman citizens who were called up for each campaign. They were divided into legions and grouped according to wealth, age and experience. The youngest were the lightly-armed *velites*, while the heavily-armed *triarii* were drawn from the experienced men.

Below, a young soldier says farewell as he leaves the family farm to join his legion for a campaign.

Roman Republican legionaries

Archaeology has shown that Rome actually began as a group of poor villages, in about 750 BC. These soon grew into a single town. At first Rome was dominated by its powerful Etruscan neighbors. But in about 510 BC the last Etruscan king, Tarquin the Proud, was driven out and Rome became a Republic.

The senate and the people

The Roman republic was far from democratic. Power was in the hands of the senate, which consisted of men from the most wealthy and powerful families.

The magistrates, who governed Rome and dispensed justice, were drawn from the senate. The most senior were the two consuls, elected each year. They commanded the armies.

Left, the consul is entering the senate house, escorted by his lictors. They carried bundles of rods and axes symbolizing his power to punish and execute people.

Ordinary citizens had few ways of resisting the senate. Peoples conquered by Rome had even fewer rights, and the growing numbers of slaves had none at all.

181

Elephants and warships

Rome's success in Italy led to wars with other strong states, especially the north African city of Carthage, which possessed a strong navy. Rome and Carthage clashed in Sicily in 264 BC.

The three terrible wars which followed, the Punic Wars, were some of the most savage in ancient times. Rome was almost brought to her knees by the famous Carthaginian general Hannibal. He took his soldiers and war-elephants by ship to Spain and from there led them over the Alps into Italy, and fought there for 16 years.

Despite enormous losses, the Romans eventually beat Carthage, even at sea. Rome had to invent new tactics, such as this boarding bridge which was lowered onto the enemy ship.

In 146 BC, Carthage was totally destroyed by Rome.

Power brings riches . . .

Rome also won wars against the powers of the Eastern Mediterranean. She was mistress of the known world, and became the greatest superpower the Mediterranean had ever seen. Soon she conquered much of the Greek world. The spoils of war made Rome rich. But her rulers were bad and often cruel. Here the Greek city of Corinth is sacked by Rome because of rebellion (146 BC). Its treasures and works of art were carried off to Italy and its citizens were sold into slavery, often to work for Romans.

. . . civil war and murder

The senatorial generals who conquered all these lands for Rome became very powerful men themselves, and their soldiers were more loyal to them than to the government. In the last century BC, several of these commanders fought the government, and each other, for control of Rome.

One of these men, Julius Caesar, defeated his rivals and took sole power. But in 44 BC a group of senators, demanding liberty, murdered him. Civil war erupted once again.

183

THE EARLY EMPIRE c40 BC-cAD 120

Julius Caesar's nephew and adopted son Octavian emerged as the unexpected victor of the civil wars following Caesar's murder. After the defeat of his last opponents, Mark Antony and Egypt's Queen Cleopatra in 31 BC, Octavian was master of the Roman world. He achieved two remarkable things. First, he brought an end to the civil wars, bringing peace and prosperity back to the provinces. Second, he held on to power for over forty years, and became the first Emperor of Rome. He was called Caesar after his adoptive father, and also took the name Augustus.

During his reign, many new provinces were added to the Empire, many cities were founded, and others were given splendid new temples and buildings. Augustus reformed every aspect of government, from the army to coinage, taxes and justice. He laid the foundations for the future.

Rebuilding Rome
Below, Augustus watches the final touches being added to the temple of Mars the Avenger in his new forum at Rome. He had sworn to build the temple when he had avenged the murder of his adoptive father, Julius Caesar. Augustus was a great builder, and introduced the lavish use of marble to Rome. He claimed that he found Rome a city of brick, and left it a city of marble.

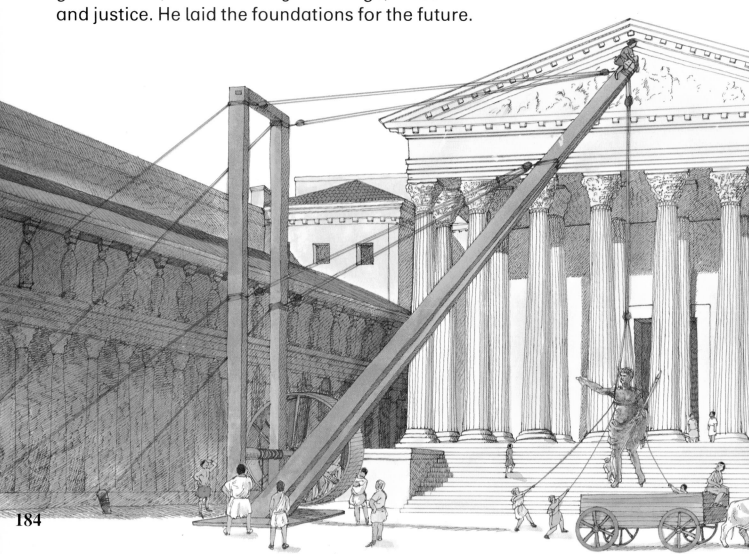

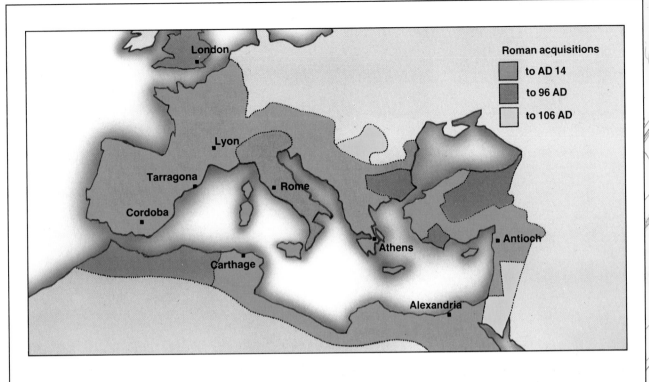

Roman acquisitions
- to AD 14
- to 96 AD
- to 106 AD

DATECHART

43 BC Mark Antony, Octavian and Lepidus jointly rule the Empire.

42 BC Civil war. Caesar's assassins, Brutus and Cassius, are killed.

31 BC War between Mark Antony and Octavian. Victory for Octavian at battle of Actium.

30 BC Suicide of Antony and Cleopatra in Egypt. Rome takes Egypt.

27 BC Octavian becomes Augustus, the first Emperor.

16-6 BC Conquest of Switzerland, Austria and Hungary.

AD 14 Death of Augustus.

AD 41-54 The reign of Claudius.

AD 43 Conquest of southern Britain.

AD 54-68 The reign of Nero.

AD 69-79 The reign of Vespasian.

AD 79 Eruption of Mount Vesuvius buries Pompeii.

AD 98-117 The reign of Trajan.

AD 101-106 Conquest of Dacia (Rumania).

AD 114-117 Parthian War. Attempt to conquer Mesopotamia (Iraq).

THE EARLY EMPIRE

The first Emperor

Augustus was a very clever politician. Although he had sole power, he was careful not to upset the senate. He lived a very modest life, and purposely behaved like a Roman magistrate rather than a king. Here, acting as High Priest, he is sacrificing to the gods.

Behind this public face, however, Augustus was building a new imperial government that was to last 300 years.

A day at the games

Games were held on many religious festivals. They consisted of theatrical performances, chariot races or exciting shows at the amphitheater.

In the great oval arena of the amphitheater, wild beast "hunts" were staged. There were also executions and fights between gladiators, often to the death. There were a few women gladiators, like these. Most gladiators were slaves or criminals. If they survived, they sometimes won their freedom.

The life of the rich

Here, a wealthy senator is giving a dinner party. The guests eat lying down, while domestic slaves bring more splendid dishes. Romans loved food; they had at least 17 ways of cooking suckling pig! But not all dinner parties were orgies. At this one, the guests are being entertained by a Greek slave, reading poems and passages from famous writers. Such well-educated slaves were very valuable and sometimes were treated as members of the family. They were often freed and a few were even adopted by former owners.

The most popular games were the chariot races. In Rome there were four teams: the Reds, Whites, Blues and Greens. They each had their stars and fans, rather like modern sports teams.

Today, many Roman amphitheaters, such as the one in the photograph in France, are still used for bullfights.

The bustling towns

Most of the Empire was made up of city states, towns with their dependent areas of farmland. Roman life was centered in towns, like Pompeii, shown in the illustration below as it was, and in the photograph as it remains today. Towns were divided into blocks by a grid or network of paved streets. Some blocks were given over to temples, public baths and the forum (the central marketplace, town hall and courts). But most blocks were patchworks of small shops, the housing of the poor and the mansions of the rich.

Roman children

Growing up was very different for rich and poor children. Here the son of a wealthy family is about to go off to school, accompanied by his pedagogue, or tutor (an educated Greek slave). It was thought that girls did not need to go to school. Children of poor families got no education at all. They had to go out to work instead.

The public baths

The baths were not just for keeping clean; they were important meeting places, like the forum. Better-off Roman men would spend the afternoon in these bustling, noisy places (women bathed earlier). After exercising, they went into the hot chamber to sweat the dirt from the pores of the skin (soap was known, but a little-used luxury). After a dip, and drying off, people might linger in the yard, chatting to friends and enjoying the sunshine. They might watch ball games, or buy snacks from vendors.

THE ROMAN PEACE cAD 120-c230

While it reduced the freedom of many peoples, the Roman Empire generally brought peace and security to the territories it conquered. Many people were probably better off, and shared in the growing prosperity of the Roman world.

When the great soldier-emperor Trajan died in AD 117, the era of expansion came to an end. His successor, Hadrian, did not go on wars of conquest, even though he was an experienced soldier. Instead, he spent much of his reign traveling through the Empire, inspecting the provinces and the armies which defended the imperial peace against attack or rebellion.

For most of the rest of the second century, the Mediterranean world was politically united, and at peace, for the first and last time in history. This was a "golden age" of relative happiness and prosperity, long to be remembered.

Planning Hadrian's Wall
Hadrian visited Britain in AD 122, and while there gave orders for the construction of the great wall. Below, the Emperor and his engineers discuss the line the wall will take, from a hill overlooking the fort of Vindolanda. Eighty Roman miles long, Hadrian's Wall ran from Newcastle to Carlisle. Much of it can still be seen today.

Provinces and frontiers of the Roman Empire

1 BRITANNIA
2 GERMANIA INFERIOR
3 GERMANIA SUPERIOR
4 GALLIA BELGICA
5 GALLIA LUGDUNENSIS
6 AQUITANIA
7 TARRACONENSIS
8 LUSITANIA
9 BAETICA
10 NARBONENSIS
11 ALPES MARITIMAE
12 ALPES COTTIAE
13 ALPES POENINAE
14 RHAETIA
15 NORICUM
16 PANNONIA
17 DALMATIA
18 MOESIA SUPERIOR
19 MOESIA INFERIOR
20 DACIA
21 THRACIA
22 MACEDONIA
23 EPIRUS
24 ACHAEA
25 ASIA
26 LYCIA AND PAMPHYLIA
27 GALATIA
28 CAPPADOCIA
29 CILICIA
30 ASSYRIA
31 JUDAEA
32 ARABIA
33 CYPRUS
34 AEGYPTUS
35 CYRENAICA
36 CRETA
37 AFRICA
38 SICILIA
39 SARDINIA
40 CORSICA
41 MAURETANIA CAESARIENSIS
42 MAURETANIA TINGITANA

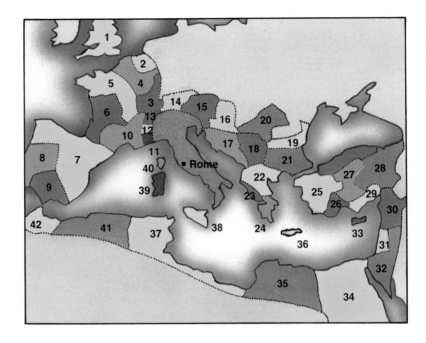

DATECHART

AD 117-138 The reign of Hadrian.

117 Hadrian abandons Mesopotamia.

121-126 Hadrian's first tour of the provinces: Greece, Turkey and the West.

122 Hadrian in Britain.

120s Building of Hadrian's Wall.

129-134 Hadrian's second tour: Egypt and the other Eastern provinces.

138-161 Antoninus Pius. His reign is remembered as a golden age of peace and plenty.

161-180 Marcus Aurelius, the "philosopher king."

161-166 Parthian War.

166 Plague spreads across the Empire. Roman envoys or merchants reach China.

167-175 Marcomannic Wars; Germans briefly break through into Italy.

180-192 The reign of Commodus.

193-7 Civil war. Provincial governors fight for the throne.

193-211 Severus founds a new dynasty, and embarks on new conquests.

195-199 Parthian War. Severus conquers part of Mesopotamia.

208-11 War in Scotland. Severus dies at York.

212 Roman citizenship for almost everyone in the Empire.

227 Parthia overthrown by Sassanid Persia.

A mosaic of peoples

The Empire was made up of peoples of many colors, cultures and languages. Most wealthy people eventually dressed in the Greek or Roman style.

1. Dacian (from modern Rumania)
2. Celtic couple (from Britain or Gaul)
3. Numidian (from North Africa)
4. Wealthy Roman
5. Greek
6. Wealthy Syrian woman
7. Jewish priest
8. Wealthy Palmyrene woman (from Palmyra in Jordan)

The rich become Romans

A wealthy Romano-British landowner rides out from his fine villa to see how the harvest is going. The tenant farmer and his family are British peasants not much affected by the Roman conquest. They still live very much like their Iron Age ancestors. The landowner lives like a Roman, and may be a Roman citizen, even though his ancestors were probably Britons.

Building – large and small

The Romans were excellent builders, especially in concrete, which they invented, and in brick.

Here we see the construction of a fine town house, and the installation of new drains.

Many Roman towns had piped water supplies and proper sewers.

The stone building beyond will have underfloor heating; hot air from a fire will circulate between the brick floor supports. On top of the floor structure, a mosaic of colored stones is being laid (inset). Mosaics were very expensive.

It took several years, and many thousands of tons of mortar and stone to build Hadrian's Wall, shown in the photograph below.

Arteries of the Empire

Having conquered an area, one of the first things the Roman army did was to build roads to let the troops move about quickly. These roads also made the movement of people and goods much easier, and helped to tie the Empire together in a political and economic network. Many Roman roads are still in use today. Some involved major works of engineering, such as this bridge at Alcantara in Spain. It still carries traffic, more than 1,800 years after it was built.

Ships and cargoes

The roads carried much of the growing trade of the Empire in the first century AD, but the cheapest way of moving goods was by water. Great ships sailed across the Mediterranean, carrying jars of wine, olive oil, and fish sauce, and also many other goods. At Alexandria in the Nile delta (below), Egyptian grain was put on freighters bound for Rome. Most of the bread baked in Rome was made from Egyptian wheat.

Camels and cults

A caravan carrying Chinese silk and other luxuries passes through the desert city of Jerash (in Jordan), past the temple of the Greek god Zeus.

Ideas, as well as goods, traveled across the Empire. By the third century, educated people from Britain to Syria all spoke Greek, or Latin, or both. Religions also spread across the Roman world. Greek cults, long known in the Middle East, now spread as far to the northwest as Britain and so did many religions, including Christianity.

A world of many gods

Most of the many religions of the Empire existed happily side by side. Most people believed that there were many gods, and Romans thought it was right to worship the gods of the peoples they conquered. They often identified local gods with their Roman gods, like Mars. This led to mixing of religions. Shown here are some Romanized Britons sacrificing to a Celtic god identified with the Roman god Mercury. Their temple is a British type built using Roman methods.

FIGHTING FOR SURVIVAL AD230-527

For much of the third century AD, the Empire was wracked by war. There were massive invasions by Germans from the north, and a new enemy, Persia, from the east. Roman generals also fought each other for the throne. There was an economic crisis. The Empire began to break up.

But then, in the nick of time, a series of soldier-emperors arose, drove out the invaders and reunited the Empire. The greatest of these men was Diocletian, who from AD 284 to 305 brought security at last. But the cost was great. The Empire was besieged, and was only kept going by force. The people in the provinces found it hard to supply the huge armies needed to keep the barbarians out. The fourth century emperors, almost all Christians, usually managed to hold the invaders at bay, but in the fifth century the Western Empire was overrun. The Eastern Empire survived – just.

Constantius visits Rome
Here the Christian Emperor Constantius II, son of Constantine, enters Rome in AD 357. Although Emperor for many years, he had never seen the ancient capital; he was too busy defending the frontiers. Rome itself now had massive walls. The Germans sometimes broke through into Italy. The forts and the soldiers of the late Empire looked more medieval than Roman.

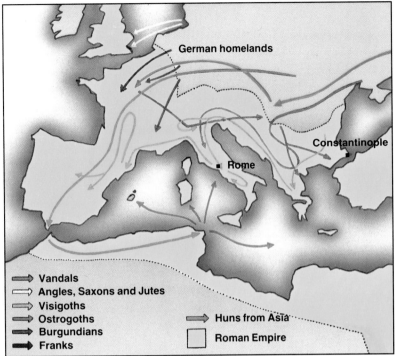

Vandals
Angles, Saxons and Jutes
Visigoths
Ostrogoths
Burgundians
Franks
Huns from Asia
Roman Empire

German homelands

Constantinople

Rome

DATECHART

AD 230s onward Wars with Persia. Barbarian invasions across Rhine and Danube.

258 Western provinces break away to form the Gallic Empire.

271 Palmyra in Jordan revolts and seizes the Eastern Empire.

272-74 Aurelian reconquers the East, Gaul and Britain.

284-305 The reign of Diocletian.

303-311 Persecution of the Christians.

306 Civil wars.

311 Edict of toleration of Christianity.

324 Constantine becomes sole emperor.

325 Council of Nicaea.

361-3 Julian, last pagan Emperor.

395 Empire permanently divided.

406 Barbarians invade Gaul.

410 Visigoths capture Rome.

c410 End of Roman rule in Britain.

410-450 Western provinces fall to Germans.

451 Huns defeated.

475-476 Romulus Augustulus, last Emperor of the West.

527 Justinian Emperor of the East.

Desperate times

The third century was a dark time for many provinces, especially those near the frontiers. They were often overrun by foreign armies. Worse, they had to support the defending Roman armies – which also fought each other! Here some soldiers are taking supplies from a farm without paying. They are from a regiment chasing barbarian raiders who have set fire to another farm in the distance. Things like this bankrupted many farmers. Many became brigands, and a great deal of land was deserted.

Rough justice

From AD 212 almost everyone in the Empire was a Roman citizen, but this did not mean everyone was equal. The gap between rich and poor widened. Poor farmers were crushed by the weight of tax and rent. The wealthy could reduce them to a state little better than slavery. Right, a powerful landowner takes a tenant to court for non-payment of rent. There was no equality even in court; the poor could be tortured to gain evidence.

Brother Emperors

When Diocletian came to the throne he knew that it was no longer possible for one man to govern the Empire. He appointed three co-rulers. This is depicted in the statues, shown in the photograph, carved in the walls of St. Mark's in Venice. Henceforth, there were usually at least two emperors at a time.

The Christian Empire

Constantine became a Christian early in his reign. He lavished wealth on the Church, which soon became an important power. But it was divided by disputes over what was true belief. Constantine intervened. His bishops met at the Council of Nicaea in AD 325 (below) and reached a compromise. However, divisions remained, and sometimes broke out into violence. Christians also began to persecute pagans, as they had been persecuted.

Collapse of the West

Soon after AD 400, the Western Empire crumbled. Germans poured into Gaul. The Goths invaded Italy, and took Rome. Below, the proud aristocrats of Rome are forced to give their riches to the Gothic king, Alaric. But there was worse to come when the savage Huns swept west from central Asia, ravaging all in their path. Under such pressures, the West disintegrated. In AD 476, the last Western Emperor was deposed.

Survival of the East

The Germans set up their own kingdoms in the old Western provinces of the Empire, but neither they, nor the Persians, could conquer the much stronger Eastern Empire.

The Greek-speaking East had lost the ancient capital, but still thought of itself as the *Roman* Empire. It controlled many of the richest provinces, in Turkey, Syria and Egypt, and had the wealth to keep a big army to defend its frontiers.

While the German peoples fought each other for lands in the West, Rome lived on in the East.

The new Rome

Constantinople, the modern Istanbul, was founded by Constantine as his new capital in AD 330. Unlike Rome, it was from the start a Christian city and was adorned with beautiful churches, the greatest of which was Hagia Sophia (right). One of the great cities of the world, it stood at an important natural junction where the main road from Europe to Asia crossed the Bosporus, the channel linking the Mediterranean and the Black Sea. Its huge walls kept the East safe from the Germans.

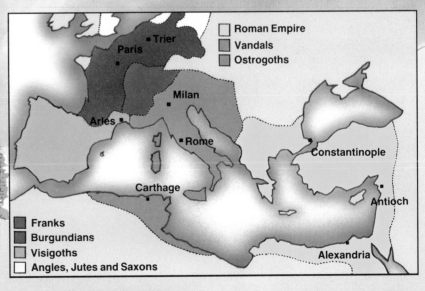

The Roman world in AD 525
Europe is a shifting pattern of German states. Rome is still strong in the East, and can resist both the Germans and the Persians.

THE LEGACY OF ROME

New states appeared on the ruins of the old Western Roman Empire. They were to become the ancestors of the modern countries of Western Europe. Modern languages such as French, Spanish and Italian grew from Latin, and many countries still use the Latin alphabet.

The Eastern Empire did not fall. It lived on, but was soon very different from the old empire of Rome, even though it was its direct descendant and still called itself "Roman." We call it the Byzantine Empire. It gave much of the Greco-Roman heritage to Russia and Eastern Europe.

Byzantium lasted for another 1,000 years, and the final fall of its capital, Constantinople, to the Turks in 1453 was still within living memory when Columbus reached America in 1492.

Inspiration from the past
The memory of Rome is still powerful. The men who drew up the constitution of the United States knew Roman history, and were influenced by it. Words such as "constitution," "republic," "senate" and "capitol" are all taken directly from Rome. Classical architecture has also been reborn in recent centuries. It was used, for example, in designing the Capitol in Washington, DC, shown in the photograph.

The French Empire

Rome also influenced Napoleon Bonaparte. He called himself Emperor and his empire was modeled on Rome. The photograph (right) of a painting by David shows Napoleon crowning his Empress. The memory of Napoleonic glory is to be seen today on the Arc de Triomphe in Paris (below), which was built as a copy of a Roman triumphal arch (right).

From Byzantium to Russia

The Greek-speaking Christian Byzantine Empire has left its own legacy. This photograph of St. Basil's in Moscow shows the Byzantine influence on architecture. Byzantium greatly influenced the development of Russia and other Eastern European states, just as the Western Empire influenced Western Europe. Both the East and the West share common roots in the Empire of Rome.

THE ROMAN FORTS

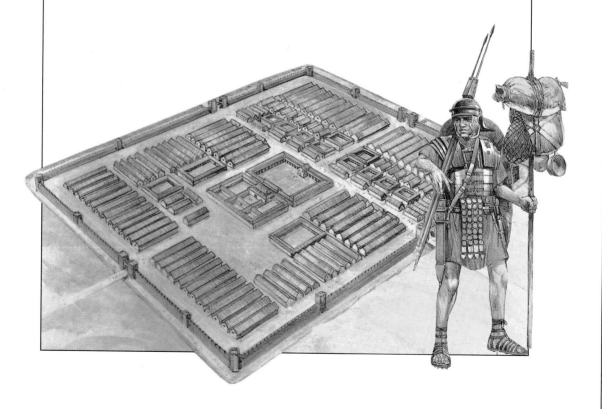

INTRODUCTION

In the cities and towns of the vast Roman Empire people of many different cultures lived as Roman citizens, their safety guaranteed by the *Pax Romana*, or Roman peace. This peace was maintained by a highly organized army. When an area came under Roman control, forts of wood and stone were built. These buildings were bases from which soldiers could patrol far frontiers and roads, and within which they could have permanent winter quarters. In this *Special Feature* we look at the important role they had to play in protecting the huge territory and great variety of peoples within the Roman Empire.

THE ROMAN ARMY

The Roman army was a well-trained and equipped body. It was organized in such a way that every soldier knew exactly what his position was and where he should fight in a battle. Augustus' army was made up of 28 legions.

The most important officers in a legion were the centurions. These captains of the Roman army carried a twisted vine stick as their badge of office – it was used for hitting legionaries – and there were about 60 centurions to a legion. Many came from the ranks and some were very brutal. There were also many technical officers, such as engineers, surveyors and medical men, as well as another army of clerks to organize how to pay, feed and equip the soldiers.

The Roman army relied on many auxiliary, or native soldiers. Numidians from Africa and Gauls from modern France were better horsemen than native Romans or Italians, and the finest archers and slingers were recruited from Crete and the Balearic Islands.

Under strict drill masters Roman recruits learned to march and run, to leap, swim and ride, and to use their weapons in attack and defense.

Every legion had a silver eagle – the symbol of the Roman Empire – as its standard. Individual units would have additional flags and badges, featuring zodiac signs or other fierce animals like wolves and boars. The loss of a standard was regarded as a disgrace and in camps and forts the legion's standards were kept in a shrine called the *sacellum*.

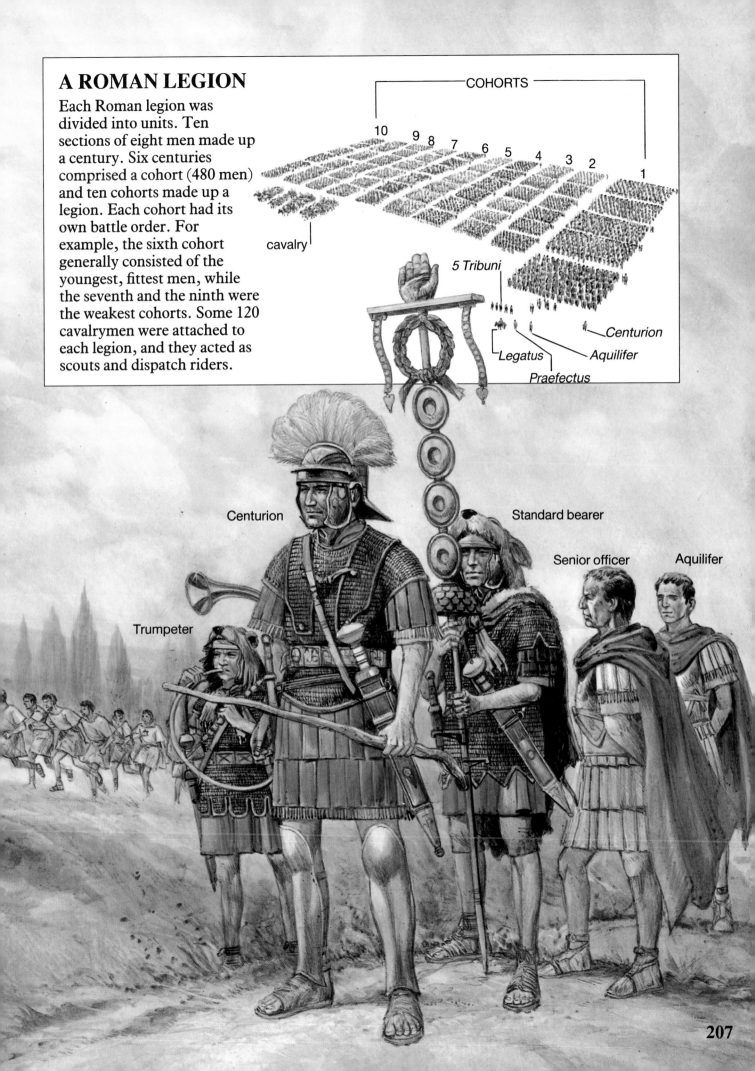

A ROMAN LEGION

Each Roman legion was divided into units. Ten sections of eight men made up a century. Six centuries comprised a cohort (480 men) and ten cohorts made up a legion. Each cohort had its own battle order. For example, the sixth cohort generally consisted of the youngest, fittest men, while the seventh and the ninth were the weakest cohorts. Some 120 cavalrymen were attached to each legion, and they acted as scouts and dispatch riders.

COHORTS

10 9 8 7 6 5 4 3 2 1

cavalry

5 Tribuni

Legatus

Praefectus

Centurion

Aquilifer

Trumpeter

Centurion

Standard bearer

Senior officer

Aquilifer

THE ROMAN SOLDIER

In the earliest days of Rome each citizen had to be prepared to fight without being paid. But soldiers in the Roman empire were paid professionals who signed on for 20-25 years of service. They had to work very hard – often marching 20 miles a day.

Living conditions were simple and very basic. In the field eight men would share a tent and a packmule; in a fort they shared just two rooms: one for sleeping in and one for storing their equipment. Much of a soldier's time was spent on patrols or on sentry duty. Soldiers would be moved around the empire as they were needed from Britain to Africa. During their army service they contributed money to a savings scheme so when they retired they could expect a gift of land or a pension. Usually the land was near the last place where they had been garrisoned. Soldiers were not supposed to marry while in service but this rule was often ignored. In time their sons might join the army as well.

Legionaries return to the fort from a patrol. During their time off duty, soldiers would play games or go to the baths. The soldiers, right, are playing with bones. Playing dice for money was not allowed but many ignored this rule. Some soldiers carried flutes and drums with their kit and whiled away the time playing music.

208

ARMOR AND WEAPONS

Over his woolen tunic an ordinary legionary wore a breastplate of metal strips, scales or rings. He had heavy studded sandals and a helmet. In cold conditions, during British winters, for example, he could stuff the thongs of his sandals with wool and fur and he would be issued with a heavy, hooded cloak. A foot soldier had his short sword, two javelins and a heavy, rectangular shield of leather and wood. Although there were repair workshops attached to each legion, much of the army's equipment came from Gaul and northern Italy. Weapons were made by the army and by private metalsmiths.

CAMPS AND FORTS

At the end of a day's march, Roman army units would build a stockaded camp. Surveying and engineering officers were sent ahead to find clear, level ground, which could not be overlooked by enemies, near a good supply of water.

Camps were usually square or rectangular in shape. A deep trench was dug around the site and the soil and turf were made into an embankment about 25 feet high. On top of this earth rampart the soldiers set up their stakes. Within this stockade the tents were pitched according to a regular pattern. In camps the headquarters complex included the commander and senior officers' tents, as well as the standards. The soldiers' tents were pitched in orderly rows around this area, with latrines and trash pits spaced around them.

The legionary bases followed the same fairly standard layout as the camps. The bases were permanent and often used as winter headquarters when the army was not on the move.

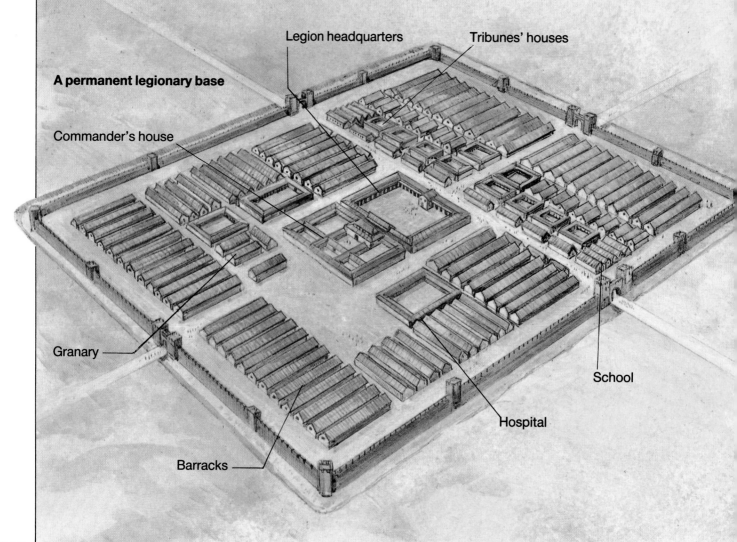

Legion headquarters

Tribunes' houses

A permanent legionary base

Commander's house

Granary

Barracks

Hospital

School

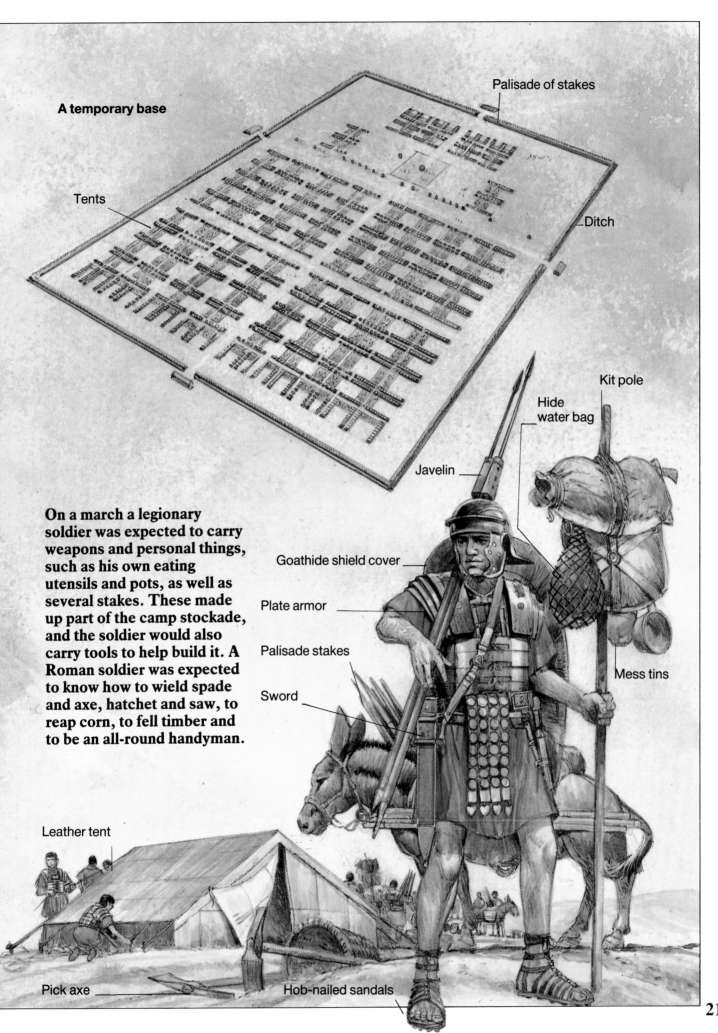

A temporary base

Palisade of stakes

Tents

Ditch

Kit pole

Hide
water bag

Javelin

Goathide shield cover

Plate armor

Palisade stakes

Sword

Mess tins

On a march a legionary
soldier was expected to carry
weapons and personal things,
such as his own eating
utensils and pots, as well as
several stakes. These made
up part of the camp stockade,
and the soldier would also
carry tools to help build it. A
Roman soldier was expected
to know how to wield spade
and axe, hatchet and saw, to
reap corn, to fell timber and
to be an all-round handyman.

Leather tent

Pick axe

Hob-nailed sandals

INSIDE A ROMAN FORT

Gradually, as the Roman Empire stopped expanding, permanent forts were built for the legions garrisoned in frontier zones. Instead of a simple stockade, these forts had stone or at least wooden walls. The ramparts were made of timber and earth. A guarded gate and watchtowers were set into each of the four walls.

As with the camps, the fort's main road led to the central headquarter (*principia*) buildings – the commander's house (*praetorium*), granaries for storing the soldiers' rations and the hospital (*valetudinarium*). In the *principia* there was often a large hall, which contained the shrine for the standards. Forts also bustled with armament workshops, stables and there was a small prison.

The basic plan had to be adjusted to take account of local conditions. In a hot African fort more room was allowed for each soldier's bed and a large courtyard served as the hall, while the British barrack block had to have a fireplace.

The Romans knew the importance of diet, exercise and hygiene for general health. Although senior officers had servants to keep house for them, the ordinary soldiers were expected to keep themselves and their quarters clean and tidy. The centurions gave out different chores, and made sure that the work was done. The soldiers below have the unpleasant duty of cleaning out the latrines.

THE BATHHOUSE

Roman soldiers were clean as well as fit. Within the bathhouses attached to every fort a soldier progressed from a tepid room to a hot room, and from the sweat room to the cold bath. The soldiers would rub oil onto their skin to clean themselves. In the hot room they would sweat and scrape the dirt off. The baths were like a clubhouse, where soldiers could enjoy a few games and a bit of gossip. Baths were usually outside the forts. This was because they needed hot water and the furnace that was used to supply the water could be a fire hazard for the fort.

DEFENDING A ROMAN FORT

Security within a Roman fort was very strict. Every day there was a different watchword which was written on waxed pieces of wood. An officer called the *tesserius* was in charge of organizing the sentries and passing on this watchword. Then, each night, four legionary cavalrymen went round to inspect the watchmen. If all was in order they took the watchwords (*tesserae*) from the sentries on duty. Then, at daybreak, the inspection party reported to the officer in charge, and handed over the wooden tablets.

If anything had gone wrong, if a sentry had been found asleep, for example, he was court-martialled. If he was found guilty he was usually sentenced to being set upon with stones and cudgels by men from his own unit. Such men usually died. If they didn't they were disgraced forever. The same penalty existed for theft. It was also considered a serious offense to lose weapons on a battlefield or to give up a position out of fear.

To communicate with other forts or units along the frontier, the Romans had elaborate signaling techniques. From special towers they issued columns of smoke from straw by day, and torch signals by night. The signaling tower had to be high enough for fire or smoke to rise clear of trees and mist. Fog made signaling impossible.

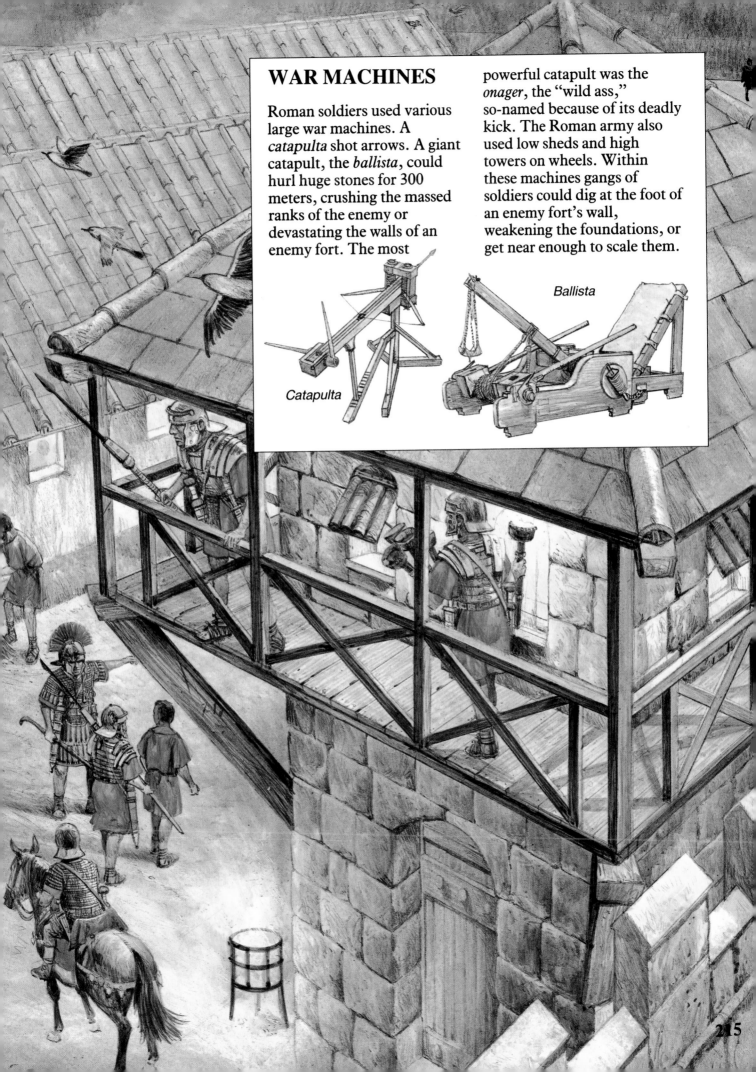

WAR MACHINES

Roman soldiers used various large war machines. A *catapulta* shot arrows. A giant catapult, the *ballista*, could hurl huge stones for 300 meters, crushing the massed ranks of the enemy or devastating the walls of an enemy fort. The most powerful catapult was the *onager*, the "wild ass," so-named because of its deadly kick. The Roman army also used low sheds and high towers on wheels. Within these machines gangs of soldiers could dig at the foot of an enemy fort's wall, weakening the foundations, or get near enough to scale them.

Catapulta

Ballista

215

OUTSIDE A ROMAN FORT

Although forts could be as large as 50-60 acres, they were strictly for soldiers and military business. Often, only the bathhouse and an amphitheater were built beyond the walls. The amphitheater was probably used for gladiator fights, parades and ceremonies, of which there were many in the army calendar. After a religious sacrifice the soldiers could feast on the carcasses of the slaughtered animals. Although their diet was good by modern standards – plenty of cereals, fresh fruit and vegetables (when available), and meat from the legion's own herds – it was also boring.

The area surrounding a fort was known as the *canabae* or booths. A large garrison acted as a magnet to local traders and they were allowed to set up their stalls outside a fort. At the stalls and taverns of the *canabae* soldiers enjoyed their leave. When they retired, soldiers were often reluctant to leave the areas they had settled in. They would join their families in their homes near the *canabae*.

Roman soldiers could buy trinkets and treats outside the fort, or get professional letter-writers to send a message home. The booths were strictly controlled by the commander, who had to make sure that the businesses didn't get in the way of the fort's defenses. Eventually, the people from the booths could apply for a charter and become a recognized settlement, or *vicus*. Many towns began like this.

AMPHITHEATER

Bear-baiting, cock-fighting, acrobatics and races were typical events in a regional amphitheater. The chance to see a real gladiator fight was a special occasion. The winning gladiator would ask the crowd if it wanted the loser's life to be spared. The crowd showed their hands and palms up for "yes" and thumbs down for "no."

CITIZENS AND SLAVES

During the reign of Augustus, Roman citizenship was a privilege. A citizen of the empire had many legal rights and privileges. Provincials or non-citizens fell under a second-class law called the *ius gentium*. However, early in the 3rd century (AD 211), all free men living within the empire became citizens. By then the empire faced threats from barbarians outside its frontiers and, by giving all men within its frontiers equal rights, hoped to inspire their loyalty.

The Roman Empire depended on millions of slaves, who both in cities and on the land did the hardest and dirtiest work. But even among slaves there were distinctions. Educated Greek slaves were often employed as teachers in noble families. Slaves did much of the clerical and administrative work of the empire. Although they were technically at the mercy of their owners, by imperial times slaves had some rights against unjust or brutal masters. More important, they could expect to become freedmen eventually.

Rome offered an orderly, prosperous life as a citizen while invading barbarians offered chaos. If a treaty could not be made, or if they could not be encouraged to settle peacefully in a fixed place within the empire, these war-like land-hungry tribes had to be overcome militarily.

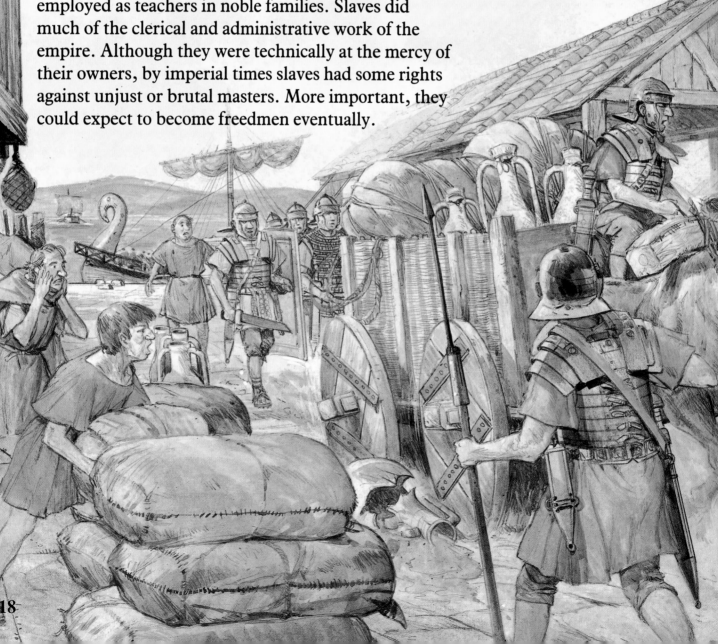

THE *TOGA*

The *toga*, a half circle of white wool or linen wrapped around the body with the end carried over the left arm, was the badge of Roman citizenship. It was hard to wear properly without pins or buttons, and it was so cumbersome and difficult to keep clean that in the days of the empire it was only worn on public and formal occasions. A great event in the life of a Roman boy was the day on which, about his 15th year, he put on the *toga virilis*, the toga of manhood. He went to the Forum where he was congratulated and his name was then added to the list of citizens.

WHAT BECAME OF ROMAN FORTS?

Under Trajan (AD 98-117) the empire grew too big to be easily defended. The next emperor, Hadrian, gave up some of Trajan's conquests and concentrated on strengthening existing boundaries.

At this time the empire was at its most peaceful and stable, but this situation did not continue. The third century saw frequent strife and disaster. The most heavily manned forts could not keep out invasions by masses of people forever. Germanic tribes were pushing over the Rhine, while Persians were pushing in from the east.

In AD 285 the emperor Diocletian had to introduce a totally new system of government. The empire was divided into eastern and western parts. Emperors had to be full-time military leaders and the army became weakened by the constant wars. In 410 the Visigoths invaded Italy and sacked Rome. Then in 476 the last western emperor, Romulus Augustulus, was deposed by his German commanders. Only the eastern half of the empire, with its capital of Constantinople, endured until its capture by Turks, in 1453.

The Romans occasionally used existing hill-forts as the basis for their own forts. When the Roman soldiers dismantled or abandoned their forts, the local people would then take over the sites and build their own towns round them.

HADRIAN'S WALL

Hadrian's Wall, which runs for 70 miles from Wallsend-on-Tyne to Bowness-on-Solway, was built in the AD 120s after a visit by the Emperor. He streamlined the empire and was concerned to protect this most northerly defense from attack by Picts. The wall was 9 feet thick and 19 feet high. It had 80 small castles and a fort every 4-6 miles. It was overrun several times, and had to be rebuilt before being abandoned in the 4th century.

THE ROMAN EMPIRE TODAY

When the empire had split in two, and its western half had collapsed, so did the legal system and the far-reaching trading networks. Rome was no longer the imperial capital and imperial buildings fell into ruins.

But, in addition to the enduring Roman legacy of Christianity, the empire lived on in countless other ways. Many modern languages – Italian, French, Spanish, Romanian – grew from a common Latin source. Latin words make up more than half of the words we use in English and came via the Normans. Among them are the words and phrases that are just the same today as they were two thousand years ago: when we speak of the salary a person receives *per annum*, for example. Then there are words that we use without realizing their origins. Arena, for example, means "sand" since the amphitheaters were usually covered with sand. Other ordinary everyday examples are "omen," "specimen," "actor," and "circus." In Britain place-names ending in "chester" come from *castrum* (camp).

For centuries and centuries after the death of the last western emperor, Rome continued to be a civilizing influence. Ruins like Dougga in Tunisia remained as a physical reminder of its grandeur, while the cultural and political legacy has been permanent.

ROMAN INFLUENCE

When people think of civilization, classical Roman buildings come to mind. Architects have continued to draw inspiration from Roman buildings. Churches were built with Roman arches throughout Europe until a new Gothic style of pointed arches became widely used in the 11th century. This library building at Oxford in England clearly owes a lot to Roman design. The founders of modern America were also influenced by Roman civilization. They used words like "senate," "constitution" and "republic."

DATE CHARTS

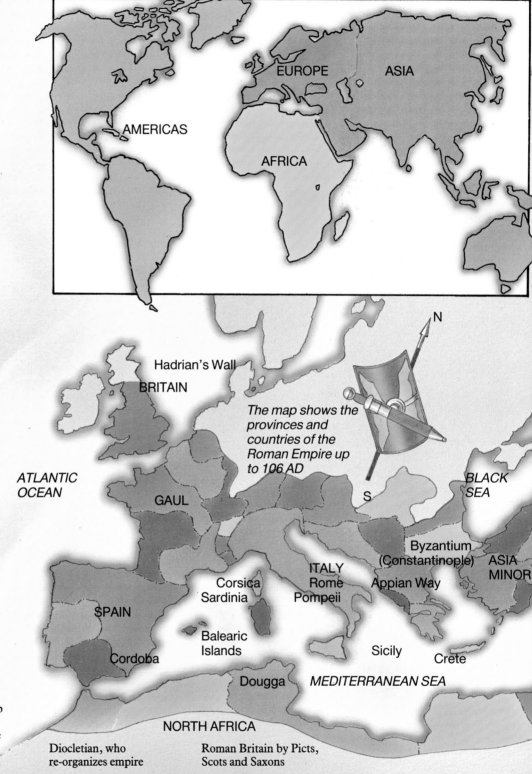

The map shows the provinces and countries of the Roman Empire up to 106 AD

31 BC Victory for Octavian at the Battle of Actium

27 Octavian becomes Augustus and the Roman empire begins

6 AD Judea made a Roman province

14 Death of Augustus

c. 28 Crucifixion of Jesus Christ

41 Emperor Caligula murdered by Praetorians

43 Roman conquest of southern Britain

64 Great fire of Rome

66 Jews in Palestine revolt against Roman rule

68 Death of Nero

70 Jewish revolt suppressed

79 Destruction of Pompeii by eruption of Vesuvius

80 Completion of the Colosseum in Rome

117 Death of Trajan; accession of Hadrian. Roman empire at its greatest extent

122 Beginning of Hadrian's Wall

161-66 War against the Parthians, followed by plague

212 Edict of Caracalla grants Roman citizenship on all free male inhabitants of the empire

230s onwards Wars with Persia. Barbarian invasions across Rhine and Danube

253-68 Germanic barbarians invade the empire

284 Accession of Diocletian, who re-organizes empire

312 Constantine is emperor

313 Edict of Milan, Christianity tolerated within empire

367 Successful attack on Roman Britain by Picts, Scots and Saxons

378 Goths defeat and kill eastern Roman emperor Valens

410 Rome captured by Alaric the Goth; around this time Roman rule ends in Britain

415 Visigoths begin conquest of Spain

476 Romulus Augustulus, last western Roman emperor deposed by Odovacar, a barbarian leader

AFRICA	ASIA	AMERICAS	EUROPE
		100 BC Beginning of the rise of Teotihuacan, great city in Mexico	
6 AD Judea made a Roman province	**6 AD** Civil servic. examination system begins in China		**27 BC** Octavian becomes emperor; the Roman empire begins
10 Kushite kingdom in Nubea in decline	**8** Radical reforms by Emperor Wang Mang in China		
c33 Crucifixion of Jesus Christ	**25** Beginning of Han dynasty in China		**14 AD** Augustus dies
66 Jews in Palestine revolt against Roman rule	**c58-75** Buddhism accepted as official religion in China		**64** Great fire of Rome
70 Jewish revolt suppressed			**79** Destruction of Pompeii by eruption of Vesuvius
	97 Chinese expedition under Kang Hin to Persian Cult		
	c100 Mongol invaders bring rice and iron to Japan; paper invented in China		**117** Death of Trajan; accession of Hadrian
			161-66 The Romans fight the Parthians
			212 Edict of Caracalla gives Roman citizenship to all free men in the empire
	220 End of Han dynasty in China		**230s onward** Wars with Persia; barbarian invasions across the Danube and Rhine
	230 Emperor Sujin rules Japan; first written records there		**253-68** Germanic barbarians invade the empire
c300 Axum conquers Nubia and becomes the dominant power in the Red Sea	**309-79** Persian power at its height under Shapur II	**300 AD** Classic Mayan civilization established in Mesoamerica	**284** Diocletian begins to re-organize the empire
	320 Gupta dynasty reunites India		**313** Edict of Milan, Christianity tolerated within empire
	c350 Pallava dynasty set up in south India		
	c360 Japan conquers Korea		
400 Axum converts to Christianity		**c400** Incas start to establish themselves on the South American coast	**410** Rome captured by Alaric the Goth
429 Vandal kingdom of North Africa is set up			**476** Romulus Augustulus, last Western Roman emperor deposed by Odovacar
560 Birth of Muhammad			

CONTENTS
THE VIKINGS

INTRODUCTION   228
RAIDERS FROM THE SEA   230
BUILDING A LONGSHIP   232
TRADING   234
HEDEBY   236
GROWING UP   238
FARMING AND FISHING   240
FEASTING   242
RELIGION   244
GOVERNMENT   246
VINLAND   248
WHAT HAPPENED TO THE VIKINGS?   250
VIKING TRACES   252
DATE CHARTS   254

ENCYCLOPEDIA OF GREAT CIVILIZATIONS

VIKINGS

INTRODUCTION

Late in the 8th century people from Scandinavia (now Denmark, Norway and Sweden) went south on raiding parties. This was the beginning of the Viking Age, which lasted until 1100. The word "viking" probably comes either from *vik* or *vig*, the Scandinavian word for a creek or battle. In the summer the sailor-warriors went "a-viking," or roving, across the seas in their wonderfully efficient ships. They searched for treasure to bring home or for new lands to settle on.

Why did these people go a-viking? One explanation was that there wasn't enough land in Scandinavia. Norway is very mountainous, Sweden is covered by thick forests and Denmark has large areas of infertile land. The Norwegians raided and then settled in the Faroe, Orkney, and Shetland islands, Scotland, Ireland, and northwest England. The Danes went to Germany, the Netherlands, France, and eastern England. Meanwhile the Swedes reached down through Russia to the Arab world.

228

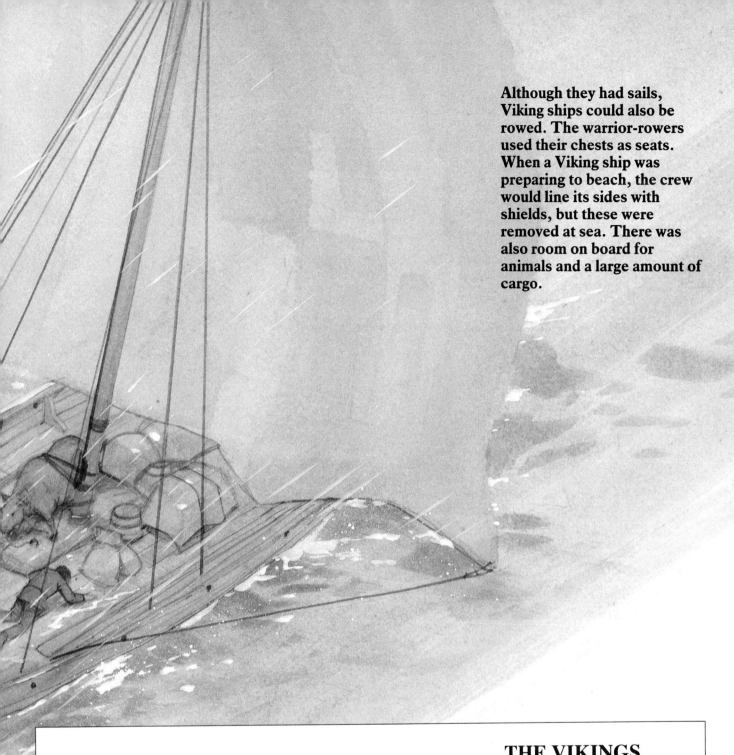

Although they had sails, Viking ships could also be rowed. The warrior-rowers used their chests as seats. When a Viking ship was preparing to beach, the crew would line its sides with shields, but these were removed at sea. There was also room on board for animals and a large amount of cargo.

THE VIKINGS

Norwegian, Swedish and Danish Vikings could all understand each other, even though they spoke different dialects. People thought the Vikings were unusually tall, and the Irish distinguished between them as either dark-haired strangers, the "dubh ghall," or blonde strangers "fionn ghall." The Germans called them ship-men, while the Arabs called them the heathen.

RAIDERS FROM THE SEA

The Vikings were not Christians and saw isolated monasteries and churches as easy targets for hit-and-run raids. In 793 longshipmen attacked the island monastery of Lindisfarne, off northeast England. They destroyed the holy place, took the church treasure, slaughtered some cattle, killed several monks and nuns and took the rest home to be slaves. Soon after these terrible raids were experienced in Ireland, Scotland, Wales, northern England and on the continent of Europe.

Although bows and arrows were used to shoot enemies at long range, Viking soldiers preferred hand-to-hand combat. Some raiders used axes, but more commonly they used spears. Both weapons were used for other purposes: axes could chop timber for houses, and ships and spears could be used for hunting and fishing.

At the time, much of Europe was ruled by Charlemagne, but after his death in 814 his sons quarreled over his empire. They were so busy fighting each other that large inland towns, such as Paris, suffered at the hands of Viking raiders. Monks described the Vikings as "a savage hurricane."

Viking warriors usually wore simple leather caps as helmets. Only the most important men wore armor, such as metal helmets and chain shirts. Vikings took great pride in their weapons but above all they prized their swords. Special swords were handed down through families, and blacksmiths were important members of Viking society.

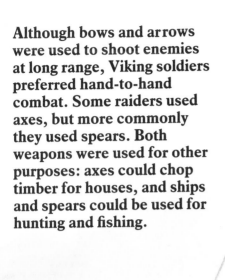

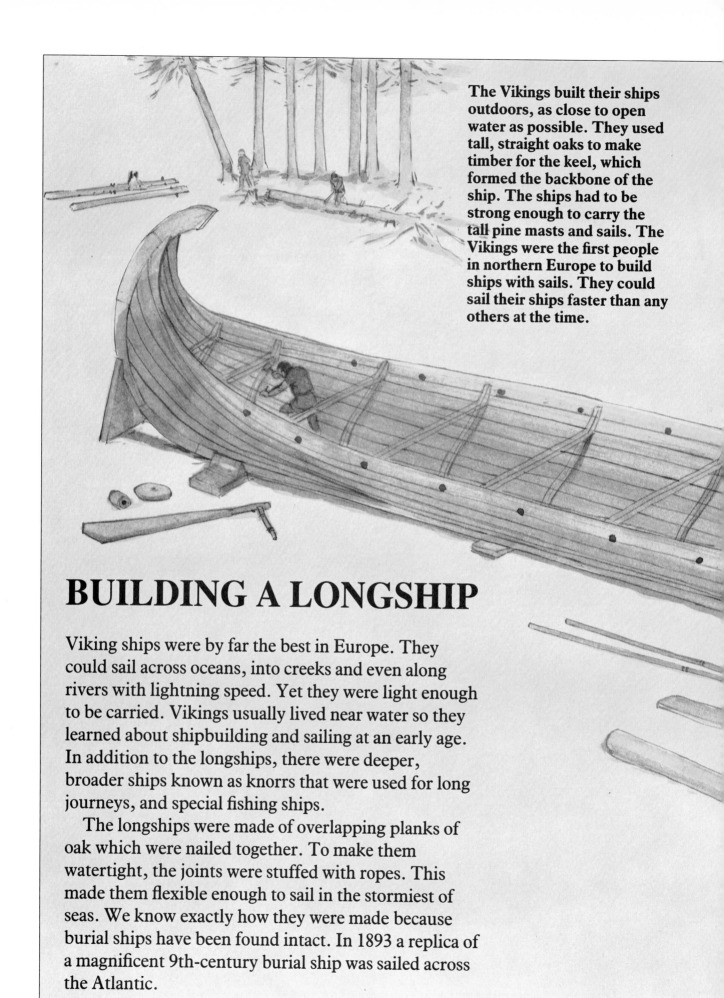

The Vikings built their ships outdoors, as close to open water as possible. They used tall, straight oaks to make timber for the keel, which formed the backbone of the ship. The ships had to be strong enough to carry the tall pine masts and sails. The Vikings were the first people in northern Europe to build ships with sails. They could sail their ships faster than any others at the time.

BUILDING A LONGSHIP

Viking ships were by far the best in Europe. They could sail across oceans, into creeks and even along rivers with lightning speed. Yet they were light enough to be carried. Vikings usually lived near water so they learned about shipbuilding and sailing at an early age. In addition to the longships, there were deeper, broader ships known as knorrs that were used for long journeys, and special fishing ships.

The longships were made of overlapping planks of oak which were nailed together. To make them watertight, the joints were stuffed with ropes. This made them flexible enough to sail in the stormiest of seas. We know exactly how they were made because burial ships have been found intact. In 1893 a replica of a magnificent 9th-century burial ship was sailed across the Atlantic.

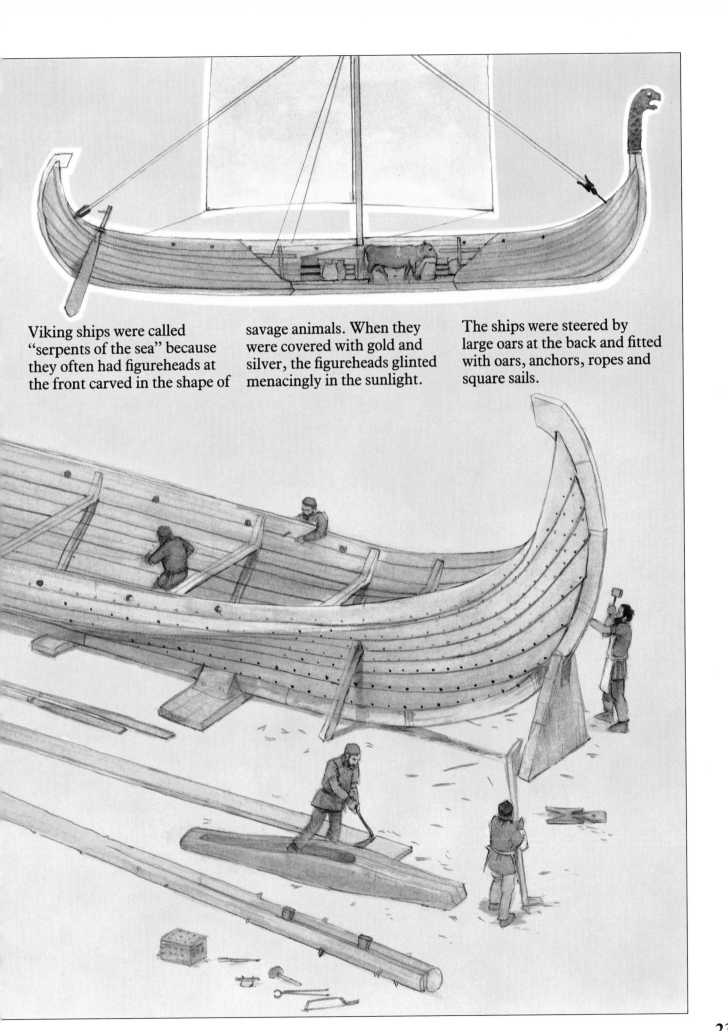

Viking ships were called "serpents of the sea" because they often had figureheads at the front carved in the shape of savage animals. When they were covered with gold and silver, the figureheads glinted menacingly in the sunlight. The ships were steered by large oars at the back and fitted with oars, anchors, ropes and square sails.

TRADING

The wandering Vikings soon became the middlemen of Europe. They took things from the cold north that were valued in the south: furs from sable, fox, squirrel and beaver, dried fish, wood, honey, amber, walrus tusks, walrus hides (for making rope), whale oil, feathers and down for quilts and mattresses. In return Viking merchants brought back wines, spices, silk and silver from the south.

Swedish Vikings traveled down through Russia to Byzantium (now Istanbul). They were interested in Arab silver coins which were valued for their silver content but they also could get hold of goods from the Far East, such as Chinese silk, oriental spices and Persian glass.

The Arabs were fascinated by the Vikings. One writer, Ibn Fadlan, noticed the great size of the "Rus men," their ruddy faces and their fearsome weapons. He also described how vain Viking men were – they loved wearing colorful clothes and precious jewelry. The Byzantine emperor was so impressed by these foreigners that he recruited them into his army to be his Varangian Guard.

Byzantium was a place of great luxury and sophistication. Viking traders were dazzled by the array of goods offered by merchants from Egypt, Moorish Spain, Damascus, Baghdad and even Tashkent. Those who came back were always able to make enormous profits from their visits.

HEADING SOUTH

Swedish Vikings sailed along the Russian rivers, using rollers, when necessary, to transport their ships overland. They went down the Dnieper River to the Black Sea. From there they sailed to Byzantium. Other ships went down the Volga River to the Caspian Sea. While they were in Byzantium, one of the Vikings carved the name "Halfdan" onto a balcony of the Hagia Sophia mosque. The word Russia comes from *rus*, which was a Finnish word for Swedes. Novgorod and Kiev were set up by the Vikings as trading bases. The Vikings also went west to England and France to get wheat, wool, tin, honey and salt.

ENGLAND

Hedeby

Volga River

Dnieper River

FRANCE

Kiev

Black Sea

Caspian Sea

Byzantium

HEDEBY

Most Vikings lived as farmers, but specialist craftworkers such as blacksmiths, weavers, silversmiths, antler-carvers and carpenters preferred to live in towns, where they could sell their products. Viking towns were near the sea.

Hedeby in Denmark was an exceptionally big and flourishing Viking town. It was surrounded by thick, high walls of earth, which were entered by tunnels. There was also a strong sea wall made of wood. Within these fortifications the merchants and craftsmen lived in wooden houses along stone-paved streets.

Merchants came from as far away as France, Russia, Spain and the Middle East. There was the usual trade in food and weapons, as well as pottery and cloth, and luxuries such as furs and spices. Hedeby was also an important slave market. Slavery was a fact of life in Europe and prisoners of war were sold to the highest bidder. Slaves owned by Vikings were known as thralls. Their owners had power of life and death over them and they were forbidden to bear arms.

In 1050 Hedeby was raided and burned by the king of Norway. There were no monks on hand to detail this event, but from the town's remains archaeologists have put together a complete picture of daily life in a busy Viking town. Whole ships were sunk in the harbor during the raid.

VIKING SILVER

Silver was highly valued and hoards of coins and silver objects have been found. At least 40,000 coins have been found in Sweden alone. In the days before banks wealthy people had to hide their valuables. The hoards were abandoned when the owners died before passing on their secrets.

237

GROWING UP

From an early age Viking children were taught to help adults. When the men were off a-viking, the women managed the farms. Some Viking women were farmers and traders in their own right. Girls had to be trained to run a household. They also had to become expert spinners and weavers so they could make clothes, ship sails, cargo bags, wagon-coverings, wall hangings and blankets. Although all marriages were arranged between families, couples could separate.

Before they were old enough to sail with the men, boys had to learn how to plow straight furrows and cut wood. Some of their work, especially hunting, fishing and boat building, would have been fun.

Little children played with model boats and wooden swords and farmsteads modeled out of clay. The Vikings liked all kinds of outdoor ballgames. In winter ice-skating and skiing were popular outdoor activities. Indoors children could hear stories of Viking adventures and play board and dice games.

A VIKING HOUSE

The Vikings built houses of wood, when it was available, stone when it was not. The houses were thatched with reeds or straw or turf, out of which grass continued to grow. Viking families usually cooked, ate, worked and slept in one very big room with a raised fireplace in the middle.

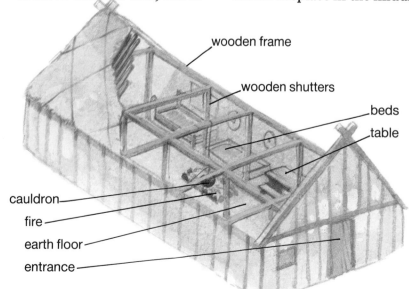

wooden frame

wooden shutters

beds

table

cauldron

fire

earth floor

entrance

As a mark of her authority a woman in charge of a household wore her keys on a chain dangling from one of her shoulder brooches. Though cozy, Viking houses must have been pretty smelly because there was only a small hole in the roof to let out smoke from the fire. The house was a center of activities, but there were also outbuildings which served as stables, barns, weaving or smithy workshops and bathrooms.

239

FARMING AND FISHING

The Vikings were very self-sufficient. They were hard-working farmers who could make almost everything they needed. They had fields of rye, barley, wheat and oats. These crops provided such everyday foods as porridge, bread and soups. Peas and beans were grown near the house, but other vegetables and nuts were gathered from the wild.

Hunting and fishing went on all year round. Apart from fishing in the sea, the Vikings used baited lines, traps and nets to catch salmon and trout in streams and lakes. Fish were dried on racks and then salted or smoked. Large sea mammals such as seals, walruses and whales were also hunted.

In summer sheep and cows were driven up to the rich mountain pastures. Then as winter approached some of them were slaughtered and their meat preserved by being salted or pickled. The salt was obtained by boiling seawater. Meat was roasted on a spit, stewed in a cauldron or cooked next to hot stones.

The whole family had to work on the farm. Thralls were slaves who worked on farms. Sometimes free born men, known as karls, who did not have any land of their own, worked on the land of wealthy farmers. There was plenty of work carrying water and collecting wood. Storing the food for the long winter was very important. Food was kept in larders. Butter was buried in tubs in the ground. Dried fish and meat could be hung on the outside walls of the house.

BONE AND ANTLER

The Vikings used bone and antler from the animals they hunted to make all sorts of everyday objects. The antlers from reindeer and deer were used to make combs (top left). Bone was used to make pieces for spinning wool (the circular objects in this picture) and pins and needles (in the center right). The other longer pieces were also made of bone and used for spinning. At the top right are fragments of Viking material.

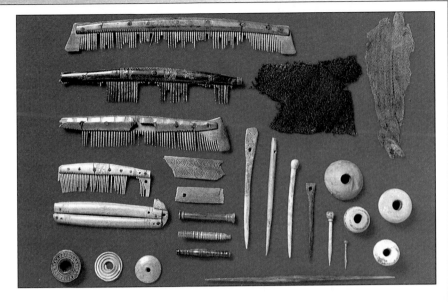

FEASTING

When they were far out at sea or isolated on their farms, the Vikings looked forward to their great feasts. At these holidays families were reunited, all the news and gossip was exchanged and weddings and deals were arranged. Not surprisingly the Vikings' idea of heaven was a permanent feast.

There were three major feasts in the year. The first took place after the winter solstice, after Christmas. The second took place in April and the third in mid-October celebrated the harvest. Before gathering in the big hall where the eating and drinking went on, the celebrators offered sacrifices to the gods. Animals and even men were killed. If it was the feast before summer, the gods would be asked for victory in the battles and raids to come. Outdoors, spectator sports probably took place with contests and races to show physical strength. All the people wore their finest clothes and their most precious jewels.

Everyone ate and drank themselves silly at a feast. The special meat eaten at the festivals was horsemeat. They drank beer, mead and, if they were wealthy, wine. Cattle horns provided drinking cups. Viking men were proud drunkards: "I leave no ale in the horn," boasted one hero, "though the warrior brings it to me until morning." Feasts were usually accompanied by entertainment in the form of poetry recitals and music.

RUNES

The borders of this casket have been decorated with runes. This was the Viking alphabet of letters made up of straight lines. Runes were easy to carve on wood, bone and even stone.

Vikings carved their names on personal things such as combs and gravestones, and on landmarks of places they visited. There were only 16 letters in the runic alphabet.

RELIGION

The Vikings did not build temples. Instead they worshipped their gods in the open air, choosing natural landmarks such as huge rocks, unusual trees or waterfalls.

The Vikings believed that there was life after death and that people would need earthly things in the afterlife. The most ordinary woman was buried with her cooking pot, some food and her favorite clothes. Wealthy people were buried with whole households. As well as food, clothes and furniture, dogs, horses and favorite slaves were killed to accompany their owners to heaven. Fortunately for archaeologists, many of the ships were buried under huge mounds rather than burned.

The Vikings who died in battle went to a special heaven. The god Odin sent warrior maidens called Valkyries to carry them off to the great hall known as Valhalla. They would spend the rest of their days there feasting and drinking. Knowing that Valhalla was their reward, Viking soldiers showed great courage.

The Oseberg ship was discovered in Norway in 1903. The ship was probably built in 800 and buried in 850. It contained the skeletons of an old rheumatic woman and a very young woman. It is not clear whether the old woman was the servant of a princess, or the young woman was the slave maid of a queen. The ship contained three beds, four sleds, a beautiful four-wheeled cart, tapestries, chests, boxes, kitchen equipment, casks, looms, riding harness, and many other things, as well as the skeletons of at least ten horses and two oxen.

VIKING GODS

The tapestry shows Odin (with axe), Thor (with hammer) and Frey (with corn). Odin was the chief god. At dawn his two ravens, Hugin and Mugin, set out to fly all over the world and returned each night to report to him on what they had seen. He was very wise and concerned himself with magic and the dead. Thor was a happy-go-lucky character who made the noise of thunder with his great hammer, and was the mother goddess Frigg's son. Frey was the god in charge of all growing things, of peace and plenty. Frigg spun gold thread on her spinning wheel and it was woven into summer clouds. The gods expected sacrifices, which were made at the festivals. In exchange the gods were supposed to give good winters, harvests, and victories in battle.

GOVERNMENT

Family ties were very important to the Vikings. When they were away at sea, they needed someone to look after their money and land. The more land and treasure a man had, the more important he and his family were. Sometimes the family ties could lead to feuds between rival families lasting several generations. If one family member was killed, then his murderer had to be punished. A relative of the murdered man would kill the murderer or one of his relatives. These kind of disputes could also be sorted out at a "Thing."

The Thing was an open air meeting of all the freemen in the district. It met regularly to discuss problems and settled arguments about thefts, divorce, murder, and the ownership of land. Things worked both as law courts and governing bodies.

Iceland did not have kings. Instead the Althing met every summer at the Thingvellir, a great plain in front of a lava cliff. Sometimes quarrels at Things were settled by duels to the death. Some had to undergo ordeals to prove they were telling the truth. In Iceland, for example, women were asked to pick stones out of vats of boiling water. Their hands were bandaged for a time and then examined. If the wound was clean it was decided that they had been telling the truth.

Every man who owned property could vote but powerful, wealthy men had more of a say than the others. Larger, national Things met in the summer. These were great social occasions, where news was exchanged and business sorted out. Things could meet for several weeks so those who attended brought tents, cooking ware and goods to sell.

Most crimes were punished by banishment or fines. These had to be paid in public. If a banished man didn't leave, he could be lawfully killed. Erik the Red was outlawed by a Norwegian Thing, only to murder another man in Iceland. He was banished from there and sailed off to discover Greenland.

VINLAND

Around 860 a Swedish chieftain was blown by a storm to the coast of Iceland and by 930 there were about 50,000 people living at the new colony. In 982 Erik the Red sailed westwards from Iceland to find another large island, which he called Greenland. This island was cold with little good farming land, but to tempt settlers he gave it a pleasant name. Eventually about 3,000 people settled in Greenland. For food and profit they hunted whales, a very dangerous activity.

Erik the Red's son, Leif Erikson, discovered a place he called Vinland, the land of grapes. With its rich pastures and forests, North America seemed an ideal place to settle. Leif stayed in Greenland but others tried to settle Vinland. Among them was Gutrid, who had been shipwrecked before arriving in Greenland. In her ship, she brought sheep, cows and one bull.

Compared with Greenland, it was easy to survive in Vinland. The cattle could survive all year outside. At first the settlers got on very well with the North American Indians, who traded with them. But after a few years the settlers and the Indians became enemies and the Vinlanders had to sail away. Though some women, including Gutrid, had had babies, there were still too few settlers for Vinland to grow into a permanent colony. Gutrid returned to Iceland, became a Christian, and even made a pilgrimage to Rome. She ended her days as a nun.

For a long time people were not sure whether the story of Vinland was a myth or history, but in 1961 archaeologists found the remains of a Viking settlement at L'Anse-aux-Meadows in Newfoundland.

Although the Indians were frightened of the Vinlanders' enormous bull they enjoyed the taste of the milk from the settlers' cattle. The Indians were keen on some red cloth from Greenland. When stocks of the cloth ran low, the Indians exchanged the same numbers of skins and furs for smaller quantities of the cloth.

WHAT HAPPENED TO THE VIKINGS ?

After about 1066 the raiding stopped, and the Vikings began to lead more settled lives as townsmen and farmers. Powerful rulers established kingdoms in Norway, Sweden and Denmark, so life became more peaceful. Most important the Vikings were becoming Christians and trading took over from raiding.

It was also harder to launch raids. England, Ireland, Germany, Holland, and France now had strong armies to resist attacks. From 911 the northern shores of France were defended by the forces of a Danish chief called Rollo. He had been granted some land by the king of France as long as he did not attack other parts of France and defended it from other Vikings. The territory became known as Normandy and Rollo's followers were soon speaking French.

It was the same elsewhere. The first settlers kept in touch with their Scandinavian family. But once they became Christian and married into the local communities, it was difficult to tell the difference between the Vikings and the locals.

In 1066 William, the Duke of Normandy, landed in southern England. His armies defeated the English king and William and his followers seized English lands. He was descended from the Viking chief Rollo, who had married a local woman. William was so well settled in France that he and his followers were called Normans.

250

THE BAYEUX TAPESTRY

This part of the Bayeux tapestry shows the invasion of England by a Norman fleet. The ships used by William were not unlike the ones Rollo would have used. It shows that the Viking ship design was so good it lasted for several centuries. The tapestry was made by Norman women to commemorate the invasion. It gives us a good record of how William the Conqueror won. It is now kept in Bayeux in northern France.

251

VIKING TRACES

From the coins, weapons, jewelry and remains of houses, ships and towns, we know a great deal about life during the Viking Age. For other evidence of Viking influence we need only look at language. Thursday is "Thor's Day" and Wednesday is "Wodin's Day." Many English words to do with trading and sailing have Viking origins. Viking sailors would have understood the words stern and starboard. The word law is also a Viking word and out of their assemblies, the Things, modern-day legislatures have developed. Legislatures are where all the important decisions about running a country are made.

Many Viking settlements became important cities and towns. The Vikings chose places near the sea or on rivers with good trading possibilities. To them we owe Dublin and Kiev. Other cities, such as York in England, were taken over and expanded by Viking settlers so that they became important trading centers.

Here are some fishermen working off the Scottish coast. The islands of Orkney and Shetland were settled by the Vikings after 872. They were under Norwegian Viking control until as late as the 15th century. They retain many Viking customs.

UP HELLYA

On the last Tuesday in January the inhabitants of Lerwick, the capital of the Shetland Islands, celebrate the Up Hellya. This elaborate festival involves a lot of celebrating and feasting. A torchlit procession is followed by the setting on fire of a longboat. Some participants actually dress up as Vikings and most people wear fancy dress.

SY.80.

DATE CHARTS

789 A.D. Viking ships off southern England.

793-95 Lindisfarne, Iona and Jarrow raided.

795 Viking raid near Dublin.

835 Beginning of 30 years of raiding on England.

843 Rus Vikings attack Byzantium (Istanbul).

845 Vikings burn Hamburg, raid Paris and Spanish towns.

around 860 Iceland discovered.

862 Vikings begin trading in Russia.

866 Danish kingdom established at York.

872-930 Norwegians settle Orkneys and Shetlands.

875-900 Colonization of Iceland.

886 Vikings control the English Danelaw.

911 Vikings granted Normandy.

934 Germans capture Hedeby.

around 965 Harold II (Bluetooth), king of Denmark, converted to Christianity.

986 Erik the Red settles Greenland.

985-86 Viking explorers sight America (Vinland).

around 1000 Norway, Iceland and Greenland become Christian.

1017-35 Reign of Canute the Great over an Anglo-Viking kingdom.

1066 English armies defeat Norwegians at Stamford Bridge; Normans defeat English at Hastings.

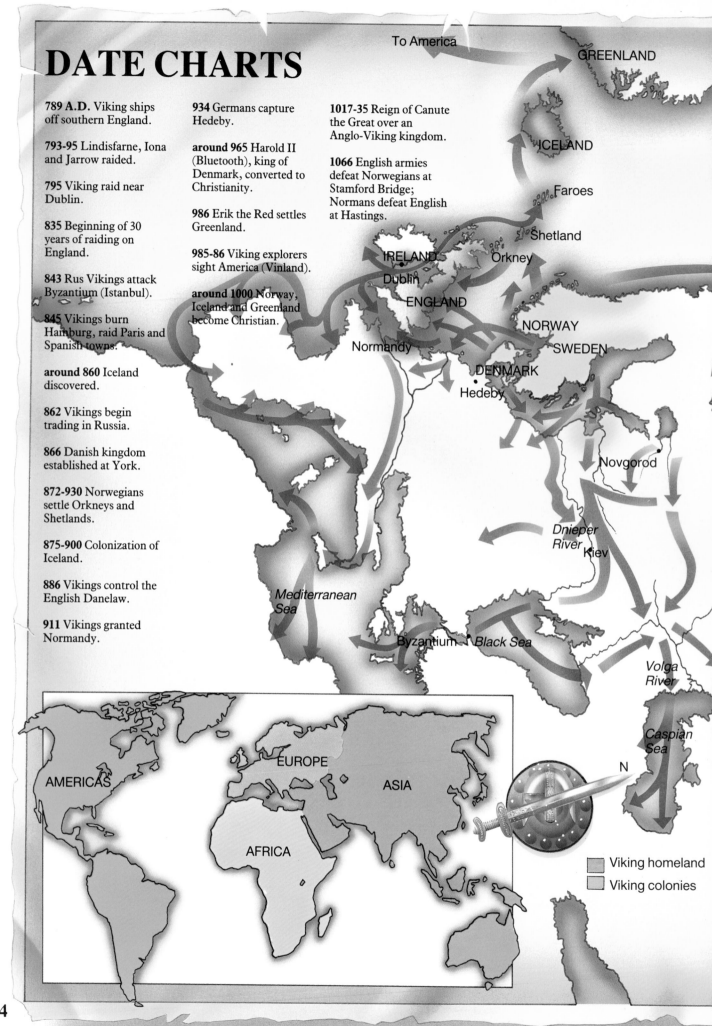

To America

GREENLAND

ICELAND

Faroes

Shetland

IRELAND

Dublin

Orkney

ENGLAND

NORWAY

SWEDEN

Normandy

DENMARK

Hedeby

Novgorod

Dnieper River

Kiev

Mediterranean Sea

Byzantium

Black Sea

Volga River

Caspian Sea

AMERICAS

EUROPE

ASIA

AFRICA

N

Viking homeland

Viking colonies

254

AFRICA	ASIA	AMERICAS	EUROPE
		600 A.D. onwards Late Classic period of the Mayan Empire.	
641 A.D. Arabs take over Egypt and overrun North Africa.	**618 A.D.** Establishment of the T'ang dynasty in China.	**650-900** Huastecan culture on Gulf coast of Mexico.	
700 Arab traders set up trading settlements in East Africa. Coptic Christians in Ethiopia.			**711 A.D.** Arabs conquer Spain, except the Asturias.
			732 Battle of Poitiers: the Arabs are defeated in southern France.
	751 Arabs defeat Chinese in central Asia.	**750** Mayan Empire declines.	**790s** Viking raids begin.
800 Beginning of Kanem Empire in central Sudan.			**800** Charlemagne crowned.
			840s Dublin founded.
850 The city of Great Zimbabwe built.			**851** Danish army winters in England.
			860s Swedish Vikings active in Russia; Vikings take over York.
		900 Beginning of Mixtec culture in Mexico.	**871-99** Reign of Alfred the Great over Wessex (west of England).
920-1050 Height of the empire of Ghana, West Africa.	**907** End of the T'ang dynasty in China.		**911** Rollo granted Normandy.
969 Fatamids conquer Egypt and found Cairo.	**960** Sung dynasty reunites China.	**980** Toltec capital set up at Tula (Mexico).	
1000s Beginning of the Yoruba Empire on the Niger.	**around 1000** Gunpowder invented in China.	**1000** Leif Erikson travels down the American coast.	**around 1000** Iceland becomes Christian.
	1037 Seljuk Turks invade Khorasian, Jurjan and Tabaristan.		**1014-35** Reign of King Canute.
1054 Ghana conquered by the Almoravid Berbers from the north.	**1055** Entry of Tughril Beg into Baghdad where he is proclaimed sultan.		**1066** English defeat Norwegians at Stamford Bridge; Normans defeat English at Hastings.
	1071 Seljuks defeat Byzantines.		**1079-81** El Cid's campaigns against Moorish kingdom of Toledo in Spain.
			1080 King of Norway converted.
			1096 The First Crusade.

CONTENTS
<u>MEDIEVAL EUROPE</u>

INTRODUCTION	258
FIGHTING AND DEFENSES	260
INSIDE THE KEEP	262
QUEEN ELEANOR	264
CASTLE PEOPLE	266
GROWING UP	268
THE CRUSADES	270
BUILDING CHATEAU GAILLARD	272
SIEGES	274
LATER CASTLES	276
TOURNAMENTS	278
FEASTS	280
WHAT HAPPENED TO CASTLES?	282
DATE CHARTS	284

ENCYCLOPEDIA OF GREAT CIVILIZATIONS

MEDIEVAL EUROPE

INTRODUCTION

In European history, the period from about 500
A.D. to 1500 A.D. is often referred to as the Middle
Ages or the medieval period. It is looked on as a
distinct time in the middle of European history,
between the civilizations of ancient Greece and Rome
and the start of Modern Times. Throughout the
period war largely revolved around control of towns
or castles. Castles served as home and fortress,
prison, armory, treasure house, and center of local
government in towns across medieval Europe. When
a country was taken over by another, the invaders
needed castles to control their new lands. This
happened in England in 1066 when the Normans
(from Normandy, France) invaded. The Saxons
(who had settled in England earlier) hated their
Norman masters for taking their land so they
attacked them. To establish rule, the Normans built
a network of castles, often at river crossings or
mountain passes.

The man with short hair on horseback is a Norman lord. He is about to go hunting with a hawk on his wrist. He is in charge and the long-haired Saxons are being forced to work for him. Behind him is his well built stone castle, where his family and soldiers lived.

DIFFERENT CASTLE TYPES

At first the Normans had wooden castles. They built a tower on a mound of earth (motte) with an open area round it (bailey).

Later castles were made of stone. They had a large stone tower or keep as well as a bailey. The walls were of stone with square towers.

Keeps were uncomfortable to live in so larger rooms were built within much stronger walls. Castles with two sets of walls were called concentric.

259

FIGHTING AND DEFENSES

Because castles were built to resist attack from an enemy, they had strong walls. As castles became larger, more than one set of walls were built. Beyond the walls there was a ditch or a moat. Moats were filled with water so that soldiers found it difficult to swim across. However it was easy to build a raft and float across the moat. So dry ditches were dug making it difficult for the attackers to get close to the walls.

When the men defending the castle started to fire arrows or stones, it became dangerous to attack the castle. If the attackers reached the walls, they would use long scaling ladders to climb over them. The defenders would then use long forked poles to push the ladders off. When the wall was taken, the defenders would move into the wall towers and continue the fight from there.

GATEWAYS

Wall towers had heavy wooden doors which were closed and barred when an attack began. Another defense was a portcullis. This was a heavy wooden and iron grating with spikes at the bottom. It was strengthened with plates of iron. To close it, the portcullis was lowered on chains by means of a winch put above it in the tower. The chains were wrapped around a large wooden roller turned by a wheel. Men working this wheel had to be strong as the whole thing was very heavy. You can still see slots and grooves cut into the stone gateways of many castles. These kept the portcullis in position and held it as it was being raised or lowered. The portcullis was part of the main gatehouse, which was heavily guarded.

As well as ladders, attackers used wooden siege towers. They had huge wheels so they could be moved up to the walls. If the attackers were too close to the walls the defenders would hurl garbage or boiling water at them. Later castles had holes in the walls through which water – or boiling oil could be dropped.

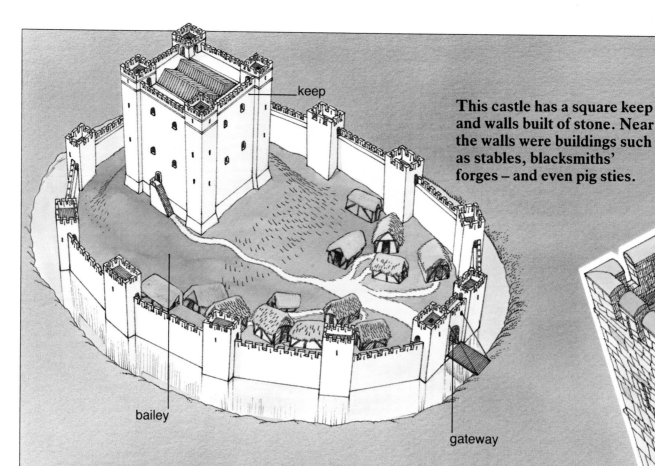

keep

bailey

gateway

This castle has a square keep and walls built of stone. Near the walls were buildings such as stables, blacksmiths' forges – and even pig sties.

INSIDE THE KEEP

The large square keeps of the 12th century had to house soldiers as well as the lord of the castle and his family. The main room was the Great Hall where everybody ate. The lord sat on a raised platform or dais. His chapel was often near the hall while above was the private room where he and his wife lived. Below the hall were the ground floor rooms for the soldiers. This was a noisy area which also contained the kitchens.

Under the ground floor was the basement. Castle supplies were stored there. Prisoners were *not* put here! They were either made to work around the castle or kept in the smaller rooms upstairs. They were held until someone paid for their release.

Each floor had at least one large fireplace. Smoke escaped through special holes in the walls. These walls were really thick – over nine feet in some castles. Notice the entrance stairs going up to the first floor. An attacker would have to fight up all these stairs to get into the keep. The well was dug inside the keep so that fresh water was available even in a siege.

In the keep the walls were made of stone and the floors of wood. The staircase for the keep was built so that the defenders had the advantage. They could use their swords more freely while the attackers could never really see their enemy. The lavatories were small rooms with chutes going down inside the walls to pits.

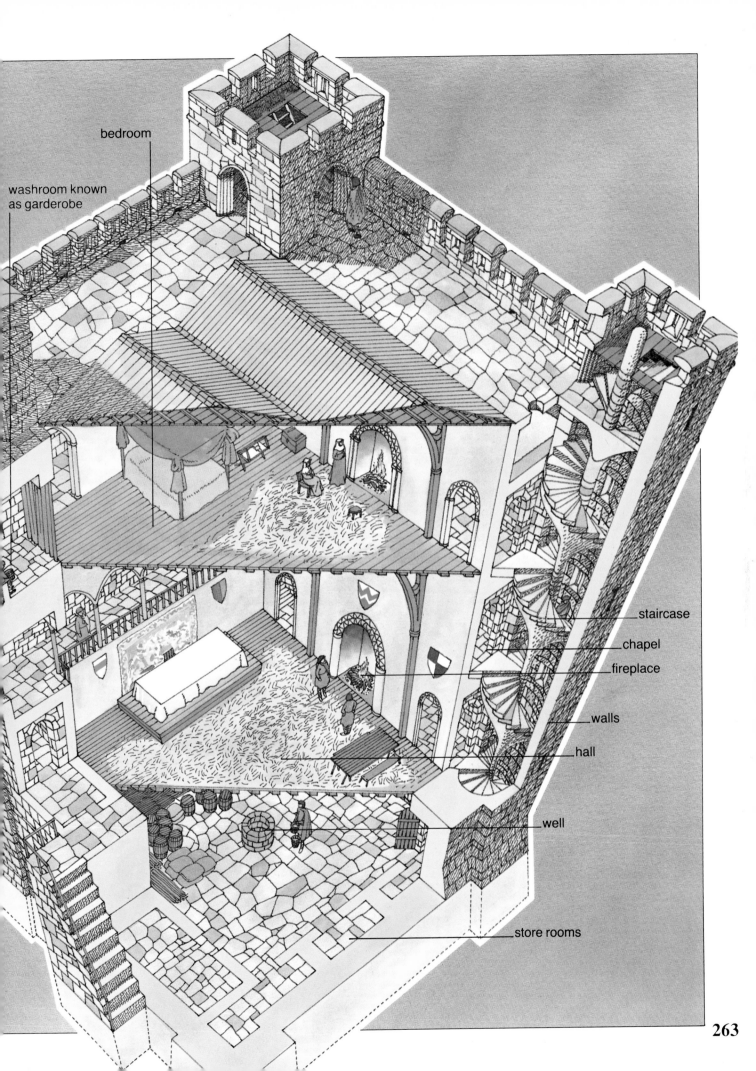

bedroom

washroom known
as garderobe

staircase

chapel

fireplace

walls

hall

well

store rooms

263

QUEEN ELEANOR

Private rooms in castles were made more comfortable with wall hangings and tapestries. Furniture was very plain, but was covered with rich material. Lords took their furniture with them from one castle to another.

Eleanor of Aquitaine was married to the English king, Henry II. She was a lively and intelligent woman, who owned much land in France. She had been married to Louis VII of France, but they were divorced by the Pope. This was very unusual at the time. She then married Henry. Henry was not the only one who wanted to control her lands. Queen Eleanor plotted against Henry with her sons. Henry won and kept her as a prisoner in various castles until he died in 1189. Then her son Richard, who had become king of England, released her. She lived for another 15 years.

The queen is shown in her private room. Henry kept her in great comfort. Here she is playing a game similar to the modern game of checkers. The pieces are made from walrus ivory. Around her she has her servants and musicians.

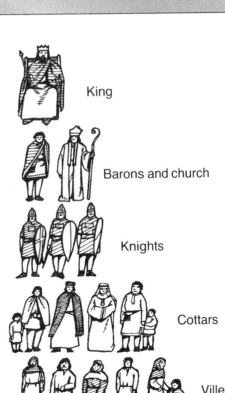

King

Barons and church

Knights

Cottars

Villeins

Serfs

THE FEUDAL SYSTEM

Kings and queens were able to rule their countries by giving land to their followers in return for their services and taxes. Land was then passed down the feudal system. Everyone owed loyalty to the one who gave them land. The serfs had no land and were bound by law to their lords.

265

CASTLE PEOPLE

A medieval castle housed the lord and his family, his soldiers as well as the servants, who looked after them. In fact, the bailey was a very busy and crowded place.

There was a lot of work involved in running a castle. Blacksmiths or armorers were very important. They had to shoe horses, repair tools and look after the soldiers' armor. The soldiers patrolled the countryside on horses. They had to be looked after in stables. Carpenters made furniture and repaired carts. Other men looked after the buildings and repaired the walls. There was usually a plumber to make new lead roofs and pipes. "Plumber" literally means someone who works with lead.

Life in the Middle Ages was hard. People had to work very hard either growing food or in someone else's service. They did not live as long as they do today – many died of diseases, like the plague, and others died in wars. A 40-year-old was considered old.

COOKING IN A CASTLE

This is the kitchen at Glastonbury Abbey. Sometimes kitchens were built in the bailey. Several men worked in the kitchens preparing food. Food was obtained from the surrounding countryside but in a siege people had to survive on animals living within the bailey or on salted or dried food. Some castles had their own fishponds and dovecots. They provided fresh food throughout the year. Women rarely worked in the kitchen but they did wash the laundry. They had to make their own soap from animal fat and water mixed with vegetable ash. Candles were also made from animal fat.

GROWING UP

Children had a part to play in the life of a medieval castle. They did errands and ran to deliver messages to people. However very few ever went to school. Bright boys would be taught by monks at a nearby monastery. Girls were usually taught how to cook and sew by their mothers. Richer families could afford to pay a teacher or tutor to educate all their children. In the poorer families, sons were trained by their fathers to do a job or craft.

Sons of noblemen were taught how to become soldiers and leaders in battle. They learned how to use weapons and were trained with wooden swords and shields. Some boys were sent to live in a powerful nobleman's house to learn leadership. They were called squires. Part of their training involved looking after their lord's armor, holding his horse for him to mount or carrying his food to him.

This covered wagon was used to carry women and young children on long journeys. A decorated covering was put over the wagon. It had no springs, so it must have been uncomfortable to travel in. Most adults went on horseback if possible.

TOYS AND GAMES

Children enjoyed games which are still popular. Boys played sports similar to modern day soccer. They also rode hobby horses. Girls had wooden dolls to dress. Both girls and boys enjoyed hoodman blind where someone was blindfolded and tried to grab the game's other players. Very young children had rattles and spun wooden tops.

THE CRUSADES

In the autumn of 1095, Urban II, Pope of the Roman Catholic church, held a meeting of church leaders in Clermont, France. He gave a stirring sermon to the assembled crowd, calling for a Crusade to the Holy Land (modern day Israel) in order to recapture it from the Muslims. He urged European Christians to unite and fight for the holy places where they believed Jesus Christ had lived.

He promised crusaders the spiritual reward of heavenly salvation for their work and thousands of people joined the cause to fight for Christianity. However, not everybody went for religious reasons; some fought to increase their own power or wealth. Over the years some Popes also used the Crusades for personal and political gain.

There were many Crusades between A.D. 1096 and 1270 with kings, nobles, knights, peasants and townspeople all taking part. The crusaders did recapture the Holy Land for a time but they eventually failed in their aim to establish lasting control. However the Crusades did bring benefits to European culture. They stimulated economic growth by bringing increased trade and introducing new foods and goods. Western Europeans learned how to build better castles and ships and make more accurate maps. They also influenced the intellectual life of western Europe in the areas of music, mathematics, and literature.

The crusades were originally called the armed pilgrims. They were armed with their religious beliefs and convictions. Many sewed the symbol of the cross of Christ on their clothing. The word crusade comes from the Latin word *crux*, meaning cross. Some crusades marched on foot. The wealthier, more important, crusades went on horseback.

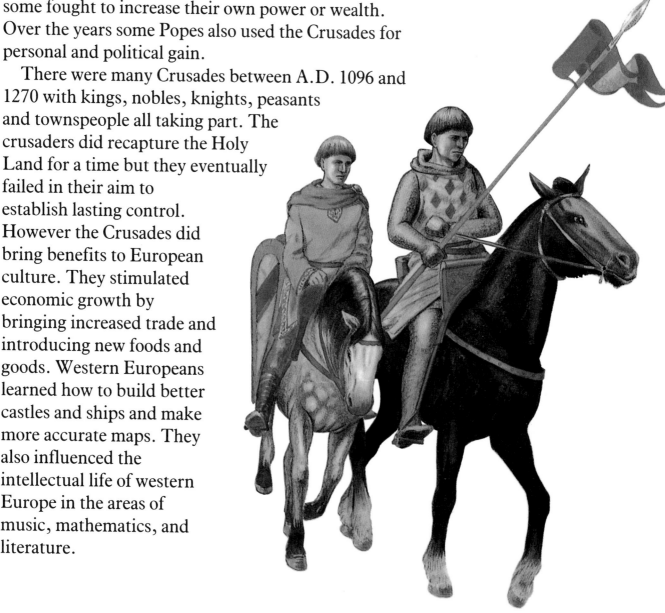

The Children's Crusade

One of the strangest and most tragic events in the history of the Crusades was the Children's Crusade in 1212. Thousands of boys and girls from about ten to 18 years of age became convinced that God would deliver the Holy City to them because they were poor and faithful. The children came from France and Germany. None of them however reached the Holy Land as many froze or starved to death during the long march. Some children returned home in shame, others got aboard ships going East and were drowned in storms or sold into slavery.

This map illustrates the Third Crusade and the routes the crusaders from different countries followed to the Holy Land. The Third Crusade began in 1189 and ended in 1192, and the leaders of this Crusade included the German emperor Frederick I (called Barbarossa), King Richard I (the Lion-Hearted) of England, and King Philip II (Augustus) of France. However, faced with the brilliant command of the Muslim leader Saladin and the development of quarrels between their leaders, the crusaders eventually realized their failure to recapture the Holy Land.

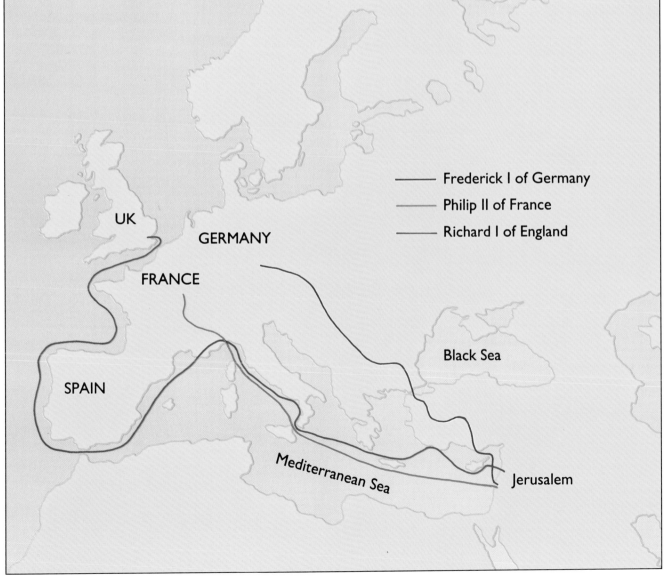

UK

GERMANY

FRANCE

——— Frederick I of Germany

——— Philip II of France

——— Richard I of England

Black Sea

SPAIN

Mediterranean Sea

Jerusalem

BUILDING CHATEAU GAILLARD

Château Gaillard was built in France on a cliff overlooking the River Seine. Château means castle in French and Gaillard was built by Richard I of England in the 1190s. He put it there to protect his lands in France from attack. The castle had strong walls which divided it into sections. Each section had to be captured before the castle could be taken. The keep was round and less likely to be demolished in a siege. Richard had learned many lessons about defending castles in the Crusades in the Middle East. Gaillard was a new type of castle and looked very hard to attack.

Even so, it was captured by the French king, Philip Augustus, in 1204. The French used towers and also undermined the walls. They got inside the castle after a soldier crawled up a lavatory chute. He helped the rest of the army get in by opening one of the windows. Shortly afterward the English had to surrender.

Richard I saw to the building of Château Gaillard himself. It was built very quickly. Carpenters, masons and plumbers came from all over Normandy. Good timber and building stone from the area were brought to the site using horse drawn wagons. The cost for all the work was considerable.

DATE CHART

1189 Richard Coeur de Lion becomes King of England.

1195 Richard has to give his castle at Gisors to the French king, Philip Augustus. Decides to replace it with a new castle at Les Andelys near Rouen.

1197-98 Château Gaillard is built very quickly.

1199 King Richard is killed at Chalus by a crossbow arrow. John becomes King of England.

1203 August – Philip Augustus begins siege of Château Gaillard with a huge army.
   September – French build banks and ditches around the castle.

1204 February – French attack begins.

   March – The French finally capture Château Gaillard. This was an unusually long siege for a medieval castle. Towns sieges could last a lot longer.

1215 Philip Augustus adds strong towers to outer walls.

1300 Importance of Château Gaillard at an end. It is neglected and becomes a ruin.

Today the ruins of Château Gaillard are a national monument and have been heavily restored. They can be visited on the banks of the River Seine.

SIEGES

Castles like Château Gaillard were built to resist attacks or sieges. Sieges were not always successful but they could go on for a long time. A siege usually only lasted a few weeks but in 1224 one lasted for three months. After that time, the food in the castle ran out and those inside had to surrender.

It was not always easy for the attackers. They had to camp in tents outside the walls until the castle surrendered. In summer both sides could be hit by disease. Sometimes the castle was relieved by soldiers friendly to those in the castle. This army would attack the besiegers' camp, set fire to their tents and drive them off.

Those under attack would also try to unnerve the enemy. They would throw bread off the walls to show that food was still plentiful. Dummies would be propped behind the defenses to make it seem that there were more soldiers than there really were.

SIEGE EQUIPMENT

Stone walls could be undermined by using battering rams or climbed using a siege tower. Bits of wood were thrown into the ditch to fill it so that the tower could be pushed right up to the walls. Where the walls were large they were attacked with stones or fireballs. A fireball used burning materials to set fire to the timber parts of the castle. They were fired from a mangonel. This had a large timber piece shaped like a huge spoon. It was held down by twisted ropes. When the ropes were released, the timber shot up with great force and fired the missile. Sometimes even dead horses were thrown from these large catapult types of weapon.

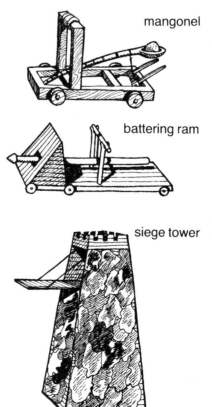

mangonel

battering ram

siege tower

274

A tunnel is being built under the wall. The tunnel is supported by timber. This would be set on fire when it had gone far enough in. The tunnel would then collapse bringing part of the wall down.

275

SAUMUR CASTLE

This beautiful castle looks over the French town of Saumur. It was built by the Duc d'Anjou at the end of 14th century. A lot of money was spent on the building. There were gilded weathercocks, bell turrets and fine carved stonework. We know what Saumur looked like because it was painted in a book called *Les Très Riches Heures*. This was finished at about the same time as the castle. Around Saumur there are vineyards. Even today the area is famous for its fine wines.

LATER CASTLES

After about 1350, castles were no longer used just for defense. People wanted to live in greater comfort so new buildings were put up, sometimes within castle walls. There was also a new way of building, known as Gothic. The old style windows and doorways had been small with round arches at the top. The new Gothic windows had pointed arches and were much larger. They let in a lot more light. Glass was expensive and most windows were closed with wooden shutters or sheets made from horn.

Toward the end of the Middle Ages, some castles became very grand. They looked like fairy tale castles with many pointed roofs and brightly painted walls. Fine stone carvings were put on arches and windows or on the walls. Rich people were becoming interested in gardens, planting roses and other flowers. The gardens had shrubs and trees trimmed to different shapes.

The people are waiting to see the lord of the castle. The man on the right is wearing a long sleeved gown and a hat based on Arab headgear. His wife has a hat with a net to tie in her hair. In about 1400 these clothes were fashionable.

TOURNAMENTS

The men taking part in a joust wore helmets with their crest or badge on top, so that everyone could tell who was fighting whom. Sometimes they wore a "favor." This was a scarf or handkerchief belonging to a lady who favored the man. The winner would present the favor to his lady, tied on his lance.

A tournament was a great occasion, which often went on for several days. It was usually held outside the castle and attracted lots of visitors. The main event was the joust. Two men would charge each other on horseback. Both wore armor and their horses were covered in richly embroidered cloth. The men held long blunt wooden lances and would try to knock each other down. Since the lances were very heavy this needed a lot of skill. They did not try to kill each other but usually everybody ended up badly bruised. Apart from jousting, there were also archery competitions, wrestling matches and sword fights at a tournament.

Tournaments began in France in about 1050 when several men took part in pretend battles. Since these were dangerous and men were killed, single combat took its place. The tournament was ideal for men to practice fighting and prove how skilled they were.

THE AGE OF CHIVALRY

This period in history is called the Age of Chivalry. You could succeed in life if you followed the rules of chivalry. Honor and fair play were taken very seriously. When a man wished to marry a woman, there were rules to follow. Men would write poems to the women they loved and try to win their love. This was known as courtly love. If a man loved someone else's woman, one way to settle the argument was to take part in a tournament.

FEASTS

Feasting and enjoying food was very important in the Middle Ages. At times, food was scarce for everybody, not just the poor. Bread was the basic food. It could be made from barley and rye as well as wheat. The wealthy used thick slices of brown bread as plates to eat on. They were called trenchers. Next to bread, fish was the most common food. Usually fish was salted or pickled to preserve it. Birds like chickens, ducks or geese were popular. On special occasions the better off ate swan and peacock. Beef and venison (from deer) were well liked, and pigs were kept for pork.

In the castle gardens, vegetables like cabbage and leeks would be grown. Herbs were used to season food or make remedies when people fell ill. During the Middle Ages, new foods, like raisins, dates, and figs were brought to Europe by the Crusaders. Before 1100 the only way to sweeten food was with honey. Spices were very expensive because they came all the way from the Far East.

Most people used their fingers to eat their food. Forks were brought in towards the end of the Middle Ages. Many people thought that using forks was silly but everyone had to behave properly at mealtimes. There were many rules on the correct way to eat and where people had to sit at the table.

EATING

The castle kitchen was quite far from the great hall so that the smell of cooking was kept away. Some castles had a small kitchen near the hall where food was reheated. This is a reconstructed medieval kitchen at Cotehele in Devon, England.

Food was cooked in metal pots called cauldrons. Meat was roasted on large spits over a fire. Since glass was too expensive, food was stored in pots or wooden barrels. The rich had bowls made of pewter or even cups of silver and gold. Plates were rarely used.

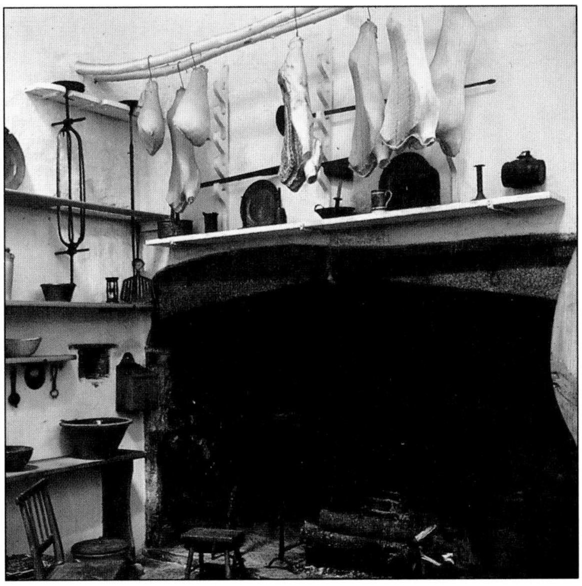

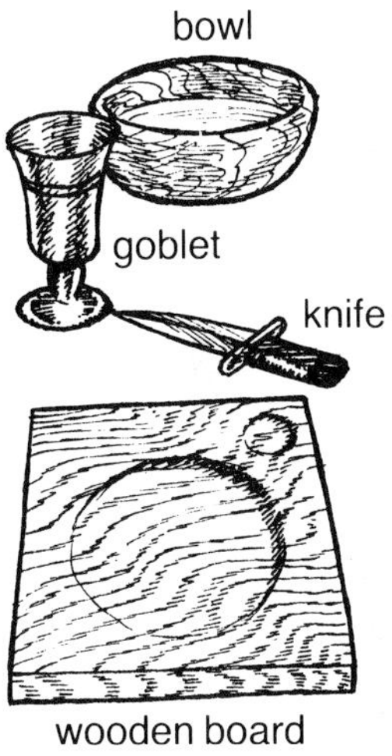

bowl

goblet

knife

wooden board

WHAT HAPPENED TO CASTLES?

As the Middle Ages came to an end, strongly defended castles became out-of-date. A few well-aimed shots from a cannon could easily knock a wall down. This was shown very clearly during 17th century wars. In central Europe the Thirty Years' War began in 1618 while in England the Civil War began in 1642. Both wars were very bloody and caused terrible damage.

In England, Oliver Cromwell's army was well organized. The soldiers had the latest type of armor and used the most powerful cannons available. However, it was not always easy to capture the larger castles. With their many towers and enormously thick walls, a lot of ammunition was used. The castles had to be captured one by one. Pembroke Castle in Wales was attacked by Cromwell himself in 1648. The siege lasted from May 22 to July 11, when the big guns had destroyed its walls.

Cromwell's army attacks one of King Charles I's castles during the English Civil War. Many castles were badly damaged during the war. If they were too expensive to repair, they were abandoned. Only castles which were still used by the army, like Dover, were kept in good condition. They were altered as new types of defense came in.

NEW DESIGNS

Tilbury Fort was built in the 15th century on the mouth of the River Thames. In the 17th century, it had new walls built according to the new designs. They were very thick to withstand cannon fire. The walls stuck out so that the defender's cannons had a clear firing area.

DATE CHARTS

1066 A.D. The Normans under Duke William conquer England. Wooden castles are built. Tower of London is started in stone.

1086 Domesday Survey carried out.

1100 About 500 castles in England.

c. 1100 Great Zimbabwe in Africa begun.

1150 Stone castles are built with rectangular keeps.

1154 Henry II is king of England and rules Aquitaine.

1180 Castle with square wall towers are built.

1200 Castles with round wall towers are built.

1271 Great Crusader castle of Krak des Chevaliers, Syria, falls to the Arabs.

1280s Concentric castles built by Edward I in England.

1295 War in Wales. Major Welsh castles built.

1370s Cannons begin to make castles dangerous to defend.

1337 Hundred Years War between France and England.

1346 Battle of Crécy. Decline in importance of castles.

1429 Joan of Arc begins French defeat of English in France. Castles built for show not defense.

1520s End of medieval castles and development of new forts.

ATLANTIC OCEAN

NORTH SEA

SCOTLAND

Doune Stirling
Edinburgh

Carrickfergus

IRELAND

Richmond

ENGLAND

Beaumaris Conway
Caernavon
Caher Harlech

WALES

Blarney

Ludlow Kenilworth
Warwick

Pembroke

Framlingham
Caerphilly Chepstow Colchester
Glastonbury
London Tilbury
Cotehele Arundel Dover
Corfe

ENGLISH CHANNEL

Caen Château Gaillard

NORMANDY

Josselin Fougères

Angers Beaugency
Langeais
Saumur Blois

Chinon

FRANCE

■ Castles
▙ Abbey
⌂ Manor House

ASIA

Kremlin (Russia) Ch'ang-an
Marienburg (Poland) (China)

EUROPE

Himeji (Japan)

AMERICAS

Krak des Chevaliers (Syria)
Baghdad (Iraq)

AFRICA

Great Zimbabwe (Zimbabwe)

AFRICA	ASIA	AMERICA	EUROPE
		500 B.C. Beginning of Mayan civilization in central America. Development of Teotihuacan.	**By 500** Roman empire in Western Europe has collapsed and is overrun by barbarians.
641 B.C. Arabs take over Egypt and overrun North Africa.	**618 B.C.** Establishment of T'ang Dynasty in China		
	751 Arabs defeat Chinese in central Asia.		**800** Charlemagne crowned emperor in the West. Vikings from Scandinavia attack British Isles. Beginning of the feudal system.
700 Arab traders set up trading settlements in East Africa. Coptic Christians in Ethiopia.			
800 The kingdom of ancient Ghana trading across to the Sudan.	**907** End of T'ang Dynasty.		**911** Vikings (Norsemen) allowed to settle in Normandy. They become Normans.
	960 Sung Dynasty in China.	**980** Toltec capital set up at Tula (Mexico)	
1054 Ghana conquered by Almoravid Berbers from the north.	**c. 1000** Gunpowder in China.		**1066** Norman conquest of England.
			1073 Gregory VII Pope. Quarrel between him and German emperor Henry IV as to who controls the church. Settled 1122.
			1096 First Crusade.
c1100 Beginning of the building of the Great Zimbabwe. Growth of the kingdom of Ife in Nigeria.	**1210** Mongols invade China under Genghis Khan.	**1151** Fall of Toltec empire.	**1295** First representative parliament in England called by Edward I.
	1279 Sung Dynasty falls to the Mongols.		**1314** Poland is reunited following Mongol raids.
c. 1235 Sun Diata Keita establishes the kingdom of Mali which lasts until c. 1500.		**1350** Beginning of Aztec empire, becoming independent after 1428.	**1348** Black Death (Bubonic Plague) sweeps across Europe.
c. 1300 The empire of Benin in Nigeria emerges.	**1368** Ming Dynasty in China takes over from the Yuan Dynasty.		**1378** Rival popes at Rome and Avignon in Great Schism (to 1417).
			1410 Poles and Lithuanians defeat Teutonic knights from Germany.
1400 Decline of Zimbabwe. Growth of state of Benin. In southern-central Africa kingdom of Great Bantu develops.			**1415** English victory over French at Agincourt, during Hundred Years War (began 1337).
	1421 Peking (Beijing) becomes capital of China.	**1438** Inca empire in Peru expands.	**1429** French begin reconquest of France.
		1450 Incas conquer kingdom of Chimu.	**c. 1450** First printing press, in Germany, during the Renaissance (a rebirth of learning and art throughout Europe).
		1521 Cortés conquers Tenochtitlàn.	
		1533 Pizarro brings down Inca empire.	**1500** Gradual end of Middle Ages.

CONTENTS
AZTECS AND INCAS

INTRODUCTION   288
GROWTH OF AN EMPIRE AD 1300-1486   290
  Aztec Beginnings – The Capital of an Empire – Gods and Beliefs

  The Emperor – Life in the Country – Food for an Empire – The Nobles
THE EMPIRE AT ITS HEIGHT AD 1486-1521   296
  Merchants and Spies – Aztec Art – Growing Up

  Science and Books – Games
GROWTH OF THE INCA EMPIRE AD 1350-1493   302
  The People Before – Armies and Conquests – The Inca Palace – Keeping in Touch

  The People of the Empire – Taxes and Welfare – Keeping Control
INCA SOCIETY AD 1493-1532   308
  Running the Empire – Farming – At Home in the Mountains

  Gods and Festivals – A Woman in Power – Building in Stone – Art to Wear
THE AZTEC AND INCA LEGACY   314

AZTECS
AND INCAS

INTRODUCTION

More than 30,000 years ago, the first people to settle in the Americas crossed over from Asia to the land which is now called Alaska. Over thousands of years more people arrived and different groups traveled south, settling in all parts of the two continents.

Over 500 years ago, there were many different groups of people living in North and South America. Some were hunters, but most were farmers. Some lived in towns and cities. Two of these groups, the Aztecs and the Incas, became rulers of great empires. The Aztecs controlled many different peoples in Mexico and parts of Central America. The vast empire of the Inca covered the land which is now the modern countries of Peru, Bolivia, Ecuador and part of Chile. The Aztec and Inca empires were thousands of miles apart, separated by mountains, rain forests and sea. They both had enormous power for about 100 years until they were conquered by the Spanish in the early 1500s.

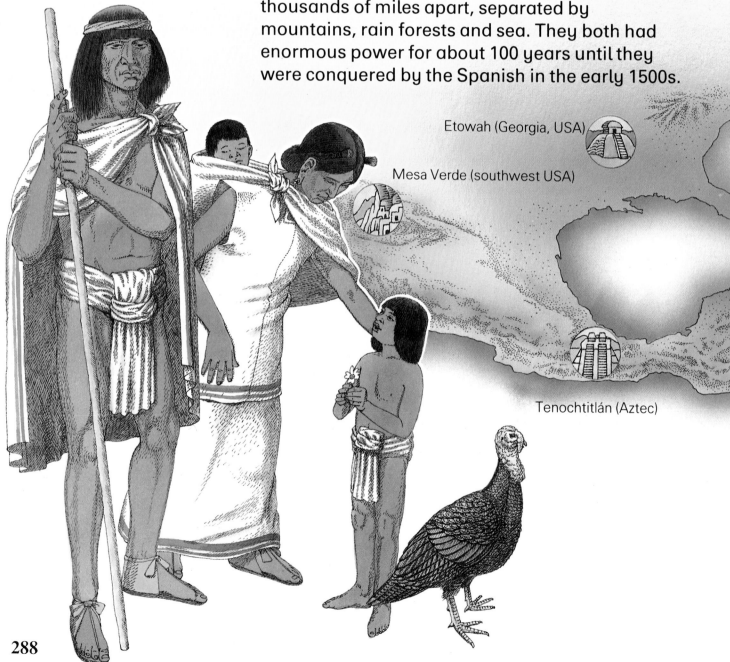

Etowah (Georgia, USA)

Mesa Verde (southwest USA)

Tenochtitlán (Aztec)

Although much of the Aztec and Inca civilizations was destroyed by the Spanish, we know a great deal about their way of life. This is because there are still remains of Aztec and Inca buildings, pottery, jewelry, books and other objects that we can look at today and study. We also have the records of the Spanish invaders who described what they saw.

This book looks first at the history of the Aztecs, where they came from, how they lived and how this small group of hunters and farmers eventually came to have a large empire. The second part of the book looks at the Inca people who successfully ruled over one of the most mountainous lands in the world.

The picture shows an Aztec family (left) and an Inca family (right). On the map are just some of the bigger places where people lived at the same time the Aztecs were in Mexico and the Incas in Peru. Today the descendants of these original Americans still live in North and South America.

Machu Picchu
(Inca)

Tupinamba
towns (Brazil)

289

GROWTH OF AN EMPIRE AD1300-1486

The Aztecs believed their ancestors were hunting people who lived in northern Mexico. Long ago they set out to find a better home. For many years they wandered, until their god Huitzilopochtli guided them to the Valley of Mexico and Lake Texcoco about 1300 AD. Other peoples had been living in this area for thousands of years and there were already many towns around the lake shore.

For a time, the Aztecs worked for some of the rulers of these towns. But finally they moved onto the marshy islands of the lake, the only land other people did not want. They began to reclaim the land. They fished, farmed and built a settlement of reed houses with a temple for their god. They eventually united with other peoples on the shore. They were then strong enough to defeat the most powerful people in the area, the Azcapotzalcos. They claimed their land. This was the beginning of the Aztec empire.

A god's prophecy
The Aztecs believed the god Huitzilopochtli told them to find the spot where an eagle stood on a cactus holding a snake. It was here they would build a city and become great rulers. The eagle was said to have been found on one of the islands of Lake Texcoco as prophesied. It was here the Aztec city of Tenochtitlán was built.

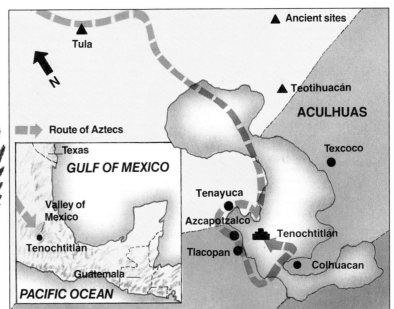

Datechart

c30,000 BC People from Asia begin to cross into the Americas to the land now called Alaska.

c1200-400 BC One of the first great civilizations in Mexico is the Olmec. Many ideas used by later peoples are developed by them.

AD 100-600 The first major city in the Valley of Mexico, near Lake Texcoco, is Teotihuacán. At its greatest, over 150,000 people live there.

AD 900-1200 A people called the Toltecs rule from their city Tula in the Valley of Mexico. The Aztecs believed they were great artists and called their own craftspeople *toltecas*.

AD 1100-1300 The Aztecs spend many years wandering in northern Mexico.

AD 1200-1323 Among the different peoples the Aztecs work for at this time are the Colhuacan. But they drive out the Aztecs when the Aztecs sacrifice a Colhuacan princess.

AD 1345 The Aztecs found their city Tenochtitlán, meaning place of the prickly pear cactus.

AD 1419 Nezahualcoyotl becomes ruler of the neighboring kingdom, Texcoco. It is one of the centers for arts and sciences in Mexico. It influences the Aztecs and other peoples. The Texcocan ruler himself is a famous poet.

AD 1428 The Aztecs defeat Azcapotzalco.

AD 1440-68 The ruler Motecuhzoma expands the empire to the coast of the Gulf of Mexico.

291

Aztec beginnings

Long before the time of the Aztecs, there had been other powerful states in Mexico. The Aztecs visited some of their ruined cities to worship at the ancient temples. The Aztecs admired and copied their style of architecture, art and religion.

The capital of an empire

Tenochtitlán (above and center) was slowly built on reclaimed land. As the city increased in size, there was a greater demand for materials not found on the lake. So the Aztecs fought to conquer new lands.

The Aztec army was feared throughout Mexico. Aztec warriors fought fiercely. Success meant they would be rewarded with gifts of slaves, cloth and land. The more prisoners a soldier took, the higher the rank he was given. Different ranks were shown by different styles of costumes, shown below.

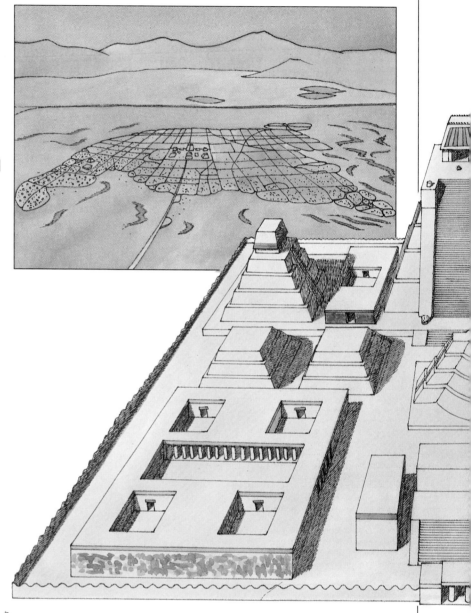

Gods and beliefs

The Aztecs believed the world had been destroyed four times. The fifth world in which they lived began when their gods sacrificed themselves to create the sun. In order to thank the gods and to help the sun in its nightly battle with the moon and stars, the Aztecs gave offerings of many kinds. The most important gift they had was human blood. In wars they captured people for sacrifice. Without this food for the gods the Aztecs thought the world would end.

There were hundreds of gods. Some, like the rain god Tlaloc, were important to all people. Other gods were special only for certain groups, such as artists or merchants. There were many religious ceremonies. A few still survive today, like the performance of *voladores* shown in the photograph in which fliers circle a pole.

GROWTH OF AN EMPIRE

The emperor

When the Aztecs were a small band of people the heads of each family made decisions together. As the empire grew, the most important people in the government, army and religion elected an emperor to rule.

People had to treat the emperor with great respect. He relied on a group of advisers to help him rule. The most important of these was called Snake-Woman. An Aztec emperor was expected to look after the welfare of his people. Emperor Motecuhzoma I gave food and clothing to the whole population. Emperor Ahuitzotl gave corn to flood victims.

Life in the country

Most people in the empire were peasant farmers. The whole family worked long hours together to grow, store and prepare the food they needed.

Aztec farmers were commoners. They had certain rights protected by law. In return they paid taxes in the form of food and clothing. Men could be made to fight and work on public projects.

Food for an empire

The whole empire depended on farming. The main food crop was corn, but other common vegetables were beans, squashes and chili peppers. The Aztecs kept turkeys, small dogs and ducks, as well as rabbits and bees for food.

The nobles

Aztec people were either nobles, common people, slaves, or they belonged to a special group such as craftspeople or merchants. A man became a noble because he had an important government job or because he was a priest or a high-ranking warrior. A woman was usually a noble if her family or husband was, but she could own property and run a business in her own right. Nobles were expected to do their work well. In return they received fine houses and servants and could afford to entertain with lavish banquets.

295

THE EMPIRE AT ITS HEIGHT AD1486-152

The market in Tenochtitlán had everything from precious stones to vegetables. Over 60,000 people sold their produce there at one time.

By the time Motecuhzoma II became ruler in 1502, the empire had become the largest it would ever be. It included millions of people in many different cities and states. These defeated states were ruled by leaders loyal to the Aztec emperor. They had to give goods to the emperor who sent ambassadors to act on his behalf and send back news. Many people were unhappy under the control of the Aztecs and there were many revolts. The army was used to stop these and to defend the empire against its enemies.

At the empire's center was Tenochtitlán, which had become a rich city of over half a million people. It had towering stone temples, beautiful public buildings, palaces for the rich and sprawling suburbs of houses. There were zoos and beautiful gardens. Streets would be full of people from all over the empire, some on government business, others bringing goods to market and others leaving for distant lands.

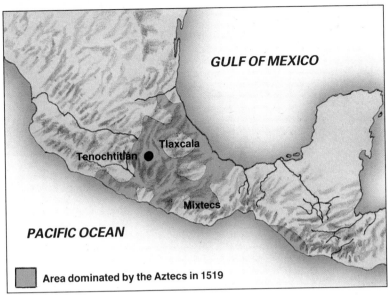

GULF OF MEXICO

Tlaxcala

Tenochtitlán ●

Mixtecs

PACIFIC OCEAN

☐ Area dominated by the Aztecs in 1519

Datechart

AD 1486-1502 Ahuizotl expands the Aztec empire as far as the Pacific coast and the borders of present-day Guatemala.

AD 1500 Tenochtitlán is flooded. Crops are destroyed and many people drown. Many houses have to be rebuilt including the emperor's palace.

AD 1502 Motecuhzoma II becomes emperor at the age of 32.

AD 1504 War breaks out between the Aztecs and the Tlaxcalans whose land is completely surrounded by the Aztec empire. The fighting continues for many years supplying both sides with prisoners for sacrifice.

AD1507 A New Fire Ceremony takes place. At the end of each 52 year period, all fires are put out. A new fire is built on

the chest of a sacrificed prisoner. If it does not take, it is thought the world will end. It is with relief the Aztecs see the flames and torches are carried to all parts of the capital to light other fires. A new period has begun.

AD 1519 (spring) Hernán Cortés and 600 Spanish land on the shore of Mexico.

AD 1519 (summer) The Spanish defeat the Tlaxcalans who become their allies against the Aztec.

AD 1520 The Spanish invaders kill many people celebrating a festival. The Aztecs rise up and drive the Spanish out of the city. Emperor Motecuhzoma II is killed.

AD 1521 The Spanish and their allies beseige Tenochtitlán for 80 days and finally defeat the Aztecs.

THE EMPIRE AT ITS HEIGHT

Merchants and spies

Under cover of darkness, lines of men loaded down with heavy packs would quietly enter the city. These were merchants and their porters returning from distant lands bringing back luxuries and other goods. Merchants were a special group of people with their own gods, laws, and customs. Trading trips could last years. They were often very dangerous but they could also be very profitable.

Some important areas for trade were the tropical lands just to the south. Here they got valuable jade, sacred quetzal bird feathers, cocoa beans, jaguar skins and other luxuries. Some merchants disguised themselves as spies to search for new trade routes and to gather information. The merchants took care not to show off their great wealth in case the ruling classes thought they were too powerful.

merchant spy

Aztec art

Artists were greatly respected in Aztec times. Even the children of royalty and nobles were encouraged to take up an art or craft. Each region of the empire had its own specialists. For instance, the Mixtec people were famous for gold and mosaic work.

Finely spun and woven cloth was produced by women. Featherworkers made brilliantly colored costumes. Artists cut and polished jade and turquoise to make religious objects and jewelry. Sculptors made stone and wooden statues for temples. Metalsmiths melted and cast gold for beautiful jewelry, like the Mixtec ornament in the photograph.

Growing up

Aztec parents were very strict with their children. Both boys and girls began to learn the skills they would need as adults at an early age.

Every Aztec boy had to go to school. A commoner's son learned how to be a warrior. A rich person's son might attend a religious school to train as a priest or leader in the government.

There were schools for girls but they were not compulsory. Girls could learn to become priestesses and were taught weaving and embroidery. After a few years most married.

Science and books

The Aztecs were interested in science. Some people were healers. They used both religion and knowledge of herbs to fight illness. Priests studied the stars so they could divide time into years, months and days. They believed that the state of their world depended on performing ceremonies or doing deeds at exactly the right time. The carving on the Aztec stone (photograph below) shows the sun in the center and the signs of the 20 days in an Aztec month.

Writing has been important in Mexico for over two thousand years. The Aztec priests wrote mainly history and religious books. The writing was picture writing. Books were made of folded sheets of bark paper or deerskin.

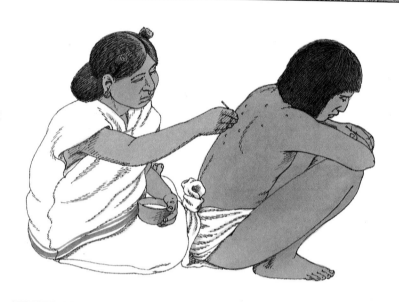

Games

The most popular Aztec gambling game was *patolli*. Colored pebbles were moved according to the throw of marked beans used as dice. Many people became addicted, often gambling all their family's belongings and their land. Some even gambled themselves into slavery.

The ball-game *tlachtli* was important all over Mexico. It was a religious game played during important festivals. It took place in special courts between two teams. To score one team had to get a rubber ball into their opponents' end. They could only touch the ball with their hips and knees. It could be a very rough game and players were often injured or even killed. One way of winning instantly was to get the ball through a stone ring on the wall of the court. The winner could take the clothes of the spectators – if he and his friends could catch them!

301

GROWTH OF THE INCA EMPIRE

About six or seven hundred years ago, several small groups of people lived in the southern Andes, a mountain range in Peru. They spent much of their time fighting each other and raiding enemy villages. One of these groups was the Incas. Eventually they became the most powerful group. They conquered some neighboring peoples and became a small state, ruled from the capital city of Cuzco.

During the next hundred years, they secured their position by defeating all the enemies in their region. The Incas then turned their forces towards the north, south and finally the powerful peoples on the coast of Peru. After long battles the Incas defeated them all and became the rulers of one of the longest empires in the world. Their empire stretched over 1,850 miles from southern Colombia to central Chile. To control the empire, the Incas built thousands of miles of roads over difficult mountainous land.

Messengers constantly traveled the roads on foot with news from all the major towns. The army used the roads to reach danger areas quickly. Storehouses of food and equipment along the way kept travelers supplied.

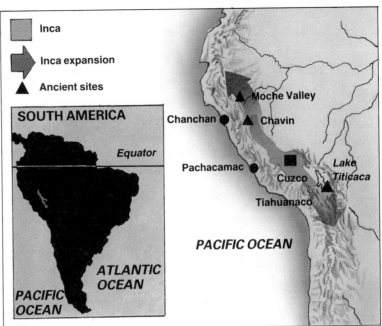

SOUTH AMERICA

Equator

ATLANTIC OCEAN

PACIFIC OCEAN

- Inca
- Inca expansion
- Ancient sites

Moche Valley

Chanchan • Chavin

Pachacamac • Cuzco

Lake Titicaca

Tiahuanaco

PACIFIC OCEAN

Datechart

c18,000 BC People are already living in the area that is now Peru. They are hunters and gatherers of wild food.

c5,500 BC People begin to farm in this area.

c800-600 BC The Chavin are one of the first people to have great influence in Peru. Their religion spreads to many places. Images of their main cat-like god appear in the art of people living hundreds of years after the Chavin disappear.

AD 100-800 Although they had no writing, the Moche people leave a wonderful record of their life and beliefs on their pottery painted with detailed scenes of daily life.

c AD 1200-1470 On the north coast of Peru the kingdom of the Chimu people extends over 600 mi. The capital is Chanchan, a huge city built of mud bricks. When the Inca, with over 30,000 people, defeat the Chimu, they borrow much of their art styles and way of life.

AD 1200 According to legend, the first Inca emperor, Manco Capac, begins his rule. The Inca also found their capital city Cuzco.

AD 1438 The Inca are attacked and almost defeated by a neighboring people, the Chanca. The emperor Viracocha runs away but Cuzco is saved by one of his sons, Yupanqui, who remains and leads the defense.

AD 1471-1493 During Topa Inca's reign the empire reaches Chile.

The people before

The early city state of the Moche of northern Peru (c AD100-800) had impressive pyramids, irrigation systems, pottery (right) and textiles. Many religions, art and building methods began long before the Incas were powerful. The Incas were quick to copy or borrow from the past and the peoples they conquered.

Armies and conquests

Inca expeditions were successful because they had a number of good leaders and a disciplined army. All men trained to fight in case they were needed. The soldiers' weapons were bronze-headed clubs, slings and spears.

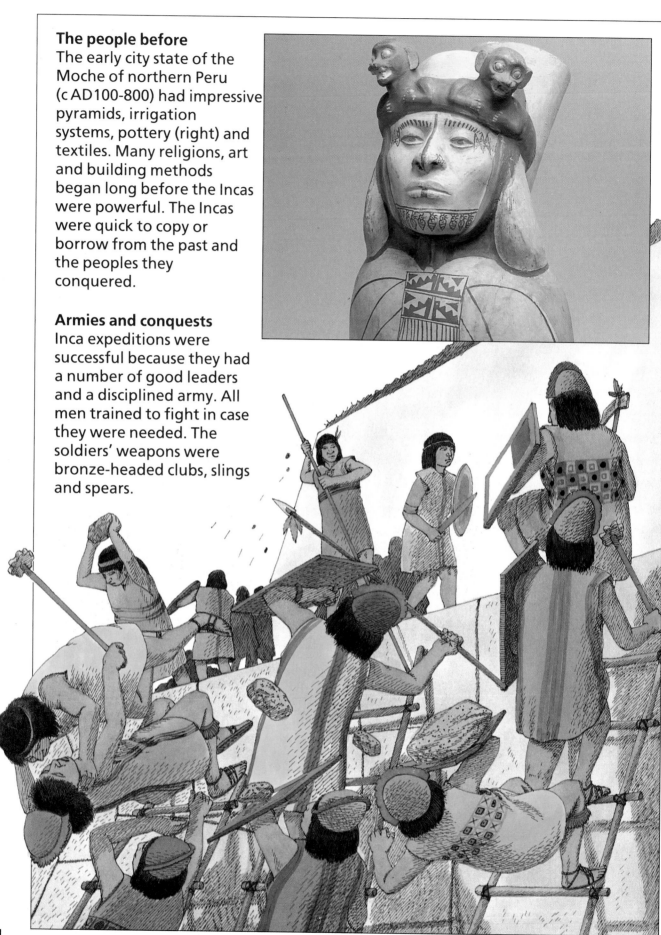

The Inca palace

The emperor's palace was a series of government offices, workshops, store rooms and public halls. Royal guards, servants and government administrators lived and worked there, as well as the royal family. This was the center from which the empire was ruled.

The rooms where the emperor and his family lived were like those of poorer people, but on a grander scale. The furniture was sparse and simple. The walls, however, were made of fine stone and often decorated with paint or plaques of gold and silver.

Keeping in touch

Although the Incas did not have a writing system, they had other methods of recording events and keeping government accounts. They used a *quipu*, a special system of knotted and colored strings. These were "read" by trained people called *quipucamayocs*. The Incas also passed on their history and religion through stories, songs and poems.

305

GROWTH OF THE INCA EMPIRE

The people of the empire

There were many different peoples in the Inca empire. Each had their own customs, which they were allowed to keep as long as they obeyed the laws of the empire. By law they had to wear their unique styles of costume so that each group could be easily identified.

The Incas believed themselves to be the superior group. True Incas were either people of royal blood or people who had been made Incas as a reward. Incas were easy to identify by their large ear ornaments.

Taxes and welfare

Most people had to pay taxes to the ruler, to the religious leaders and to the local community. Taxes were paid in the form of food, goods such as cloth, and work. Every year each village sent men to the mines, to build roads and public buildings, or to be soldiers. Farmers had to work the fields of the emperor and priests as well as their own lands.

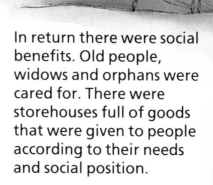

In return there were social benefits. Old people, widows and orphans were cared for. There were storehouses full of goods that were given to people according to their needs and social position.

Keeping control

When a new region was conquered, an Inca of royal blood would be chosen to govern it. Under this ruler, the local leaders were allowed to keep their posts as long as they were loyal to the emperor. By allowing this the Incas believed the conquered people would be less likely to revolt.

Often the defeated leaders' children were taken as hostages to Cuzco. The children would be treated and educated like other nobles. But they were insurance for their fathers' cooperation.

In the same way statues of local gods were brought to Cuzco to prevent rebellions. The Inca would also send whole communities of troublemakers to live in more secure areas, and loyal people were moved to live with newly conquered groups.

INCA SOCIETY AD1493-1532

By the end of the 15th century, the Inca empire had become a very rich state. Vast quantities of copper, gold and silver were being mined. There were many successful trading expeditions to other parts of South America. The storehouses of the empire were full.

But this wealth had little effect on the majority of the common people. For them life was much the same as before the Incas – except they had to pay more taxes and had less freedom. They were not allowed to travel long distances, wear fine clothing or have riches like gold and silver.

In contrast the nobility became very wealthy. They used gold and silver objects, their clothes were made of the finest wool and cotton, and they wore jewelry of precious metals. They lived in well-built houses with servants to look after them. Commoners could be punished by torture, but a noble would only receive a public warning. A commoner's life had the same value as a noble's honor.

The Inca people believed the emperor, called Sapa Inca, was the descendant of the sun. This gave him the right to rule. When he died, his preserved body was kept in his palace where servants continued to wait on him. On important occasions the mummies of the dead Sapa Incas would be paraded with great honor.

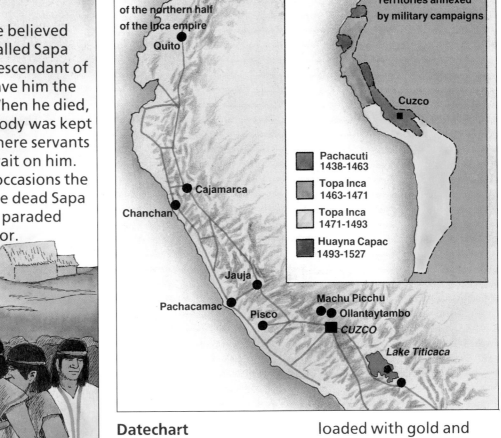

Main roads and towns of the northern half of the Inca empire

Quito

Cajamarca

Chanchan

Jauja

Pachacamac

Pisco

Machu Picchu
Ollantaytambo
CUZCO

Lake Titicaca

Territories annexed by military campaigns

Cuzco

Pachacuti
1438-1463

Topa Inca
1463-1471

Topa Inca
1471-1493

Huayna Capac
1493-1527

Datechart

AD 1493-1527 The emperor Huayna Capac extends the empire as far north as the modern borders of Colombia and Ecuador. During Huayna Capac's reign, an adventurer called Alejo Garcia is the first European to visit the Inca Empire. He travels from Brazil.

AD 1527 Huayna Capac hears that foreigners have been seen on the coast. These are the Spanish led by Francisco Pizarro exploring the region. Soon after, the emperor dies, possibly of smallpox. This disease was brought by the Spanish.

AD 1527 Pizarro captures an Inca ocean-going raft loaded with gold and silver ornaments and other riches for trading.

AD 1527-1532 There is civil war between two rivals for the Inca throne – Huascar and Atahuallpa. The latter finally wins.

AD 1532 (spring) Pizarro leads his soldiers into the Inca empire.

AD 1532 The Spanish capture Atahuallpa. The Incas fill a large room full of gold and a hut twice full of silver to pay for his ransom. Despite this, the Spanish kill him. After his death the Incas still fight back. Many Incas flee into the eastern forests and keep up resistance for several years.

INCA SOCIETY

Running the empire

The population of the Inca empire was organized like a pyramid. At the top was the Sapa Inca. The ordinary people were at the bottom. In between there were leaders responsible for a certain number of taxpayers. The least important leader was in charge of 10 taxpayers, the next 100, and so on. The four most important men below the emperor each governed a quarter of the empire.

This system meant that laws and orders could be passed down through the chain of leaders to the ordinary people. And information about the commoners could be passed up to the Sapa Inca.

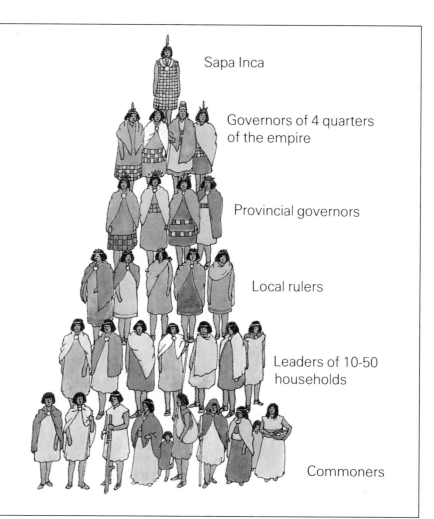

Sapa Inca

Governors of 4 quarters of the empire

Provincial governors

Local rulers

Leaders of 10-50 households

Commoners

Farming

Farmers in the Inca empire helped each other with plowing, planting and harvesting, just as they do in Peru today. In the mountains where the land was steep, they cut terraces to make flat fields. Canals were built to direct water down the slopes to dry areas. A sharp pointed digging stick was used for plowing and planting. It is still used today (photograph right).

Different crops were grown at different heights – tropical fruits and vegetables in the low valleys, grains and some root vegetables higher up.

At home in the mountains

This family is preparing its main meal. The son brings in the fuel. His sister grinds the corn for cakes. A vegetable stew and soup are cooking on the clay stove. Peasant families would eat very little meat as their animals were too valuable to kill frequently for food.

Living in the mountains could be very cold. The house has thick stone walls and a thatched roof. There are no windows and the one room is dark. There is little furniture. As most of the time is spent out of doors there is little need for comfort. On the floor guinea pigs eat scraps, keeping the house clean. They may also be eaten.

Alpacas and llamas were kept

People fished the sea and lakes

311

Gods and festivals

The Incas believed the world was created by the god Viracocha. But they thought other gods affected humans most – the gods of the earth and sky. The Incas made offerings of animals and sometimes human sacrifices to them.

All the gods were thought to help increase crops and animal herds. Important religious festivals would be held at the beginning of each growing season. In this picture royalty are taking part in the ceremony of the planting of the first corn. The men make the first holes in the earth and the women follow them planting a few corn seeds. A festival with drink, food and dancing would follow and then the farmers would begin the real planting work.

A woman in power

The Coya, the emperor's wife, had an important role in the running of the empire. She was connected with the female god, the Moon. She sometimes took the place of the ruler in Cuzco when he was away. She also took part in many agricultural ceremonies and had a great interest in nature. Her own gardens were full of different kinds of plants and animals. Here the Coya is shown having her hair combed by her women attendants.

Building in stone

The Incas had excellent engineers and architects. In the picture a clay model is being used to plan a new building. Stonemasons are shaping the blocks for the walls. Stoneworkers used hand tools such as bronze and stone chisels, mallets and crowbars. They cut stone so well that blocks fitted tightly together without mortar.

Many Inca walls are still standing, despite many earthquakes. The stones used were often rounded at the edges or polished to catch the bright light and make patterns. One of the Inca achievements was to build in mountainous areas. The most famous example is Machu Picchu (photograph above), built on a high steep slope.

Art to wear

Beautiful cloth was very valuable to the Incas. The finest cloth was made of the wool of alpaca or its cousin, the wild vicuña, woven by highly trained men and women.

The girls and women shown here are in a special school or convent where they spent much time spinning and weaving. They were selected from all over the empire to be priestesses or wives of nobles or royalty.

313

THE AZTEC AND INCA LEGACY

The Spanish arrived in Mexico and Peru in the early 1500s. They were amazed by the splendor and sophistication of the cities. They wanted the great riches they found and so they attacked both empires.

They were fiercely resisted but after several years they conquered both empires. Shiploads of gold and silver objects were melted down and sent to Spain. The Aztec and Inca religions were stopped and sacred objects and temples were destroyed. The American peoples had new masters.

CONQVISTA DE MEXICO POR CORTES 7

The conquerors

The photograph above shows a 17th century painting of the final Spanish attack on Tenochtitlán. Enemies of the Aztecs such as the Tlaxcalans helped the Spanish win.

After both conquests, most people of the old empires were made slaves. Thousands died in wars, or due to overwork or European diseases like smallpox.

Aztec and Inca today

Evidence of Aztec and Inca cultures still survive, such as the Inca walls in Cuzco that support Spanish colonial buildings (top right).

The descendants of the Aztecs and Incas are a living link with the past. Many are trying to improve living conditions and to protect their rights and land. They are proud of their past and many still follow ways of life that can be traced back to before the conquest. The Mexicans in the photograph (center right) are honoring their dead during 'The Day of the Dead' festival. Others take part in a religious procession (bottom right). Both festivals have European and native American origins. And below, Peruvian villagers still hold markets on ancient Inca sites.

INDEX

abacuses 74, 102
Abu Simbel 23, 25, 52
Abusir 11, 12
Adams, William 101
Aeschylus 173
afterlife, belief in
  Chinese 68
  Egyptians 51
  Vikings 244
Age of Chivalry 279
Agincourt 285
agriculture
  Aztec 294
  Chinese 65, 84-5
  Egyptian 15
  Greek 156
  Inca 310
  Japanese 96
  rice cultivation 84-5, 96
  Viking 240
Akhenaten 22, 23, 25
Alaska 291
Alexander the Great 29,
  32, 33, 147, 166-7,
  168,170, 171
Alexandria 32, 167, 168,
  169, 194
Alfred the Great 255
alphabets 154, 242
Althing 246
Amenemhat I 16, 17
Amenhotep I 23
Amenhotep III 23
American Declaration of
  Independence 143
amphitheaters 186, 187,
  216, 222
ancestor worship 69
Antoninus Pius 191
Anyang 65
Arabs 29, 234, 255, 285
architecture
  Byzantine 203
  Gothic 276
  Greek 173
  Inca 313
  Roman 202, 203, 222
Arkhimedes 169
Arkhimedes' screw 169
armies
  Aztec 292
  Egyptian 20, 22
  Greek 155, 164
  Inca 304
  Japanese 136-7
  Roman 177, 180, 206-
    217

arms and armor
  Egyptian 20
  Greek 164
  Inca 304
  Japanese 103, 123,
    124-5
  Roman 209, 211
  swords 103, 123, 124,
    231
  Viking 231
Assyrians 28, 32
astronomy 31, 64, 74,
  155, 300
Aswan Dam 34, 35, 52
Athens 155, 159, 160,
  161, 162, 164, 165
Augustus, Caesar 184-6
Aztec Empire
  agriculture 294
  army 292
  beginnings of 288, 290
  crafts 298
  datecharts 291, 297
  defeat by the Spanish
    297, 314
  education 299
  emperors 294
  expansion 296, 297
  festivals 315
  government 294
  human sacrifices 57,
    293, 297
  legacy 315
  maps 291, 297
  nobility 295
  pyramids 57
  religion 290, 293
  science 300
  social classes 295
  spies 298
  taxation 294
  trade 298
  writing system 300

barbarians 196, 197, 218
bards 152
Bayeux Tapestry 251
Bell beaker culture 59
Black Death 143, 285
blacksmiths 231
Britain
  Norman invasion 250-1
  Roman occupation 179,
    190, 191, 192, 195,
    197
  Viking raids 230
Bronze Age 59

bronze casting 64, 65, 67
Bullet Train 119
burial customs
  Chinese 64, 68, 70-1,
    73
  Egyptian 8, 26, 40, 50-1
  Greek 149, 151
  Inca 309
  Japanese 95, 97
  Viking 244
Byblos 11, 21
Byzantine Empire 33,
  202, 203
Byzantium 234, 235

Caesar, Julius 33, 178,
  179, 183
calendars 31, 300
camps, Roman 210-11
canals 11, 70, 71, 74-5,
  310
Canute 143, 255
caravans 21, 80-1, 195
Carthage 179, 182
castles
  Château Gaillard 272-3
  datechart 284
  defense of 260-1, 272
  gateways 261
  inhabitants 266
  Japanese 104, 137
  keeps 259, 262-3
  kitchens 267, 281
  later architecture 276,
    283
  moats 260
  motte and bailey 258,
    259
  Norman 259
  private rooms 262,
    264-5
  sieges 260-1, 274-5,
    283
centurions 206, 212
Chanca people 303
Chanchan 303
Changan 78
chariot races 187
chariots 21, 22
Charlemagne 231, 255
Château Gaillard 272-3
Chavin people 303
children
  Aztec 299
  Children's Crusade 270
  Egyptian 19, 47
  Greek 163

Japanese 133, 140
  medieval period 268-9
  Roman 189
  samurai children 133
  Viking 238
Chile 303
Chimu people 303
China
  agriculture 65, 84-5
  ancestor worship 69
  Boxer Rebellion 87
  burial customs 64, 68,
    70-1, 73
  civil service 76, 77
  court life 73
  crafts 65, 67, 73, 85
  datecharts 65, 71, 77,
    82
  emperors 69, 72, 73,
    84-5
  entertainment 79
  family life 68-9
  first empire 70-5
  golden age 76-81
  Great Wall 71, 72
  Han dynasty 70, 71
  inventions 71, 74-5
  justice and punishment
    79
  literature and the arts
    76, 81, 82
  Manchus 82, 83
  maps 65, 71, 77, 82
  Ming dynasty 77, 82, 83
  modern China 88-9
  nobility 64, 73
  Opium Wars 82, 87
  People's Republic of
    China 82, 88
  philosophy 62, 65, 66,
    68-9, 72
  prehistoric forebears 63
  Qin dynasty 64, 65, 71,
    72
  Qing dynasty 82, 83, 87
  religions 76, 80, 86
  science 64, 74
  Shang dynasty 65
  Song dynasty 76, 77
  Tang dynasty 76, 77
  terracotta warriors 70-1
  town life 78-9
  trade 80-1
  voyages of exploration
    82, 86
Warring States era 64-5
women 79

writing system 64, 67
Zhou dynasty 65
Chinatowns 89
Claudius 185
Cleopatra 33, 167, 184, 185
cloth-making 45, 109, 158, 298, 313
clothes
  medieval 277
  Roman 219
coinage 155, 171, 237
Colhuacan people 291
Columbus, Christopher 143
Commodus 191
compasses 74, 86
Confucius 62, 65, 66, 68-9
Constantine 199
Constantinople (Istanbul) 33, 171, 201, 202
Constantius II 196
Corinth 179, 183
Cortés, Hernán 297
Cotehele 281
crafts
  Aztec 298
  Chinese 65, 67, 73, 85
  Egyptian 27, 44-5
  Greek 150
  Japanese 95, 96, 109
  Viking 236, 241
Crete 59, 149
Cromwell, Oliver 283
Crusades 255, 270, 285
Cuzco 302, 303, 307, 315

Dacia (Rumania) 185
Danes 228
Darius III 166, 167
Deir el Medinah 27
democratic government 156, 162, 164
Diocletian 196, 197, 199, 220
Domesday Book 143
Dover Castle 283

Edo (Tokyo) 106, 107, 114, 135
education
  Aztec 299
  Egyptian 19
  Greek 163
  Japanese 110, 133

medieval Europe 268
  Roman 189
Egypt
  agriculture 15
  army 20, 22
  burial customs 8, 26, 38-9, 40, 50-1
  court life 13
  crafts 27, 44-5
  datecharts 11, 17, 23, 29, 58-9
  decline 28-9, 32-3
  education 19
  family life 47
  games and toys 19, 46
  government 11, 18
  houses 14-15
  Inundation 9, 15
  inventions 15
  legacy 34-5
  maps 11, 17, 23, 29
  Middle Kingdom 16-21, 59
  mummification 26, 50-1
  New Kingdom 22-7, 59
  Nile 9, 35, 52-3
  Old Kingdom 10, 11, 59
  pharaohs 13
  Ptolemies 29, 33, 167
  pyramids 11, 12, 38-43, 45, 54, 59
  religions 13, 23, 25, 30, 32, 33, 38, 47, 51
  Roman province 33
  royal cities 30
  royal crowns 13
  scholarship 30, 31, 48
  taxation 42
  trade 11, 20-1, 23, 24
  unification of 10-11
  Valley of the Kings 23, 27, 55
  writing system 18, 19, 48-9
El Cid 255
Eleanor of Aquitaine 264-5
engineering 74, 194, 302
English Civil War 282, 283
Erik the Red 247, 248
Eskimos 59
Ethiopia 255
Etruscans 181

family life
  Chinese 68-9

Egyptian 47
  Japanese 117
feasts
  medieval 280-1
  Viking 242-3
festivals
  Greek 147
  Inca 312
  Japanese 119
  Viking 253
feudal system 265
food and drink
  Aztec 294
  Egyptian 47
  Inca 311
  medieval 267, 280-1
  Viking 240, 242
Forbidden City 82, 83
forts
  hill-forts 220
  Roman 196-7, 212-17, 220, 221
Frederick I (Barbarossa) 270
French Empire 143, 203
French Revolution 143

games and toys
  Aztec 301
  Egyptian 19, 46
  medieval 265, 269
  Roman 208
  Viking 238
Gaul 197, 200
geisha 111
Genghis Khan 285
Ghana 255, 285
Giza 11, 12, 40, 43
gladiators 186, 216
glass 276
gods and goddesses
  Aztec 290, 293
  Celtic 195
  Egyptian 13, 25, 30, 31, 32, 38
  Greek 157
  Inca 312
  Japanese 92
  Roman 195
  Viking 244, 245
gold 24, 150
goldsmiths 27, 45
Goths 200
Grand Canal 70, 71, 74
Great Bantu 285
Great Schism 285
Great Wall of China 71,-2

Great Zimbabwe 255, 285
Greece
  agriculture 156
  architecture 173
  aristocracy 150
  army 155, 164
  Athens 155, 159, 160, 161, 162, 164, 165
  burial customs 149, 151
  children 163
  coinage 155
  colonies 154, 155
  crafts 150
  dark age 154-5
  datecharts 149, 155, 161, 167
  demokratia 156, 160, 161, 162, 164
  education 163
  entertainment 162, 172-3
  Golden Age 160-5
  Hellenistic Age 166-71
  inventions 169
  language 172
  legacy 171, 172-3
  literature and the arts 152-3, 155, 161, 162, 173
  maps 149, 155, 161
  medicine 168
  Myceneans 148-53
  Olympic Games 172
  Peloponnesian War 161, 165
  Persian Wars 155, 159
  philosophy 155, 162
  the polis 156
  religion 157
  rural life 156
  scholarship 155, 168-9, 172
  science 168-9
  ships 164-5
  Sparta 159, 160, 161, 163, 165, 166
  states 156
  trade 149
  tyrants 155
  women in 158
  writing systems 151, 154
Greenland 247, 248
gunpowder 255
Gutrid 248, 249

317

Hadrian 190, 191, 220, 221
Hadrian's Wall 190, 191, 193, 221
Hannibal 179, 182
Hastings 255
Hatshepsut 23
Hedeby 236-7
helots 163
Henry II 265
Hiroshima 113, 115
Hittites 22, 59
Holy Land 270
Homer 152
hoplites 155, 164, 166
hostages 24, 106, 307
houses
  Egyptian 14-15
  Inca 311
  Japanese 109, 117
  Roman 193
  Viking 238-9
Huayna Capac 309
human sacrifices 57, 293, 297, 312
Hundred Years War 285
Huns 197, 200
hunting 9, 52, 150, 240, 259
Hyksos 17, 21, 59

Iceland 246, 255
Iliad 152-3
Imhotep 48
Inca Empire
  administration 305, 306, 307, 310, 312
  agriculture 310
  architecture 313
  army 304
  beginnings of 288, 302
  burial customs 309
  Coya (emperor's wife) 312
  datecharts 303, 309
  defeat by the Spanish 309, 314
  emperors 309
  expansion 302-7, 309
  festivals 312
  houses 311
  justice 308
  legacy 315
  map 303
  nobility 308
  palaces 305
  peoples of 306, 307

pyramids 57, 304
religion 312
road systems 302
Sapa Inca 310
social classes 308, 310
taxation 306, 310
India 22, 143, 167, 170-1
Indus Valley culture 59
inventions
  Chinese 71, 74-5
  Egyptian 15
  Greek 169
  Roman 193
irrigation 59, 64
Issos 166, 167

jade 73
Japan
  Age of Strife 100-5
  agriculture 96
  armies 136-7
  Black Ships 107, 114-15, 138
  burial customs 95, 97
  castles 104, 137
  children 133, 140
  Chinese influences 95, 98
  the common people 102
  court life 95, 99
  crafts 95, 96, 109
  daimyos 100, 102, 104, 106, 110, 134 135, 137, 138
  datecharts 95, 101, 107, 113, 142-3
  earliest civilization 94, 95, 96
  education 110, 133
  emperors 94, 95, 99, 100
  entertainment 111
  family life 117
  festivals 119
  fishing 103
  Fujiwara 95, 99
  Gempei War 95
  Heian period 95, 99
  houses 109, 117
  industry and technology 116
  isolation 106-11
  kamikaze 126
  literature and the arts 95, 98, 107, 110, 130-1, 134

maps 95, 101, 107, 113, 142
martial arts 103, 123
modernization 112-19, 138
Mongol invasions 101, 126
myths 92, 93
nobility 99
Olympic Games 112, 113
Portuguese, arrival of 101, 104
religions 95, 97, 98, 100, 101, 104, 128
samurai 100, 101, 103, 108, 110, 122-40
shogunates 100, 101, 102, 106, 114, 115, 134-5
shrines 97, 128
social classes 108
taxation 96, 102, 134
tea ceremony 140
towns and town life 104
trade 106, 107, 116
traditions 118, 140
women in 132-3
world financial center 118
World War II 112, 113, 115, 126
writing system 98
Jesuits 86
Jesus Christ 225
jewelry 45, 298
Julian 197
justice and punishment
  Chinese 79
  Inca 308
  Roman 198, 214
  Viking 246, 247
Justinian 197

Kanem Empire 255
karls 240
Kiev 235
Knossos 149
Kublai Khan 77, 126
Kush 22

lacquerware 109
L'Anse-aux-Meadows 249
latrines 212-13
lavatories 262
legionaries 177, 180, 208, 209, 211

legions 206, 207
Leif Erikson 248, 255
Lindisfarne 230
literature and the arts
  Chinese 76, 81, 82
  Greek 152-3, 155, 161, 162, 173
  Japanese 95, 98, 107, 110, 130-1, 134
  Luoyang 65, 70

Machu Picchu 313
magic 30
Magna Carta 143
Mali 285
mangonels 274
Mao Zedong 88
map-making 155
Marathon 155, 159
Marcomannic Wars 191
Marcus Aurelius 191
Mark Antony 33, 184, 185
mathematics 31, 155, 169
Mayan civilization 225, 255, 285
medicine
  acupuncture 74
  Aztec 300
  Chinese 74
  Egyptian 30
  Greek 168
medieval Europe
  Age of Chivalry 279
  castles 259, 260-5, 266-7, 272-3
  children 268-9
  courtly love 279
  Crusades 255, 270, 285
  datecharts 273, 284
  feasting 280-1
  feudal system 265
  map 284
  tournaments 278-9
Memphis 10, 30, 38
Mentuhotep II 16, 17
merchants 107, 108, 236, 298
Mesopotamia (Iraq) 59, 185, 191
metalworking 59, 150, 298
Mexico 59, 288, 291, 292
Middle Ages 258
  see also medieval Europe

Mixtec culture 255, 298
Moche people 303, 304
Mogul Empire 143
Mongols 76, 77, 101, 126
Montezuma I 291, 294
Montezuma II 296, 297
Mozambique 143
Muhammad 225
mummification 26, 50-1
Mycenae 59, 148, 149, 150, 155
Nanking 77
Napoleon Bonaparte 143, 203
Nefertiti 25
Nero 185
Nicaea, Council of 197, 199
Nile 9, 35, 52-3
Normans 250, 251, 258-9
North America 248-9
Norwegians 228
Novgorod 235
Nubia 11, 16, 21, 22, 24, 28, 32, 34, 225

obelisks 34
Octavian 184
Odyssey 152-3
oligarchs 156
Olmec civilization 291
Olympic Games 112, 113, 172
opera, Chinese 79
opium 87
ordeal, trial by 246
Orkney 252
Osaka 104, 108
ostracism 164
outlaws 247

palaces
  Greek 148
  Inca 305
Palestine 225
parliaments 285
Parthenon 160-1, 173
Parthian War 185, 191
Peking 82, 83
Peking man 63
Peloponnesian War 161, 165
Pembroke Castle 283
Perikles 147, 164, 165
Persian Empire 32, 155,

159, 166, 167
Persian Wars 155, 159
Peru 59, 143, 302, 303
Pharos of Alexandria 168
Philip Augustus 270, 272, 273
Philip of Macedon 166
philosophers
  Confucius 62, 65, 66, 68-9
  Laozi 66
  Mencius 66
philosophy
  Chinese 62, 65, 66, 68-9, 72
  Greek 155, 162
  Legalism 72
  Taoism 66
physics 155
Pizarro, Francisco 309
Poitiers 255
Poland 285
Polo, Marco 77, 81, 143
Pompeii 185, 188
Pompey 178, 179
porcelain 85
Poros 170
pottery 59, 95, 96, 303, 304
Priene 171
printing 74, 285
public baths 189, 212
Punic Wars 179, 182
Punt 11, 23
pyramids
  at Giza 11, 12, 40-1, 43, 45
  construction 40-1, 42-3, 53
  Great Pyramid 40-1, 43
  modern pyramids 56
  purpose 38
  pyramid complexes 40
  South American 57, 304
  step pyramids 11, 12, 38
  straight-sided pyramids 11, 12, 38
  tomb-robbers 27, 43, 54-5
Pythagoras 155

Qin Shihuang 72
quipu 305

Ramesses II 22, 23
Ramesses III 23, 24

religions
  Aztec 290, 293
  Buddhism 76, 80, 95, 98
  Chavin 303
  Chinese 76, 80, 86
  Christianity 29, 33, 86, 101, 104, 106, 107, 197, 199, 225, 285
  Egyptian 13, 23, 25, 30, 32, 38, 47, 51
  Greek 157
  Inca 312
  Islam 29
  Japanese 95, 97, 98, 100, 101, 104, 128
  Roman 195, 197
  Shinto 97, 98, 128
  Viking 244-5
  Zen Buddhism 100, 101, 103, 128
Renaissance 285
Richard I 265, 270, 272, 273
road-building 74, 194, 302
Rollo 250, 255
Roman Empire
  architecture 202, 203, 222
  army 177, 180, 206-17
  citizenship 191, 198, 218, 225
  city states 188
  datecharts 179, 185, 191, 197, 224-5
  decline of 196-201
  Eastern Empire 196, 197, 200, 202, 220
  emperors 186, 199
  expansion 184, 185
  extent of 176
  forts 196-7, 212-17, 220, 221
  houses 193
  justice 198, 214
  Latin language 202
  legacy of 202-3
  maps 179, 185, 191, 197, 201
  peace and security 190-5
  peoples of 192
  provinces and frontiers 191
  religions 195, 197
  road-building 194

slaves 181, 187, 218
towns 188, 189, 193, 216
trade 194
Western Empire 196, 197, 200
Rome
  army 180
  children 189
  citizens 180, 181
  civil wars 178, 179, 183, 184
  consuls 181
  foundation of 178, 179, 180-1
  games 186-7
  public buildings 184
  Punic Wars 179, 182
  Roman Republic 179, 181
  sack of 200, 220
  senate 181
  superpower 178-83
  wealthy Romans 187
  see also Roman Empire
Romulus Augustulus 197, 220
Romulus and Remus 180
Rosetta Stone 35
Russia 235

Saladin 143, 270
Salamis 159
salt mining 74
samurai
  abolition of 138
  arms and armor 123, 124-5
  battles 136-7
  code of honor 122
  defeat of the Mongols 101, 126
  religion 128
  ritual suicide 123, 139
  samurai legends 140
  sashimono (personal flag) 131
  skills 103, 122, 123, 130-1
  way of life 103, 122
  women and children 110, 132-3
Sappho 155, 158
Saumur 276
Saxons 258, 259
scribes 18, 45, 48, 49
Sea Peoples 23, 24

Seleucid Empire 179
Seljuk Turks 255
Senusret II 17
Senusret III 17
Seti I 22, 23, 26, 27, 50
Severus 191
shaduf 15
Shetlands 252, 253
ships and boats
  Egyptian 53
  Greek 164-5
  Norman 251
  ship burials 244-5
  triremes 164, 165
  Viking 228-9, 232-3
sieges 260-1, 274-5, 283
silver 237
slaves 21, 156, 171, 181,
  187, 218, 236, 240
smallpox 309, 314
Sokrates 162
space technology 116
Sparta 159, 160, 161,
  163, 165, 166
squires 268
standards, Roman 206
stone circles 59
Stonehenge 59
sumo wrestling 111
Swedes 228, 234, 235
Syracuse 155, 161

tableware 280, 281
taxation
  Aztec 294
  Egyptian 42
  Inca 306, 310
  Japanese 96, 102, 134
temples
  Buddhist 119
  Egyptian 23, 25, 30, 31,
  52
  Greek 160-1
  Romano-British 195
Tenochtitlàn 57, 290,
  291, 292-3, 296, 297,
  314

Teotihuacán 225, 291
terracotta warriors 70-1
Texcoco 291
theater
  Chinese 79
  Greek 162, 173
  Japanese 111, 130
Thebes 17, 27, 28, 29,
  30, 55, 166
Thera 154
Thirty Years' War 282
thralls 236, 240
Tilbury Fort 283
Tlaxcalans 297, 314
Tokugawa Ieyasu 106,
  107, 135
Tokyo 118
  see also Edo
Toltecs 255, 285, 291
tomb paintings 45, 48
tombs
  beehive tombs 149, 151
  Chinese 68, 70-1
  Greek 149, 151
  Japanese 95, 97
  mastabas 10, 12, 40
  tomb robbers 27, 43,
  54-5
  see also pyramids
tools
  Chinese 64, 65
  Egyptian 45
  Inca 313
tournaments 278-9
towns
  Chinese 78-9
  Japanese 104
  Roman 188, 189, 193,
  216
  Viking 236
trade
  Aztec 298
  Chinese 80-1
  Egyptian 11, 20-1, 23,
  24
  Greek 149
  Japanese 106, 107, 116

merchants 107, 108,
  236, 298
  Roman 194
  Viking 234-5, 236
Trajan 185, 190, 220
Trojan War 149, 152,
  153
Tutankhamun 23, 34
Tuthmosis I 23
Tuthmosis III 23
tyrants 155, 156

Up Hellya 253
Ur, Royal Graves of 59
Urban II, Pope 270

Valhalla 244
Valley of the Kings 23,
  27, 55
Vespasian 185
Vikings
  agriculture 240
  burial customs 244
  coinage 237
  crafts 236, 241
  datechart 254-5
  feasts 242-3
  festivals 253
  feuds 246
  government 246-7
  houses 238-9
  justice 246, 247
  legacy 252-3
  longships 228-9, 232-3
  origin of word 228
  physical characteristics
  229, 234
  raids 230-1, 250
  religion 244-5
  settlements 248-9, 252
  Things 246, 247, 252
  towns 236
  trade 234-5, 236
  weapons 231
  women and children
  238-9
  words of origin 252

writing system 242
Vinland 248-9
Visigoths 197, 220
voladores 293

warfare
  samurai battles 136-7
  sieges 260-1, 274-5,
  283
  war elephants 170
  war machines 169, 215,
  261, 274
  see also armies; arms
  and armor
weaving 45, 109, 158,
  298, 313
William the Conqueror
  250-1
women
  Aztec 295
  Chinese 79
  Greek 158
  Japanese 132-3
  Viking 238, 239
wood-block printing 107,
  111
writing materials
  clay tablets 149, 151
  paper 71, 74-5
  papyrus 9, 18
  reed pens 18
writing systems
  Aztec 300
  calligraphy 67, 110,
  131
  Chinese 64, 67
  Egyptian 18, 19, 48,
  49
  Greek 151, 154
  hieroglyphs 19, 35, 48,
  49
  Japanese 98
  Linear B script 151
  runes 242
  Viking 242

Zheng He 86

With special thanks to the following photo libraries:

Hutchison Library, Michael Holford, Greg Evans Library, George Hort, Robert Harding Library, Scala, Photosource, Ancient Art and Architecture Collection/Ronald Sheridan, Tony Stone Associates, Richard and Sally Greenhill, Anglo-Chinese Society, Zefa, National Trust Picture Library, Bridgeman Art Library, Mansell Collection, Allan Cash, John Cleave, British Museum, Chloe Sayer, Rex Features, International Society for Educational Information, Jorvik Centre/York, Archeological Trust, Werner Forman Archive, Popperfoto, Japanese Information Center, Eastern Images, British Film Institute, C. M Dixon/Photosource, Spectrum, Leo Mason, J. Allan Cash Library.